CREATED EQUAL

Elizabeth Cady Stanton

Created Equal

A BIOGRAPHY OF ELIZABETH CADY STANTON

1815-1902

BY

ALMA LUTZ

OCTAGON BOOKS

A DIVISION OF FARRAR, STRAUS AND GIROUX

New York   1974

Reprinted 1974
by arrangement with the original publisher, The John Day Company, Inc.

OCTAGON BOOKS
A DIVISION OF FARRAR, STRAUS & GIROUX, INC.
19 Union Square West
New York, N. Y. 10003

Library of Congress Cataloging in Publication Data

Lutz, Alma.
  Created equal; a biography of Elizabeth Cady Stanton, 1815-
1902.

  Reprint of the ed. published by the J. Day Co., New York.

  Bibliography: p.
  1. Stanton, Elizabeth Cady, 1815-1902.   2. Woman—Rights of
women.   I. Title.
JK1899.S7L88   1974   324′.3′0924 [B]   74-6500
ISBN 0-374-95167-5

Printed in USA by
Thomson-Shore,Inc.
Dexter, Michigan

TO A. MARGUERITE SMITH

WHOSE HELP AND ENCOURAGEMENT

HAVE BEEN INVALUABLE

PUBLISHED IN CELEBRATION OF

THE SEVENTY-FIFTH ANNIVERSARY

OF

VASSAR COLLEGE

AND

IN HONOR OF

HENRY NOBLE MACCRACKEN

IN THE TWENTY-FIFTH YEAR

OF HIS PRESIDENCY

FOREWORD

EVERY woman who cherishes freedom owes a debt of gratitude to Elizabeth Cady Stanton. Every man who recognizes that the unhampered co-operation of men and women is necessary for the building of a better civilization, will admire her determination to gain a fuller, freer life for women.

Elizabeth Cady Stanton lived in an era when the law cast the shadow of a "defect of sex" over women, and not only was this "defect of sex" reflected in the laws relating to women's property, their children, their work, and their marriage, but in the traditions which had grown up regarding their mental ability and their place in society.

Elizabeth Cady Stanton's life, in addition to making a good home and bringing up seven children, was devoted to changing these laws and traditions. She was essentially a torchbearer for women. She saw far ahead when other women were taking their first steps of freedom. It was this quality which made her the moving spirit in calling the first Woman's Rights Convention in 1848 and gave her the courage to make the first public demand for woman suffrage against the advice of her most liberal friends. From then on, every woman's rights convention demanded the ballot. After the Civil War, when the campaign to enfranchise the Negro began, she saw this as woman's great opportunity to win suffrage, and, with Susan B. Anthony, stood out against the great majority of men and women who insisted that women must step aside for the Negro. The struggle for women's enfranchisement in the United States continued from 1848 for seventy-two years, finally ending in victory in 1920.

Elizabeth Cady Stanton's interest in woman's emancipation went far beyond woman suffrage to equal rights under the law and in all human relationships. She asked for equal educational opportunities for women and recommended coeducation. She recognized women's need for economic independence and rejoiced when they entered new fields in business and the professions. Realizing how much women suffered under prevailing marriage laws, she publicly advocated liberal divorce laws at a time when divorce was a forbidden subject for good women to discuss.

She saw that before women could be completely free, there must be a great change in their own thinking. She urged them to discard false traditions, to be wary of cultivating so-called womanly qualities which had been held up to them in the past as virtues and as substitutes for equality, to question the edicts of the Church regarding woman's sphere and to recognize that only man-made doctrines, not true religion, gave women an inferior rating. She was eager to widen women's interests and to have them think in terms of the nation and the world.

Independence of thought, self-respect, courage to enter new fields, loyalty to other women, recognition of women's contribution in building up this country, devotion to the ideal of freedom, and no compromise—these were the qualities which Elizabeth Cady Stanton held up to women.

Her life is a challenge to women to finish the work she began.

ALMA LUTZ

CONTENTS

ix

ILLUSTRATIONS

CREATED EQUAL

I

"A DEFECT OF SEX"

JUDGE CADY's law office was a place where things happened, things that Elizabeth, only ten, could not quite understand. But they fascinated her. Even as a very young child she had liked nothing better than to wander in and sit on her father's knee while he explained points of law to his clients.

Her father, she knew, was a man of importance. He had been a member of Congress and now was a judge. She had seen him in court, sitting there like a king while other men argued before him. He was dignified and distant, and she feared him a little, but there was a bond between them, and she wanted his love.

Today as she stood in his office, alone, a bright splash of color in her red flannel dress, she surveyed the book-lined walls and planned. Yes, the books she had marked were still upside down. Some night while the family slept, she would steal in with her scissors and cut out all the laws that made women cry.

So many women came to her father and begged him to help them — poor farm women, some old and wrinkled, some looking tired and worn, bringing their babies with them. She had listened while they told their stories. Husbands, she discovered, were often unkind, even cruel, and the law upheld them. It was wrong for a husband to take the money his wife earned at the washtub and spend it on drink when his children were hungry. But the law, her father declared, said a wife's wages belong to her husband. There was old Mrs. Brown whose husband had willed her farm to her stepson and now she had no home to go to, although she had toiled on that farm all her life.

Touched by their sorrow and eager to help, Elizabeth always hoped that her father would send them away happy, but he never did. He only shook his head sadly, and when it was hard to make them believe that such injustice could be upheld, he patiently took

3

a volume from his shelves and read from the statute. She kept her eye on the book and the section he read, and taking it from him when he had finished, spelled out the words for herself, marked the place, and put the book back on the shelf upside down so she could find it again.

As she stood there thinking this over, making her plans, her father came in. Flora Campbell was with him and sat down in the chair by the desk. For years Flora had brought butter, eggs, chickens, cider, and other good things to the Cady home and Elizabeth loved her. She went over to her and stood by her side for a time, while, with tears streaming down her cheeks, Flora told Judge Cady her troubles. Her husband without her consent had mortgaged the valuable farm which her father had left her. His creditors were taking it over. What could she do?

Elizabeth watched her father, hoping this time he could help. She saw that his face was saddened and strained as he patiently explained to Flora what the law said. And because it was hard to make Flora understand, he took a book down from the shelves and read her the law. Elizabeth knew what that meant. He couldn't help Flora. But maybe she could.

She heard her father explaining again in a stern voice, "The law plainly states that on marriage a woman's property becomes her husband's." Then he added, "As long as I live, Flora, I'll not allow you or your children to want. I'll put you on one of my very best farms. You can have all you make from it and stay there as long as you live."

But this was no comfort to Flora. She wanted her farm. She left the office in despair, her last hope gone. Elizabeth ran after her, sensing her anguish, and, throwing her arms around her, cried impulsively, "Dear Flora, don't cry another tear. I have all those wicked laws marked and I will cut every one out of the books tonight."

As soon as she could, Flora hurried back to the office to warn Judge Cady of Elizabeth's plan. That night after supper, when it was time for the evening story, he took Elizabeth to his office, and, as they sat by the fire, he told her how laws were made without letting her guess that he had discovered her secret. He explained carefully how many lawyers there were and how many law books, that, if his library should burn, it would in no way help women.

"When you are grown up," he continued, "and able to prepare a speech, you must go to Albany and talk to the Legislature; tell them all you have seen in this office—the sufferings of these women, robbed of their inheritance and left dependent on their unworthy sons, and if you can persuade them to pass new laws, the old ones will be a dead letter."

Thus the law books were saved, and Elizabeth saw that for a time at least she was helpless. Yet quite unwittingly that night Judge Cady mapped out a career for his daughter.

When Elizabeth was born, November 12, 1815, women lived under the shadow of a "defect of sex," as Blackstone described it in his *Commentaries*. Not only was this "defect of sex" reflected in the laws relating to women's property, their children, their work, and their marriage, but in the conventions and traditions which had grown up about their mental ability and their place in society.

Again and again through her childhood, Elizabeth came face to face with the challenge of a "defect of sex" and rebelled. She was a sensitive, imaginative child with a mind far above the average. She observed life, thought about it, and questioned. Instinctively she resisted unquestioned authority, craved freedom to develop and resented being relegated to an inferior sphere because she was a girl. Yet there was no more fun-loving, daring, or good-natured playfellow than Elizabeth Cady.

The Cadys lived in a comfortable white frame house on the corner of Market and Main Streets, in Johnstown, a small, prosperous town in northern New York. There were three children in the family older than Elizabeth—Tryphena, Harriet, and a son, Eleazer—and two younger sisters, Margaret and Catherine.

Elizabeth's mother was always busy looking after the housework and servants. Elizabeth admired her secretly, for she was beautiful to look at—tall and commanding, much like her father, Colonel Livingston, who served in the Revolution, so everyone said. But she was in awe of her, and there really was no one to talk to about things that perplexed her.

Nurse was so stern. She watched over the three younger children, Elizabeth, Margaret, and Catherine, and sent them to school in bright red flannel dresses, just alike, with stiffly starched white ruffles around their necks and black alpaca aprons to keep their dresses clean. She always, so Elizabeth thought, called them away from their play at the most exciting moment, and when they displeased her, told them terrifying tales of hell-fire where they would burn for their sins unless they reformed.

But nurse was not always in command. There were happy hours spent with Abraham, Jacob, and Peter, the Negro servants of the family, who brought laughter and light-heartedness into their lives. Never was Elizabeth so carefree as when she romped through games with them or listened to their singing and the strumming of their banjos.

Yet, even in her happiest moments, the threat of hell-fire hung like a cloud over her. Everything connected with religion filled her with gloom. The church was bare and cold. There was no organ to send out its mellow tones and relieve the austerity which pervaded the congregation. The sermons were long, the chanted psalms doleful. To be restless or fall asleep was sure evidence of total depravity, and as she was often guilty of this, she suffered for fear the devil would some day drag her off to hell-fire. He was a real person to her, and she imagined him crouching in the corner of the nursery waiting to pounce upon her. Often at night, terrified by the thought of her sins, she stole out of bed and sat shivering on the stairs, comforted somewhat by the light of the hall lamp and the sound of voices in the parlor.

In spite of all this, the most loved friend of her childhood was the gray-haired, high-cheeked Presbyterian parson, the Reverend Simon Hosack. Somehow, she did not associate him with the religion he preached but with his garden, which adjoined theirs and where she could always find him early in the morning and in the cool of the evening. She spent hours with him there, asking him endless questions as he worked. Together they went on his parish rounds, jogging along the country roads in his well-worn buggy, she driving the old white mare. Unhappily married and lonely, he found solace in her companionship, and she in turn found in him the understanding and affection that she craved.

When she was eleven, her brother Eleazer died. Eleazer had been so promising, had only that summer graduated with honors from Union College. Her father, stunned by the loss of his only son, was inconsolable. Bowed with grief, he sat in the darkened parlor beside the casket. Elizabeth, yearning to comfort him, stole quietly into the room. He took no notice of her for a long time. Finally she went over to him and sat on his lap. As he held her close and she struggled to know what she could do to comfort him, he exclaimed suddenly, "Oh, my daughter, would that you were a boy!"

It was then that she made a firm resolve. She would be the boy that her father longed for. The rest of the day and most of the night she pondered the matter, wondering why a boy seemed so much more important to her father than all or any of his five daughters. She mapped out her course of action—what she must do to be like a boy. She must study Greek and ride horseback. She must give less time to play and stand at the head of her class. She would do all this, and then her father would smile at her and say, "My daughter, you are just as good as a boy after all."

With these high hopes, she got up very early the next morning and hurried over to Dr. Hosack. He was in his garden, hoeing. "Dr. Hosack," she cried breathlessly, "which do you like best, boys or girls?"

"Why girls, to be sure," he replied, smiling down at her. "I would not give you for all the boys in Christendom."

"My father prefers boys," she continued, her blue eyes still troubled. "He wishes I were one, and I intend to be as near like one as possible. I am going to ride horseback and study Greek. Will you give me a Greek lesson now? I want to begin at once."

"Yes, child," replied Dr. Hosack, throwing down his hoe. "Come into my library."

She followed him eagerly, watched him take down from the bookshelf a worn old grammar, and sat down beside him while he explained that he had studied from that same book many years ago at the University of Glasgow. By breakfast time, she had learned the Greek article. Then, triumphant, she scampered home across the gardens, hesitating a moment at the door, reluctant to leave the bright sunshine for the sadness which she knew awaited her within.

These plans helped her somewhat through the sad days of mourning. For several months until winter came, she went with her father at twilight to the cemetery, and while in his grief he threw himself upon his son's grave with outstretched arms, she leaned against a poplar near by, her desire to comfort him struggling with the fear and dread that surged over her. She was filled with indefinable fears of the future, of what had become of her brother, of what might become of her. It took many years before she was able to wipe out the mind pictures of her brother's death, and never in her life could she bear the sound of a tolling bell.

Her love of study and exercise steadied what might have been a morbid adolescence. The plump, rosy-cheeked little girl, vigorous physically, soon learned to ride horseback well, even to leap a fence and a ditch. Proud of her accomplishments, she longed desperately to hear her father say, "Well, a girl is as good as a boy after all." He never did. When Dr. Hosack came over to spend an evening, she whispered to him, "Tell my father how fast I get on," and Dr. Hosack, sympathetic and proud of his pupil, always praised her highly. But in answer, Judge Cady only paced the room and sighed.

Soon after she began her lessons in Greek with Dr. Hosack, she joined a class of boys at the Academy who were studying Latin, Greek, and mathematics. That she was the only girl troubled her not at all. In fact, it never entered her mind that only an unusual girl studied these subjects or that people in general thought girls incapable of absorbing anything beyond the reading, writing, and arithmetic of the elementary schools. For three years she ranked second in the class, although most of the boys were older than she. Secretly she cherished the ambition to win one of the two prizes offered in Greek, confident that this could not fail to impress her father. When the great day came and she was awarded her prize, a Greek Testament, but one thought filled her mind, that at last her father would see that a girl was as good as a boy.

She ran all the way from the Academy to his office and proudly displayed her prize. He examined it, asked her questions about the class, and seemed greatly pleased. But as she was waiting for her reward, longing to hear him acknowledge the equal worth of sons and daughters, he handed the book back to her, kissed her on the forehead, and said with a sigh, "Ah, my daughter, you should have been a boy!"

With those words he cruelly and unwittingly robbed her triumph of all its joy and impressed upon her more deeply the tragedy of "a defect of sex."

There were always many young law students getting their training in Judge Cady's office. Two of these students, Edward and Henry Bayard, sons of Senator James A. Bayard of Wilmington, Delaware, were favorites of the family. Edward had been one of Eleazer's classmates at Union and a frequent visitor at the Cady home during his college course. Soon after Eleazer's death, he and his younger brother, Henry, came to Judge Cady for instruction, and began at once in some measure to fill Eleazer's place.

Henry Bayard was a great tease and nothing delighted him more than to read Elizabeth the worst laws that he could find relating to women and then laugh gaily at her dismay. He read her passages from the Bible and *The Taming of the Shrew* to taunt her and she hated Petruchio as if he were a real man. One Christmas morning when, bubbling over with joy, she displayed her new coral necklace and bracelet, he admired them, told her how becoming they were, and then solemnly and pompously announced: "If you in due time should become my wife, these ornaments would be mine. I could take them and lock them up and you could never wear them without my permission. I could even exchange them for a cigar and you could watch them evaporate in smoke." And so it continued, until she dashed off in desperation, unable to bear it any longer. Everything pointed to the divine headship of man, but she would not consent to it.

Edward Bayard was different. He did not tease. He loved children and understood them, and gradually became her confidant and very best friend, filling the place that Dr. Hosack had held in her childhood. The energetic, determined little girl with her winning smile, her rosy cheeks, fair skin, and curly brown hair, appealed strongly to him. She, ten years younger, adored him, and was very happy when he became one of the family by marrying her older sister, Tryphena.

When Elizabeth was fifteen, she finished the course at Johnstown Academy. The only girl in the class of higher mathematics, Latin, and Greek, she fully expected to go with the boys to Union College. It was a day of bitter disappointment when she learned that girls were not admitted at Union.

Then in family conference it was decided that she be sent to the best school for girls in the country, Emma Willard's celebrated Female Seminary in Troy, New York. Her work at the Academy had advanced her far beyond what was taught at the Troy Female Seminary, but there was no other school to attend, as no college admitted girls in 1830.

She spent two years at the Seminary studying music, French, and dancing, when her keen mind was eager for college courses. But by this time she had cultivated the philosophy of making the best of things, and while there were days when she rebelled at the injustice of being shut up in the Seminary, missing the advantages of Union College, she had her good times.

When her two years at the Troy Female Seminary were over, she returned to Johnstown eager for the freer life that lay ahead. She left the Seminary with great admiration for Madame Willard, for her intellect and her dignity. Here was a woman who had accomplished something which men as well as women must respect. And yet Madame Willard's persuasive words regarding the duty of every young woman to be a teacher aroused no response in her. She was conscious of no particular ambition, of no great purpose in life.

The Cady home was filled with young people. Elizabeth's friends from Troy came on long visits. Margaret and Catherine, now students at the Troy Female Seminary, brought home their friends for the holidays. The law students joined them and occasionally boys from Union College. There were long walks and sleigh rides in the winter and evenings of games, music, and dancing. There were early morning horseback rides along the Mohawk Valley and toward the blue hills.

Edward Bayard enjoyed to the full the genial social life of the family. He was in his element when he could gather about him in the evening a group of Seminary girls and start a philosophical, religious, or political discussion, or read aloud to them from Scott, Bulwer, Cooper, or Dickens.

In that circle of eager young faces, just one stood out for him, Elizabeth's. The appealing little girl who had turned to him so naturally in her troubles, whom he had guided and loved as a younger sister, was now a woman, beautiful, spirited, infinitely desirable. The ten years between them had melted away. Elizabeth took his affection for granted. He had always been her very best friend. There were younger boys who sought her companionship. There were temporary romances, but Edward Bayard stood out head and shoulders above them all and nothing was as sweet as praise from him.

Like most of the girls in Johnstown, she did her share of church work. One of the objects of the Presbyterian Girls' Club, of which she was leader, was to raise money to educate a young man for the ministry. The girls industriously sewed and baked, held fairs and sociables to pay the way of a promising young student at Auburn Theological Seminary. When he graduated, they sent him money to buy a new black broadcloth suit, a high silk hat, and a cane, and invited him to preach a sermon in their church.

This was a great event. Everyone turned out to hear him. When the church was filled with an eager congregation, the girls, dressed in their very best new spring clothes, filed into the front rows which were reserved for them. Their young minister stood before them in the black broadcloth suit which he had bought with their hard-earned money. He stood there on display as the product of their industry, and thundered out these words as his text, "But I suffer not a woman to teach, nor to usurp authority over the man, but to be in silence." (I Tim. 2:12)

The girls looked at each other a moment in amazement and dismay. Then, marshaled by Elizabeth, they arose and two by two marched down the long aisle to the street, not waiting to hear one word of the long-anticipated sermon.

From that day on, nothing could induce Elizabeth to sew one stitch or devote one thought to the education of young men for the ministry. She never forgot this experience. It stayed in her mind along with the stories she had heard from the farm women in her father's office, along with the dictum that colleges were closed to girls; and rebellion smoldered.

II

PETERBORO AND HENRY B. STANTON

No YEAR was complete without a visit to Peterboro with Cousin Gerrit Smith and his family. Judge Cady frowned on these visits but seldom forbade them, for although he regarded Gerrit Smith as a dangerous radical, he respected his honesty of purpose and his genuine goodness. The two families were so bound together by relationship and friendship that no difference of opinion could really estrange them.

Elizabeth always approached Peterboro with excitement. The large square house with pillars across the front was inviting. The wide lawn, the stately elms, the gardens, and many buildings gave the place the air of a Southern plantation. As she drove up in her carriage, she looked first for Cousin Gerrit, who was invariably waiting on the porch to welcome her with a kindly smile and open arms. Cousin Nancy was close beside him—the most beautiful woman she had ever seen—and their daughter Elizabeth, always called Libby, who was her very best friend.

Libby was a most satisfying playmate ready to romp or to canter over the fields and eager to talk over seriously the subjects they heard discussed by their elders. There was slavery, so abhorrent to Gerrit Smith and equally so to Libby. She told heart-rending stories of fugitive slaves, hidden in the barn or garret until her father could get them safely on their way to Canada and freedom. Occasionally Elizabeth saw them herself, and their terror and helplessness made an impression she never forgot.

Instinctively she rebelled against slavery. A Negro to her was a friend—just as Peter had been in her childhood. She had never thought of his color. Hand in hand they had walked to school and all about Johnstown. She had sat with him at church in the Negro pew. She could not bear to think of him as a slave, sold perhaps to a cruel master. But at home abolition was never discussed and Abolitionists were regarded as fanatics stirring up strife.

At Peterboro she heard enough to keep her thinking throughout the year. There was much talk of William Lloyd Garrison, who, mobbed and dragged through the streets of Boston, had barely escaped with his life. She read his *Liberator* whenever she could. James G. Birney, the Southerner who freed his slaves; George Thompson, the English Abolitionist, harassed by mobs in this country; Wendell Phillips, the eloquent young orator; Frederick Douglass, the Negro, all became heroes to her. She heard of Lucretia Mott, the Quaker, who spoke at an antislavery meeting where women were supposed to keep silent. She listened with pride to praise of Angelina and Sarah Grimké, courageous young Southern women, who, defying convention, spoke against slavery. Sometimes she heard of Theodore Weld and Henry B. Stanton, students at Lane Seminary in Cincinnati, Ohio, who left college to deliver fiery lectures for the antislavery cause.

But slavery was not the only subject made vital at Peterboro. All subjects were thrashed out—from politics, temperance, and religion to woman's rights and dress reform. The house was always filled with guests from all walks of life, for Gerrit Smith's generosity, his hospitality, and genuine love of mankind drew people of all sorts to his door. In the little village in the hills, scholars, statesmen, and reformers gathered, and friendly Indians stopped for a day or two of good living. Every wayfarer was welcome. They all sat down to dinner together, and if there were more than the dining room would hold, another table was spread in the long hall. Cousin Gerrit, carving the meats, led the conversation in his genial way, making all feel at home. And Elizabeth, looking on, her eyes bright with interest, felt that nowhere else could society be so stimulating.

From Cousin Gerrit she learned an entirely new philosophy of life. In spite of his wealth and his vast landholdings, inherited from his father, Peter Smith, fur trader and friend of the Indians, he lived very simply. He would have nothing in his home which would make his humblest visitor feel out of place. Believing that land should be free as air and that he had no right to keep what he had not earned and could not improve, he gave away hundreds of farms to needy men and women. "God gives me money to give away," he often remarked to Elizabeth, and she loved him more and more for the happiness which she saw him bring to others.

When he discussed religion, she listened to every word. It was a subject that still troubled her. He had been a strict Calvinist, but the Church's attitude toward slavery had made him question traditional beliefs. He had broken away from religious organizations and now urged a practical Christianity expressed in daily life. Every morning the family gathered while he read from the Bible and offered a short simple prayer. For the first time, she realized that religion might be a comfort, and often read with fresh assurance the framed text, "God is Love," which hung over his bedroom door.

Temperance was another cause important to Cousin Gerrit. No wine was served at his table. Elizabeth, remembering the worn mothers who came to her father's office with tales of drunken husbands, was readily converted to temperance.

Woman's rights were often discussed, and Elizabeth listened to this as to nothing else. Women, growing bolder and feeling duty bound to help free the slaves, were forming female antislavery societies. The churches protested, believing that women were straying out of their God-ordained sphere. Abolitionists differed regarding the wisdom of allowing women to take part in the movement. Some welcomed them gladly. Some, although they acknowledged that women had a right to take part, thought it best not to entangle the antislavery cause with such an unpopular issue. Others stormed and quoted the Bible, and raved like fanatics at the thought of women presuming to enter the sphere of men.

A prominent lawyer, Judge Hurlburt, it was reported at Peterboro, prepared a paper against the rights of women and found he could refute every argument he had drawn up. The result was a telling work called "Human Rights" in which he favored political equality for women. Then Judge Hertell introduced in the New York Legislature (1836) a bill granting married women property rights. It found little support, even among women. Ernestine Rose, a beautiful Polish woman and an eloquent lecturer, circulated petitions for it with the help of Paulina Wright Davis. The results were discouraging. Only five women signed. Some feared they would be laughed at for signing; some said they had rights enough; and others agreed with the men that they had too many rights as it was.

All this Elizabeth discussed with Libby and often with Cousin Gerrit, who agreed that law and tradition both oppressed women. He believed in one code of law, one code of morals, one standard of education for men and women. But the Negro, he said, needed help far more than the women. Women must fight their own battles. The fault lay with them. They lacked self-respect. How could they hope to be free and develop while they were such slaves to fashion as to wear clothes which injured their health and made them inactive?

There was truth in all that he said and Elizabeth acknowledged it sadly. But women were breaking down barriers and hope lay ahead.

After a visit to Peterboro, Johnstown seemed drab for a time, especially after Edward and Tryphena had left to settle in Seneca Falls where Edward opened a law office. There was no one with whom she could talk things over now that Edward was gone.

When her father went West on a business trip, she traveled with him to Seneca Falls. How good it was to see Edward again! And Edward, finding Elizabeth more beautiful and companionable every time he saw her, fell desperately in love.

He tried to keep this to himself. He threw all his energies into the study of homeopathy which had become his new interest. Eagerly he told her of his experiments and his hopes of becoming a homeopathic physician.

Then one day off guard, he impetuously revealed his secret, told her that he loved her, and she knew that she had always loved him. It was all so joyous and yet so tragically involved. What could they do? She must be loyal to her sister. But Edward needed her. Halfstarved for affection and understanding, he had turned to her, and she longed to pour out to him all the love in her heart.

She thought it all over again and again. There was no way out. She would always love Edward, but no one must know, only he. She went home sadly, determined to put this beautiful, tempestuous, impossible thing out of her life. But it was hard to do this, for just as she thought she had conquered, Edward would stop over in Johnstown on his way to New York, and an understanding glance and a smile from him would make her heart pound and bring back longings that she had vowed to suppress.

Often he persuaded the family to send her and Madge to New York with him to visit their sister Harriet, who had married a successful merchant, Daniel C. Eaton. Sometimes they went by stage, sometimes by boat down the Hudson, and occasionally in their private carriage. After the quiet of Johnstown, New York with its bustle and wealth, its theaters and fashions, its ships in the harbor sailing to foreign ports, cast a spell of romance over Elizabeth.

On moonlight nights Edward strolled with her along the Battery and told her of his love. She longed for these walks, although she knew that she should not. How proud she was to be with him! He was so handsome and attentive. As they walked on together arm in arm, soothed by the lapping of the waves, looking out at the ships softly outlined in the moonlight, he begged her to sail away with him. Why sacrifice their love any longer? There was adventure ahead, love, and undying devotion. Torn between her love for him and loyalty to Tryphena, she struggled to know what to do. In New York everything was different; family ties seemed to vanish; love and adventure beckoned. But in her heart she knew what had to be done, and she went back to Johnstown.

At home she was desolate, and her thoughts turned continually to Cousin Gerrit, Cousin Nancy, and Libby. They would help her forget. Finally she arranged a visit to Peterboro.

There was more than usual to talk over with Libby, but her love for Edward she kept to herself, and as Libby now had her own romance, she listened sympathetically to eulogies of Charles Dudley Miller. The house was full of young people, and determined to ease her heartache, she was one of the liveliest, a ringleader in the boisterous, practical jokes they continually played on each other.

Then Henry B. Stanton came to hold a series of antislavery meetings in Madison County and made Gerrit Smith's home his headquarters. His arrival brought news of the dissension in antislavery ranks, of the dissatisfaction of the New York Abolitionists with the policies of Garrison's group. Garrison now strongly urged his no-human-government doctrine, calling the Constitution, "a covenant with death and an agreement with hell." Flaunting his motto "No Union with Slaveholders," he hoped to persuade the North to dissolve the Union. He and his loyal followers were refusing to vote, not wishing in any way to imply that they acknowledged or supported the Constitution.

Practical men like Stanton, Birney, Weld, Whittier, and many Abolitionists of the New York group, among them Gerrit Smith, had no sympathy with the no-government doctrine. To them the way to reform lay in the ballot. They preached political action, urging every Abolitionist to go to the polls as a religious and moral duty, to voice there his opposition to slavery by choosing a candidate pledged for reform and against the extension of slavery. Henry B. Stanton, with his ability as a speaker and an organizer, had soon become the moving force of the political group. Unfortunately Garrison took as a personal affront this opposition on the part of Stanton. Garrison was a hero not easily opposed. People followed him blindly. But Stanton, convinced of the danger of the no-government doctrine, held his ground courageously in the face of Garrison's censure.

Elizabeth listened with interest to all this discussion of political action. Henry Stanton stood out as a hero to her. He was a fine-looking man, tall, friendly, most interesting to talk to. From others she heard of his untiring devotion in pleading the cause of the slave, of his courage as he faced cruel and harassing mobs. Some called him the most telling orator on the antislavery platform. She soon was to judge this for herself.

Every morning two carriage loads started off over the hills, bound for an antislavery meeting. Sometimes they drove for ten miles in the crisp October air through trees of flaming color. They returned in the moonlight, tired and happy, inspired by what they had heard. Elizabeth never forgot those drives nor those meetings. She had a passion for oratory. She listened spellbound to Henry B. Stanton, as he moved his audience first to laughter and then to tears. Carried away by the enthusiasm of the people, the fiery oratory, and the clear arguments of the speakers, she was an ardent convert to the antislavery cause. Life took on a new meaning, filled with purpose and work for mankind. All sorts of new ideas surged through her mind. Many half-formed thoughts which had been simmering for a long time now became articulate. Never was so much happiness crowded into one short month. Edward Bayard was being forgotten.

By this time Henry Stanton was not interested wholly in the antislavery cause. Elizabeth Cady began filling his thoughts, and he spent as much time as possible with her. One morning when there was no meeting, they went for a horseback ride. It was a beautiful morning of Indian summer when the sun was warm and the leaves were pure gold. They were gone a long time, and when they returned, both radiant, they had news for Cousin Gerrit.

Cousin Gerrit, though secretly pleased and with nothing but praise for Henry, knew only too well how Judge Cady would feel about Elizabeth's engagement to a young Abolitionist. He warned her of this, and tried to impress her with the seriousness of the step she was taking and the folly of being too hasty. Elizabeth, wanting only to cherish her happiness, was bewildered by all this advice from Cousin Gerrit, who usually understood so well. Little he knew what a refuge Henry was after Edward's persistent pleading. With love awakened by Edward and then repressed, she found Henry a godsend. He too was ten years her senior, a man of accomplishment who appealed to her mind as well as her heart. His need of her and dreams of work together for the antislavery cause made life seem very worth while.

Cousin Gerrit suggested that she write her father about her engagement. But Judge Cady, indignant at Gerrit Smith as well as

Elizabeth, did not deign to reply to her well-worded letter. He would stamp out this folly when she returned home.

She lingered on at Peterboro in her new-found happiness. Henry had gone to Cleveland, Ohio, to an antislavery convention, but his letters came often, filled with pledges of undying devotion. She thought over all he had told her about his life, preparing herself to convince her father. There could be no objection to his family for he was descended from Elder Brewster. She thought of how hard he had worked for his education, how he sacrificed his course at Lane Seminary in Ohio when the ruling was made that students no longer could debate or discuss the question of slavery. He had told her of his friendship with James G. Birney and with Theodore Weld, who had recently married Angelina Grimké, whom she looked up to as a prophet among women. He had told her of his lecture tours with Whittier, the young poet, of their lobbying together at the State House in Boston, of his happy visits at the cottage in Amesbury, of their work together on the *Antislavery Standard*. He had shown her the volume of antislavery poems which Whittier dedicated to him.

Surely her father could not object to a man so respected as this. Yet she knew that he would. An Abolitionist, a radical, would find no place in Judge Cady's esteem. And so, leaving Peterboro with all its happy memories, leaving Libby who understood so well, she summoned her courage to meet her father in Johnstown.

Judge Cady was adamant in his objections. Austere and unapproachable, he made it difficult for her to plead her case. An antislavery lecturer, radical and impractical, could never, he maintained, earn enough to support a wife. He painted a sordid picture of poverty and disillusionment.

Discouraged and almost ready to give in to her father's unrelenting opposition, she gained courage and hope with every letter from Henry. He wrote as he spoke, vividly and persuasively. She wrote him frankly of her father's objections. But Henry was used to opposition. He could and would support her and make her life happy. He had his salary as an antislavery agent. He was writing for the papers, now a series of articles for the *New York American*.

Judge Cady, however, was not convinced. And Edward Bayard came and joined forces against Elizabeth. She must give Henry up, he said, and not ruin her life and his. Edward loved her. She knew it. He would not let her go. Edward was there on the spot. His passion compelled. It was all so bewildering. He loved her and Henry loved her. She loved them both. She could not marry Edward. They would not let her marry Henry. Her courtship had been so happy. Now they had turned it into a tragedy and had filled her with doubt until she was fearful of taking the step she longed to take. Was it wise to oppose those who had always loved her and looked out for her welfare? Even Cousin Gerrit had warned her. Before this her friends had continually suggested suitable matches, had painted glowing pictures of marriage. Now they said men were deceivers, not to be trusted. Through all this, memories persisted of the women who had come to her father's office, poor, downtrodden, and oppressed by the law. Husbands could be despots and the law upheld them. Now she was free. Was it wise to take a step that would bind her?

All in all the pressure was so great that she gave in. She broke her engagement. Very sadly she wrote Cousin Nancy in March:

> I cannot tell you dear Cousin with how much pleasure and how often, in memory I go back and enjoy again the many weeks I spent with you.... Memories like these bind me to the dear ones who shared these joys with me, cast a spell that cannot soon be broken. You have heard, dear Cousin, I suppose, that my engagement with S. is dissolved and I know you wonder and so do I. Had anyone told me at Peterboro that what has occurred would come, I would not have believed it, but much since then has convinced me that I was too hasty. We are still friends and correspond as before. Perhaps when the storm blows over we may be dearer friends than ever.

Edward Bayard was persistent. The situation was intolerable. She could not run away with him and sacrifice Tryphena to her love. The scandal would be nothing to her in comparison with disloyalty to Tryphena. What would life hold for her with Edward? Passionate love for a time perhaps, new scenes, but always regret.

Henry still pleaded his case. He would not give up. With him she would escape from the austere, conservative atmosphere of her family. Her friends would be those she met at Peterboro, reformers and idealists. She could throw herself into this new life with enthusiasm. Her mind looked forward to this. Her heart held back a little for Edward. She was so used to him. He had been such a sure refuge. But she loved Henry, she knew, and must put Edward out of her mind.

Then came a letter from Henry telling her he was to sail for London in May as a delegate to the World's Antislavery Convention. Birney was going, and Garrison, and Lucretia Mott. She must marry him and go with him. He would not put the ocean between them.

She made her decision. She would marry Henry. She was no longer a child to be buffeted about by others' opinions. She was twenty-five now, old enough to make her own choice, to live her own life. Her mother had married at sixteen. She would turn her back on the past and Edward, and make the best of the future. Because she was so determined, her father yielded, though he still disapproved.

They planned their marriage for Thursday, May 9, 1840. The time was too short for the usual preparations—an elaborate trousseau and wedding festivities, but these meant little to Elizabeth. The main thing was to have made up her mind.

Henry Stanton, coming up from New York by boat, was stranded for hours on a sandbar in the river so that the ceremony had to be postponed until Friday.

The Scotch clergyman begged them to wait until Saturday and not begin their married life on such an unlucky day, but they overruled his objections. Elizabeth then had to convince the clergyman that the word "obey" must be omitted from the ceremony. She had her own ideas about marriage. It was an equal relation, a real partnership. She refused to put her life wholly into the hands of another and lose her identity. She knew she was the equal of any man, and while she did not draw up a marriage protest as did Lucy Stone and Henry Blackwell some fifteen years later, nor insist on keeping her own name, she did not enter marriage blindly or without the reservations of an independent woman. Finally the clergyman consented, and on Friday, May 10, in a simple white evening dress, before a few friends, Elizabeth Cady was married. She had put Edward out of her life.

Edward, defeated, turned more resolutely to homeopathy and became a prominent, kindly physician. And it is said that after Elizabeth's marriage, he never allowed himself to be left in a room with her alone. He loved her to the end of his days.

III

LUCRETIA MOTT

S AILING out into the ocean with Henry, Elizabeth felt as if she had left her old self behind her. The thought of going to London, of traveling through England, Scotland, and Ireland, and perhaps seeing Paris, the prospect of meeting Lucretia Mott, William Lloyd Garrison, and Wendell Phillips—all this kept her in the highest spirits. The voyage itself was an adventure and she loved every minute of it. She made friends with the captain, explored the ship, and was even hoisted to the masthead in a chair.

Her exuberance was a strain on James G. Birney, who was on the *Montreal* with them. A very proper Southern gentleman, he felt that "ladies" should be seen and admired but not heard, and he feared very much that she would make a poor impression in conservative England. He did his best to train her for the part she should play as the wife of a delegate to the convention, and she took his corrections good-naturedly, asking him every night what her sins for the day had been. And he would reply, "I heard you call your husband, Henry, in the presence of strangers, which is not permissible in polite society," or "you went to the masthead in a chair, which I think is very unladylike."

Both he and Henry gave her thorough instruction in antislavery doctrines so that she would be intelligent on the subject and not disgrace them in London; and as they discussed slavery and social questions, Mr. Birney respected her intellect more and more and began to overlook some of her gaiety and banter.

To set foot on English soil, to drive through the beautiful green English countryside on the top of a coach was like living in a storybook. But when they reached London and she entered their lodging house, Mark Moore's at 6 Queen Street, Cheapside, she thought it was the gloomiest place she had ever seen. The next day, however, when the women delegates from Boston and Philadelphia arrived—Emily Winslow, Abby Southwick, Elizabeth Neal, Mary Grew, Abby Kimber, Sarah Pugh, and Lucretia Mott —the atmosphere was charged with new life and interest, and she looked forward to happy stimulating companionship.

She met them all at dinner, wondering if they would have a feeling of hostility toward her because her husband and her Cousin Gerrit Smith represented the "Birney faction," which did not want women to take an active part in antislavery meetings. But Lucretia Mott greeted her cordially and she was seated beside her at the table. Before long the Baptist ministers in the party began to joke about the way the women delegates had caused division among the Abolitionists in America and were preparing to do the same thing in England. The repartee was quick and keen and on the surface good-natured, but Elizabeth could see that there was a battle ahead on woman's rights and that she by marriage was on the wrong side. However, her sympathies were with the women, and she was soon taking an active part in the conversation, combating the men. She was delighted to find the women delegates so charming, for Mr. Birney had described them in most uncomplimentary terms. Now she realized how prejudiced he was against women who were active in antislavery organizations. Mrs. Mott's manner aroused her admiration, as calmly and skillfully she parried all the attacks of the men, turning the laugh on them by her quiet humor and silencing their ridicule and sneers by her earnestness and dignity. The look of recognition she gave Elizabeth when she saw that she comprehended the problem of woman's rights and wrongs made her feel that she was no longer an outsider. How beautiful Lucretia Mott looked to her that day, and how wise!

And Lucretia Mott wrote in her diary, "Elizabeth Stanton gaining daily in our affections."

As the day for the opening of the convention drew near, it became more and more evident that there was going to be a heated contest over the admission of women delegates. They were approached again and again with requests and suggestions that they conform to English customs and not force themselves upon the convention. Their admission as delegates, they were told, would cause the press to ridicule the convention and rouse prejudice against the cause. But they stood firm, maintaining that they had been chosen as delegates, had traveled 3000 miles to serve, and that their exclusion was inconsistent in a convention called in the interests of liberty and equality. They counseled with George Thompson and Wendell Phillips, and Wendell Phillips agreed to champion them at the convention.

Knowing that a battle which concerned her and all women would be fought out on the convention floor, Elizabeth, tense with excitement, entered Freemasons' Hall with her husband on the morning of June 12. Delegates from all parts of the world were assembling—an interesting sight at any time, but doubly so now to Elizabeth as she wondered how they felt about women.

Little groups gathered here and there, talking earnestly and emphasizing their words with vehement gestures. American clergymen kept the English opposition at white heat. English Friends, usually tolerant toward women's activities, joined their clerical brethren because they could not take the same side as the unorthodox Lucretia Mott, a Hicksite Quaker.

Elizabeth joined the other women in the space marked off for them at the far end of the hall. There, screened off by a rail and a curtain like a choir, they were secure from the gaze of the men and could listen with all modesty while their lords expounded at length on the question of their admission as delegates. Here Quaker gray, white caps, and kerchiefs predominated, brightened by Elizabeth's stylishly cut silk and the gowns of the well-dressed ladies from Boston and London.

As Elizabeth sat down beside Lucretia Mott, Wendell Phillips came up with his lovely young wife, Ann Phillips, a delegate from the Massachusetts Society, who sent him away with the warning, "No shilly-shallying, Wendell! Be brave as a lion!"

The air was electric with the impending contest. Impatiently Elizabeth sat through the preliminaries and the address of the veteran English Abolitionist, Thomas Clarkson. Finally Wendell Phillips rose to speak. Her eyes appraised him approvingly as he stood there before them, handsome and commanding. In a clear, well-modulated voice he proposed the motion that was to inflame the convention: "That a Committee of five be appointed to prepare a correct list of the members of this Convention, with instructions to include in such a list all persons bearing credentials from any antislavery body." He urged the acceptance of the fully qualified women delegates sent to the convention by American antislavery societies.

Dr. John Bowring was the next to champion the women. "I look upon this delegation from America," he said, "as one of the most interesting, the most encouraging, and the most delightful symptoms of the times. I cannot believe that we shall refuse to welcome gratefully the co-operation which is offered us."

By this time the opposition was fully aroused. The Reverend J. Burnet, an Englishman, after appealing to the American ladies to conform to English customs, shouted, "It were better that this Convention be dissolved at this moment than that this motion should be adopted."

An American, the Reverend Henry Grew of Philadelphia, then took the floor to fight the women. "The reception of women," he thundered, "as a part of this Convention would, in the view of many, be not only a violation of the customs of England, but of the ordinance of Almighty God, who has a right to appoint our services to His sovereign will."

"I have no objection," added the Reverend Eben Galusha of New York with complacency, "to woman's being the neck to turn the head aright, but do not wish to see her assume the place of the head."

Then George Bradburn of Massachusetts pleaded for the women, recounting all they had done for the cause in America. George Thompson, after praising the work of American women, proposed that Wendell Phillips' motion be withdrawn with the consent of all parties.

Elizabeth, listening breathlessly to the debate, heard this with dismay. But Wendell Phillips still stood firm. Eloquently he defended his position. "When we have submitted," he declared, "to brickbats, and the tar tub and feathers in America, rather than yield to the custom prevalent there of not admitting colored brethren into our friendship, shall we yield to parallel custom or prejudice against women in Old England? We cannot yield this question if we would; for it is a matter of conscience.... We stand here the advocates of the same principle that we contend for in America. We think it right for women to sit by our side there, and we think it right for them to do the same here. We ask the Convention to admit them."

The women in their corner of the hall thrilled to his words.

The opposition, now plainly excited, began to flourish their Bibles and announce what was God's will about the whole matter.

"I have certain views," declared the Reverend A. Harvey of Glasgow, "in relation to the teaching of the Word of God, and of the particular sphere in which woman is to act.... If I were to give a vote in favor of females, sitting and deliberating in such an assembly as this, I should be acting in opposition to the plain teaching of the Word of God."

Other clergymen joined him, waxing eloquent over woman's sphere and the Word of God, and their duty to see that God's will was fulfilled.

Screened from the conflict by the rail and the curtain, the women listened with growing indignation while their sphere and God's will were bandied about by pompous men. How Elizabeth longed to hear Lucretia Mott plead her own case, but Lucretia remained silent beside her.

Then George Bradburn stood up and towering over his fellow delegates, expressed his impatience with the conceit and bigotry of the clergy. "Prove to me gentlemen," he cried, "that your Bible sanctions the slavery of women—the complete subjugation of one-half the race to the other—and I should feel that the best work I could do for humanity would be to make a grand bonfire of every Bible in the universe."

After this, James Birney, in all his dignity, rose to speak, and to Elizabeth's disgust and disappointment joined forces with the opposition. She hardly expected more from Mr. Birney. But now Henry was on his feet. Would he feel that he must support his colleague? Henry, she knew, believed women had a right to take part in the convention but deplored the animosity this issue stirred up. To her great joy, he made a telling speech in favor of admitting the women delegates. How proudly now her eyes met Lucretia Mott's!

The stormy debate continued for several hours, but Wendell Phillips' motion was defeated and the women delegates were excluded by an overwhelming majority. That they were even admitted as visitors was a concession, for women never before had been admitted to a business meeting.

All this roused Elizabeth far more than the antislavery questions which the convention was called to discuss. Never before had she faced such bitter opposition to women. She could not understand how Abolitionists, who felt the wrongs of the slave so keenly, could fail to comprehend the wrongs which women suffered. Although the legal status of their mothers, wives, sisters, and daughters was similar to that of slaves, they felt no concern. Instead the very mention of the fact stirred up a fury it was hard to explain.

Young and impatient, she wanted to do something about it, and as she and Lucretia Mott walked home that night arm in arm, they made their plans. They would hold a convention in America to advocate the rights of women.

At Mark Moore's the women, deprived of an opportunity to speak at the convention, voiced their views freely; and often there were heated, bitter discussions, so much so that Mr. Birney, who had made himself unpopular with the women at the convention, sought more peaceful quarters.

Through the long days of the convention, women who had worked untiringly for the abolition of slavery, who had sacrificed to make the long ocean voyage, listened to the platitudes of men who had no real comprehension of the meaning of liberty.

Then William Lloyd Garrison arrived, delayed at sea and five days late. Learning of the exclusion of the women delegates, he resolved to take no part in the convention, and no amount of persuasion could alter his purpose. "After battling so many long years for the liberties of African slaves," he declared, "I can take no part in a convention that strikes down the most sacred rights of all women."

So the World's Antislavery Convention continued, while the greatest and most consecrated antislavery worker of the age sat silent in the gallery. For him it was a great sacrifice. It would have meant much to him to take part in the discussions. His opponents called it "play-acting," all done for effect. But from the women he won undying gratitude. To Elizabeth he was a greater hero than ever. She thought him the noblest man she had ever known.

Garrison, lodging at Mark Moore's and talking daily with Elizabeth, wrote home to his wife, "Mrs. Stanton is a fearless woman, and goes for women's rights with all her soul."

There was much to see in London, and Elizabeth and Lucretia Mott often set out together for a sightseeing tour, but became so absorbed in conversation that the object of their expedition was quite forgotten. One day, going with a large party of fellow Abolitionists to the British Museum, they sat down on a bench near the door to rest for a few minutes while the others went on ahead. Three hours passed and the sightseers returned to find them in the same spot completely absorbed in each others' views of religion and social life.

Lucretia had been telling Elizabeth about the doctrines and divisions among the Friends, of the "inward light," of Elias Hicks, of Channing, of practical religion. They talked of women's legal disabilities, of their lack of educational opportunities, their submission to tradition and Bible interpretation, their stupid indifference, their inherent rights as human beings, and of the glowing examples of women's independence and ability. They discussed Mary Wollstonecraft's social theories and her demands for equality for women. Elizabeth had been reading Mary Wollstonecraft's writings, Combe's *Constitution of Man* and *Moral Philosophy,* and Channing's works—all of which were banned except among liberals. She had thought much over what she had read, and now to hear Lucretia Mott freely discussing what she had scarcely dared think was such joy that the wonders of the British Museum paled in comparison. Never before had she met a woman with sufficient confidence in herself to form her own opinions on political, religious, and social matters and to express them courageously.

These two women spent hours together, Elizabeth, young, eager, vivacious, and Lucretia Mott, twenty-two years her senior, with the riper judgment of a mature woman and a well-thought-out scheme of life. Between them grew a love and understanding which endured through the years.

To Elizabeth, Lucretia Mott was everything that a woman should be. She was beautiful in her plain Quaker dress and the white cap which almost covered her smooth brown hair. Her intelligent face with its high brow and clear eyes, lighting up when she talked, was kindly and understanding. Her naturalness and self-possession made her stand out among other women.

They met many prominent, charming English women, interested in the antislavery cause, among them Elizabeth Fry, Amelia Opie, Lady Byron, and Elizabeth Pease, but most of them seemed very placid and indifferent about the convention's insult to women delegates. They alone were stirred to action, and although that action was of necessity deferred for eight long years, the flame kindled at the World's Antislavery Convention continued to burn steadily.

Elizabeth heard Lucretia Mott preach in a Unitarian church. She had never before heard a woman speak in public, although for a long time she had believed women had a right to address public assemblies and speak in church and had often championed this innovation among her more conservative friends. Now to see Lucretia in the pulpit, to hear her preach earnestly and impressively, was like the realization of a happy dream.

Religion still puzzled Elizabeth. The impressions and fears bred in childhood were not easily erased. Again and again she turned to Lucretia Mott for help in this direction. Man-made creeds meant nothing to Lucretia, nor was anything too sacred to be questioned. She had thought out her religion, had refused to abide by the literal interpretation of the Scriptures, and had tried to rule her life by the principles taught by Jesus. This was all like manna in the wilderness to Elizabeth, who rebelled at theological dogma and yet feared it.

William Lloyd Garrison also was a liberal influence in helping
Elizabeth adjust her religious beliefs. At Mark Moore's on Great
Queen Street, she heard him tell what a strict Calvinist he had once
been, how he had lost theology and found religion, and how, because he could no longer believe in the Bible as the direct word
of God, he was called an infidel, although he loved the Bible for
the fundamental truths it contained.

Knowing two religious liberals whom she repected so highly,
gave her courage to think for herself and to measure theological
dogmas with reason and free herself from fear. She could talk
more freely with Lucretia than with Garrison. From her she got
a clearer working knowledge of religion, and she was getting a
woman's interpretation. Little wonder that when she was asked
on her return to America what interested her most in Europe, she
replied unhesitatingly, "Lucretia Mott."

When the Antislavery Convention was over, Henry Stanton
filled lecture engagements in England, Scotland, and Ireland. As
he and Elizabeth were entertained in the homes of the nobility
and wealthy Quakers, they had an unusual opportunity of observing English home life. Elizabeth was intensely interested in their
way of living, and they in turn were curious about her as she was
the first American woman many of them had seen. It troubled her
to hear her beloved Lucretia Mott so often criticized in Quaker
families. Because she was a Hicksite, Orthodox Quakers looked
upon her an an infidel, a heretic, a disturber of the peace. They
said it was she who had made all the trouble at the World's Convention. They accused her of quoting Mary Wollstonecraft and
Thomas Paine. They warned Elizabeth to beware of her influence.
But Elizabeth's faith in Lucretia never wavered. She knew she had
found the woman of her times.

From York, Elizabeth wrote her Cousin Gerrit Smith:

Mr. Birney, Mr. Scoble, Henry and myself are going through all
the principal towns in the Kingdom. These gentlemen lecture almost
every evening—horrifying the British public with the enormities of
our slavery system. Loud cries of shame! fill the House wherever the
negro is mentioned, and the bursts of indignation that follow some of
Henry's graphic descriptions are music to our antislavery ears. We

are kindly and warmly received everywhere. We find it is no disgrace to be an Abolitionist in England, but requires some courage not to be one, as many of our eloquent clergy have found.... Night after night we hear many of the British clergy of all sects declare most solemnly that an American clergyman who is not an Abolitionist in America both in theory and practice shall never enter their pulpit again. At all these meetings we have some great personage in the choir, some member of the royal family, or a Sir or the mayor of the town, in which we may be. Tell Libby that Mr. Birney is much admired by all the ladies young and old and indeed he is a noble man and I like him very much, though he lectures me occasionally through Henry for my want of discretion. He is almost too discreet I think, too fearful of what "the people" may say.... However it will do me no harm to be checked occasionally, and as we are among strangers and on such a mission we cannot be too serious. I feel that I am a little too gay, and much too ignorant on the subject of slavery for the circumstances in which I am placed. I hope Cousin Nancy will write me one of her long serious letters often. Henry often wishes that I was more like her. I console him by telling him that Cousin Nancy was quite gay and frolicsome once.

They went to Paris for a month. As Henry was sending articles about his trip to New York papers and to the *National Era* in Washington, they were eager to collect as much interesting and accurate information as possible. The great difference between the two countries impressed them, the difference in the temper of the people: the uproar, confusion, and enthusiasm of the French; the silence, the order, the cleanliness of the English. Brought up to a strict, solemn Puritan Sunday, Elizabeth was delighted with the gay festive Sunday of the Parisians, but so deep were the impressions of childhood that the first time she took part in these festivities, she felt very guilty and would not have been surprised had she been struck down by a chastening bolt of lightning.

In Scotland they were alone for a time and took long walking trips, reveling in the beauty of the country. They were in Dublin when enthusiasm for the Repeal of the Union was at its height and dined one evening with Daniel O'Connell. Elizabeth revered him for his devotion to the liberation of Ireland, but even more for his noble attitude toward women at the World's Antislavery Convention. When she asked him if he hoped to carry the Repeal measure, he replied, "No, but it is always good to claim the uttermost and then you will be sure to get something." She remembered this and made it her policy for the future.

She spent a few happy days in the home of Hannah and Richard Webb in Dublin, and Hannah Webb, writing to Sarah Pugh, said, "Elizabeth Stanton, with whom we were highly delighted, is a brave upholder of woman's rights," while Richard Webb added, "She is better than a whole third of that portion of the Pledged Philanthropy which assembled in Freemasons' Hall."

In November, after six months of travel, she and Henry boarded the *Sirius* of the Cunard Line, bound for Boston. It was one of the first transatlantic steamships and not yet considered seaworthy, but the shorter voyage during those dreary November days appealed to them both. After eighteen long stormy days, they landed in Boston and hurried to New York by rail, arriving there just in time to spend Christmas with the Eatons. It was joyous to be at home again. To Elizabeth the sky was clearer, the air more refreshing, the sunlight more brilliant than in any other land.

She had been very happy with Henry in Europe. What life held for them now, she did not know, but their love was cemented by common interests. She had great confidence in Henry. She was wiser and surer of herself. There was work to be done for women, but the way was not yet clear. Life was very good, very satisfying. The future beckoned alluringly.

IV

JOHNSTOWN, BOSTON, AND SENECA FALLS

AFTER spending the holidays in New York with the Eatons, Elizabeth and Henry set out by stage-sleigh for Johnstown, Elizabeth, jubilant at the prospect of seeing her family and friends after her long eventful journey, and Henry, happy in her happiness —proud that he was not bringing back a sorrowful, disillusioned bride as had been prophesied.

At Judge Cady's suggestion, Henry took up the study of law in his office, and so marked were his legal talents that much of the Judge's prejudice against his "abolition-mad" son-in-law wore away. For a little over a year, Henry and Elizabeth lived in the Cady household.

It was a far more serious and forceful Elizabeth who returned to Johnstown. She had gained poise and a wider interest in life. Her decision to marry Henry in spite of the opposition of her family had been a turning point in her mental life. From then on she had confidence in her ability to think things out for herself. Lucretia Mott's influence encouraged this confidence and showed her the possibilities of liberated womanhood. Even then she realized that she owed Lucretia as great a debt of gratitude as one mind could owe another.

Woman's rights were still her main interest and she discussed the subject whenever she could. She wrote Lucretia:

> The more I think on the present condition of woman, the more I am oppressed with the reality of her degradation. The laws of our country, how unjust they are! Our customs, how vicious! What God has made sinful, both in man and woman, custom has made sinful in women alone.

She kept up a correspondence with the friends she had made in England, especially with Elizabeth Pease, sending her the latest antislavery news and explaining her own position as a Third Party

Abolitionist—why she could not follow Garrison all the way, although she admired him greatly. She wrote her:

> It may be that my great love for Henry may warp my judgment in favor of some of his opinions but I claim the right to look at his actions and opinions with the same freedom and impartiality that I do at those of any other man. Well, then, as I am not yet fully converted to the doctrine of no human government, I am in favor of political action, and the organization of a Third Party is the most efficient way of calling forth and directing action. So long as we are to be governed by human laws, I should be unwilling to have the making and administration of those laws left entirely to the selfish and unprincipled part of the community, which would be the case should all honest men refuse to mingle in political affairs. Many of Garrison's party are in favor of political action, but not of the Third Party. A party formed and candidates nominated, afford a rallying point, a nucleus around which the Abolitionists may gather, which gives a reality to antislavery principles.

Then for a time, another interest absorbed her. Her first child was born March 2, 1842, and was named after her father, Daniel Cady Stanton.

Eager to bring her baby up in the best possible way, she read every book she could find on the subject, but they were, as she expressed it, "as confusing and unsatisfactory as the longer and shorter catechism." She then realized that she would have to rely very largely on her own intelligence and common sense.

The nurse had her own very firm ideas about bathing and bandaging babies, about temperature and fresh air, about covering their faces, and dosing them with herbs, and nothing that Elizabeth could say would impress her in the least. Had she not borne ten children and nursed countless others, while this was Elizabeth's first baby!

Although Elizabeth did not want the child bandaged, the nurse insisted on swathing him thoroughly every morning lest he fall apart, and Elizabeth, determined that his little body be left free to develop, as regularly removed the bandages. Fully converted to homeopathy through Edward Bayard, she refused to allow the baby to be dosed with herbs. She insisted on regular feedings, fresh air, and sunshine, but it took constant watchfulness to see that her plans were carried out.

The doctors were as ignorant as the nurses in regard to the care of babies, and when after four days it was discovered that Daniel's collar bone was bent, the doctor put on a tight bandage which noticeably interfered with his circulation. Elizabeth took it off and called another doctor who announced that the bandage would have crippled the child. He tried a mode of bandaging which proved to be no better, and she in despair decided to handle the matter herself. To the consternation of the nurse and her family, she again took off the doctor's bandage and invented one of her own which corrected the difficulty.

When the doctors smilingly commented, "Well, after all, a mother's instinct is better than a man's reason," she replied tartly that there was no instinct about it and that she had done some hard thinking before she saw how she could get pressure on the shoulder without impeding the circulation.

"I trusted neither men nor books absolutely after this," she confessed, "either in regard to the heavens above or the earth beneath, but continued to use my 'mother's instinct' if reason is too dignified a term to apply to a woman's thoughts."

In the fall of 1842, Henry Stanton went to Boston to open a law office. Elizabeth stayed on with her family until he was established and spent most of the winter with them in Albany. Here she met many lawyers and legislators and became very much interested in the married woman's property bill which Judge Hertell had been persistently introducing in the legislature since 1836. From him she learned something of the opposition such measures encounter. Women, he explained, because of their ignorance, were not asking for the bill, but its advocates were the wealthy Dutch aristocracy who hated to see their property pass into the hands of dissolute sons-in-law.

In her limited way, she did her best to work for the bill asking every legislator she met to vote for it and urging Governor Seward to give it his support. But not until six years later, in 1848, did it become a law.

Late that winter she and the baby finally joined Henry in Boston, and there an active stimulating life opened before her. She renewed her acquaintance with the antislavery workers whom she had met in Peterboro and London. She attended all the antislavery conventions and fairs, all the temperance, peace, and prison-reform conventions, and as many lectures, theaters, and concerts as possible.

Still searching for an understandable, intelligent religion, she found Theodore Parker's sermons and lectures most satisfying. One of her antislavery friends, Oliver Johnson, was a Parker enthusiast, and together they attended his lectures at Marlborough Chapel. It was a long journey on Sunday from her home to Marlborough Chapel, a two-mile walk, as no public conveyances were available, and she was often so tired when she sank into the pew that she slept through all the preliminary service so as to be fresh for the sermon. Spellbound, she listened through the two hours and left the chapel fired with enthusiasm to make religion a living force in her life. Theodore Parker's rejection of miracles appealed to her intelligence, and she loved to hear him pray to God as "the Father and Mother of us all."

Brook Farm was flourishing at this time. With Marianna Johnson, Oliver Johnson's wife, she spent two days there and met the Ripleys, William Henry Channing, Charles A. Dana, and Mrs. Horace Greeley.

She was now as ardent an Abolitionist as Henry and would not have thought of missing the stirring meetings and conventions at Tremont Temple and Faneuil Hall. She never tired of hearing William Lloyd Garrison and Wendell Phillips hurl their denunciations on the institution of slavery. She was enthralled by the Hutchinson family—the four brothers in blue broadcloth with white turn-down collars and pretty sister Abby in silk and lace, whose antislavery songs always quieted an unfriendly audience. There were times when the mob was menacing and excitement ran high, when the speakers were pelted with rotten eggs and the din was deafening. Northern merchants whose fortunes depended on Southern cotton were as eager to suppress the Abolitionists as were the slaveholders themselves. They fanned the mob spirit. Garrison and Phillips were never safe from their vengeance. In Elizabeth's eyes the heroism of these two men mounted day by day. And she was proud of her husband. He was as eloquent as Phillips. He spoke at the conventions and before Lyceums in near-by towns. He too was a veteran at facing mobs.

At these conventions she made many new friends among men and women whom she had idealized from afar, Lydia Maria Child, Abby Kelly, Maria Chapman, John Pierpont, Parker Pillsbury, and Stephen S. Foster. Here too she first saw and heard Frederick Douglass. Vividly describing the impression he made on her she said:

> He stood there like an African Prince, conscious of his dignity and power, grand in his physical proportions, majestic in his wrath, as with keen wit, satire, and indignation he portrayed the bitterness of slavery, the humiliation of subjection to those who in all human virtues and capacities were inferior to himself.

She had a long talk with him after their first meeting. He was honored to have her sit by his side. She spoke of the subject, ever dear to her heart, woman's rights, and convinced him that it was a most worthy cause. From then on a warm friendship grew between them, and it survived in spite of the differences which sprang up in the years that followed.

During the winter of 1844, she was obliged to give up this busy, interesting life and return to her family in Albany to await the birth of her second son. Busy with his law practice, Henry was unable to be with her when his namesake was born, and he wrote, "I can hardly realize that I have got a new son....I long to see you, my lovely Lee. I am lonesome, cheerless, and homeless without you."

Several months passed before she was able to rejoin him, and then she returned to a new house which her father had bought for her in Chelsea. With everything spic and span, housekeeping was an adventure. She entertained frequently. Whittier was often their guest. He and Henry with their common interest in the antislavery cause and the Liberty party had much to talk over, and her friendliness made the shy, reserved poet feel at home.

In September 1845, another son was born, and because Cousin

Gerrit and Nancy were spending a few days with them at this time, he was named Gerrit Smith Stanton much against Elizabeth's wishes. Although she loved her Cousin Gerrit, she wanted her son to have his own name, a beautiful musical name. She saw no reason for labeling children with family names just to please others. She had a list of perfect names for sons and daughters and as yet had used none of them.

Henry Stanton was now achieving success as a lawyer. It was inspiring to practice in the courts with such men as Rufus Choate, Samuel Hoar, Daniel Webster, and Jeremiah Mason. He could not keep out of politics, was nominated as a Liberty party candidate for Congress from Massachusetts, and defeated. He was regarded as a man of promise. But his health was poor and he began to fear more and more the effects of the damp, raw winters in Boston. He advised with Whittier, Judge Cady, and other friends about moving to a healthier, drier climate. It was hard to think of leaving when he and Elizabeth were so contented and everything pointed to a successful law career for him in Boston. Finally, however, a change became imperative, and they decided on Seneca Falls, New York, for their next home. They chose Seneca Falls not only because they thought it was one of the healthiest regions of the state, but because they had friends there, made when they visited Edward and Tryphena Bayard, and because it was in central New York where a powerful group of liberals and antislavery workers held sway and the political prospects for Henry were good.

Judge Cady owned considerable land in and about Seneca Falls, and when he found that Henry and Elizabeth seriously contemplated living there, he gave Elizabeth a house on the outskirts of the town and a check to help her make it liveable. "You believe," he said, "in woman's ability to do and dare; now go ahead and put your place in order."

As business affairs kept Henry in Boston longer than he anticipated, Elizabeth went on to Seneca Falls alone in the spring of 1847 to open their home. For a month she kept carpenters, painters, paper hangers, and gardeners busy. When she needed advice regarding prices of materials or workmen's wages, she consulted with her neighbors, Judge Sackett and Ansel Bascom. Both came over frequently to see how the house was progressing, and invariably became involved in long and interesting political and woman's rights discussions. New York was revising its constitution at this time and as Mr. Bascom was a member of the constitutional convention, she did her best to show him the need of revising the laws which affected the status of women. Seated on a box, her long, full skirts trailing in the shavings, she pleaded with him to propose an amendment to that article in the state constitution which limited suffrage to men. It would be very simple. All they needed to do was to strike out the word male, and women would be eligible as voters. Mr. Bascom listened sympathetically. He had great respect for this intelligent, eager advocate of woman's rights, and while he admitted that he agreed with her fully regarding the political equality of woman, he would not consent to make himself the laughingstock of the convention by proposing the amendment. However, he aided woman's cause in other ways, and her talks were not completely in vain.

When the house was finished and she was settled there with her family, life soon became humdrum. Henry was away a great deal on business. As the house was far from the center of the town, and there were no sidewalks and the roads were often muddy, she felt very much isolated. Her servants were inexperienced and trying, her three boys, growing up together, were full of mischief and were always outgrowing their clothes. Care of them and the house was unending. She read as much as she could and this made life bearable, but she was hungry for the stimulating companionship she had had in Boston. She began to understand the practical difficulties of women in the average household and how impossible it was for them to develop to advantage when in contact most of their lives with servants and children. The worn anxious look on the faces of most of the women she met made her realize that something must be done to better their condition. If intelligence were applied to the problem, perhaps housekeeping and caring for children could be made easier. Possibly community life or cooperative housekeeping was the answer. She had no intention of being resigned to what was supposed to be woman's sphere, and she thought often during those days of the woman's convention which she and Lucretia Mott had planned in London and rediscussed one memorable day in Boston. If women could only get together to discuss their problems and their needs, it would give them courage to improve their condition. They would see the need of more education, of more opportunities to earn a living, of better pay for the work they did. They would recognize the importance of the married woman's property bill and an improved legal status. They could pool their experiences so as to simplify their housework and learn to take more intelligent care of their children. The possibilities were unending. Although the convention still seemed a long way off, she kept the subject of woman's rights alive wherever she was. Long ago she had asked her friends to direct her letters to Elizabeth Cady Stanton as she saw no reason why she should be addressed as Mrs. Henry B. Stanton and lose her identity. Now she discussed the question of a married woman's name with her friends in and around Seneca Falls. She wrote to one of them:

> Last evening we spoke of the propriety of women being called by the names which are used to designate their sex and not by those assigned to males. You differed with me on the ground that custom had established the rule that a woman must take the whole of her husband's name, particularly when public mention is made of her. ...I have very serious objections, dear Rebecca, to being called Henry. There is a great deal in a name. It often signifies much and may involve a great principle. Ask our colored brethren if there is nothing in a name. Why are slaves nameless unless they take that of their master? Simply because they have no independent existence.... Even so with women. The custom of calling women Mrs. John This and Mrs. Tom That... is founded on the principle that white men are lords of all. I cannot acknowledge this principle as just; therefore I cannot bear the name of another.

Great was her rejoicing when word came in April 1848 that the married woman's property bill had finally passed the legislature. Under its provisions a married woman could now hold real estate in her own name. Heretofore all property owned by a woman at marriage and all received by gift and inheritance had at once become her husband's. He had had the right to sell it or will it away without her consent, to collect the rents and the profits, while all that had been allotted to her was a life interest in one-third of his real estate after his death.

She felt that she had had a small part in this victory for women. She rejoiced for the farm women who had told such heart-rending tales to her father years ago. Their daughters would now never suffer their mothers' humiliation. She was proud that her state was among the first to grant women a small measure of freedom and would set an example for other states. The satisfaction in her own personal gain or freedom was nothing in comparison with her overwhelming desire to win complete freedom for all women.

V

THE FIRST WOMAN'S RIGHTS CONVENTION

A FEW months later, in July 1848, when Elizabeth had been in Seneca Falls barely a year, word came from Lucretia Mott that she would soon be near-by in Waterloo and Auburn. Eagerly Elizabeth accepted an invitation to visit her at the home of Jane and Richard Hunt in Waterloo. Here she made three more Quaker friends, Jane Hunt, Mary McClintock, and Martha C. Wright, Lucretia's sister. They all soon felt intimately bound together by common interests. The four younger women looked up to Lucretia Mott as a leader, seeking enlightenment from her wealth of experience. What Elizabeth lacked in experience, she made up in enthusiasm. She poured out to her new friends all the thoughts about women that had been surging through her mind for months. They freely added their rebellious ideas to hers. None of them were embittered by hard experiences or filled with antagonism toward men. All of them were happily married and were bringing up children. All were intelligent and felt keenly their inferior position before the law, in education, and in the thoughts of the world.

When Elizabeth proposed a convention to consider what steps women should take to improve their status, she had four enthusiastic allies. As they sat around the tea table that evening, the four in their quiet, gray Quaker dress with white kerchiefs and white caps, and Elizabeth in her stylishly cut full skirt and tight basque with touches of lace, they planned to hold a convention a week later in Seneca Falls, and drafted the following call which they sent to the *Seneca County Courier* for publication:

WOMAN'S RIGHTS CONVENTION

A Convention to discuss the social, civil, and religious condition and rights of women will be held in the Wesleyan Chapel, at Seneca Falls, New York, on Wednesday and Thursday, the 19th and 20th of July current; commencing at 10 o'clock A.M. During the first day the meeting will be exclusively for women, who are earnestly invited to attend. The public generally are invited to be present on the second day, when Lucretia Mott, of Philadelphia, and other ladies and gentlemen, will address the convention.

The call was not signed and the public could only guess who was responsible for such a bold undertaking.

Once the call was issued, there was no turning back, and there were but a few days to formulate the plan of action. The five insurgents gathered about the mahogany table [1] in the McClintock home the next morning to draft their Declaration of Principles and Resolutions and to agree on subjects for speeches. They used as models reports of antislavery and temperance conventions with which all of them were more or less familiar. How mild and ineffectual these reports sounded in contrast to the high-sounding declarations of freedom which should issue forth from this convention! When they tried to condense their tumultuous thoughts into the three or four concise lines of a resolution, they encountered unexpected difficulties. Finally Elizabeth, seeking inspiration, picked up the Declaration of Independence and dramatically read it aloud. At once they decided to use this as a basis for their Declaration of Rights and the result was a telling variation of that historic document. They worked hard over it that afternoon, and over the resolutions, and when Elizabeth returned to Seneca Falls, she continued to work over both, and with Henry's help collected a list of eighteen legal grievances from the statute books to correspond with the eighteen listed by the signers of the original Declaration of Independence.

She had discovered when she helped write the Declaration and resolutions that she had real facility of expression. She liked the rhythm and sound of her phrases and knew how to put life into words. Lucretia Mott was a natural orator, but writing for her was laborious. So the burden of the composition fell on Elizabeth's shoulders. After all, the convention was her idea, was to be held in her town, and she felt very responsible.

[1] This table is on exhibit at the Smithsonian Institution, Washington.

She was planning a speech which would sum up all she had been thinking about, women through the years. She drafted a resolution wholly her own. No one else had anything to do with it or knew anything about it. It was to come ninth on the list and it read: "RESOLVED, That it is the duty of the women of this country to secure for themselves their sacred right to the elective franchise." It seemed so important and so basic to her that she could not imagine anyone questioning or opposing it.

When she talked it over with Henry, who had been so ready to help with the list of grievances, he vehemently opposed it, and urged her to give up all idea of proposing anything so revolutionary. But she had come to the conclusion that there was one thing which women needed more than anything else—the right to vote. Through the exercise of the ballot, they would be revalued and could more readily win their freedom. If this was the basic need, the short cut, why not ask for it? Had not the veteran reformer, Daniel O'Connell, said to her, "It is always good policy to claim the uttermost, and then you will be sure to get something." She would not listen to Henry's protests, and he, feeling just as keenly about it as she did, told her that since she was bound to turn the proceedings into a farce, he would wash his hands of the whole business. He threatened to leave town and attend none of the meetings, and he kept his word.

It was hard not to have Henry's support, and she eagerly awaited Lucretia Mott's arrival, longing for her advice and approval. Then Lucretia sent word that on account of James's illness she might not be able to come to Seneca Falls. This was almost more than Elizabeth could bear. There were moments when she was so gripped by terror, when the thought of directing such a convention and addressing a large audience was so appalling that she longed to run away. But a principle and an ideal were involved, and she turned her back on her fears. Lucretia arrived after all with her husband and Martha Wright, and as soon as she could, Elizabeth read her the resolution. Even Lucretia discouraged her and exclaimed almost impatiently, "Oh Lizzie! If thou demands that, thou will make us ridiculous! We must go slowly."

Still Elizabeth was not convinced. Frederick Douglass was coming. She would consult him. The fiery apostle of an enslaved people would understand the need of a downtrodden class. When she asked him what he felt the Negroes needed more than anything else to put them on the right plane, he promptly replied, "The ballot."

"And I see," she exultingly retorted, "that the ballot is exactly what we women need."

She read him her resolution and begged him to speak for it. He assured her that he would. She was skeptical of her own ability to win over her many opponents.

On the morning of July 19, carriage loads of curious men and women drove into Seneca Falls and gathered in the Wesleyan chapel, where the convention was to be held. Although only women were expected to attend the first day's meeting, so many men appeared and expressed real interest that they were allowed to stay.

As Elizabeth watched the audience grow and heard the animated hum of their conversation, the realization of the bold, unprecedented step she had taken swept over her, and she began to battle heroically with stage fright and a numbing sense of hopelessness.

At eleven o'clock James Mott took the chair, for the women had decided that since they were inexperienced in conducting meetings it would be well to have a man in charge for the first time. They could trust James Mott. Tall and dignified, in his Quaker costume, he gave the meeting an impressive air. Mary McClintock was appointed secretary. Lucretia Mott, the one woman in the group accustomed to public speaking, then told the expectant crowd why the convention had been called and what its objects were. She pictured for them the humiliating condition of women throughout the world and explained how important it was that their status be raised. She urged all the women present to set aside the tradition that it was unladylike to speak in public, and to take part freely in the discussion.

Then Elizabeth Cady Stanton in a clear, unfaltering voice read the Declaration of Sentiments, putting all that she felt into the reading. The ringing passages, written by Thomas Jefferson and now pleading for the freedom of women, were very telling as they came from the lips of one so earnest and attractive:

> We hold these truths to be self-evident that all men and women are created equal; that they are endowed by their Creator with certain inalienable rights; that among these are life, liberty, and the pursuit of happiness; that to secure these rights governments are instituted, deriving their just powers from the consent of the governed. . . .
> The history of mankind is a history of repeated injuries and usurpations on the part of man toward woman, having in direct object the establishment of an absolute tyranny over her. To prove this, let facts be submitted to a candid world.

She enumerated in phraseology appropriate to the Declaration eighteen startling grievances. Women were deprived of the ballot, of property rights, of the right to their persons, of rights over their children. Married women were civilly dead and single women property owners were taxed without representation. Women were deprived of educational opportunities and hampered in earning a living. They were degraded by a double standard of morals and by man's assumption that he could map out their sphere. She concluded:

> Now in view of this entire disfranchisement of one-half the people of this country, their social and religious degradation —in view of the unjust laws above mentioned, and because women do feel themselves aggrieved, oppressed, and fraudulently deprived of their most sacred rights, we insist that they have immediate admission to all the rights and privileges which belong to them as citizens of the United States. In entering upon the great work before us, we anticipate no small amount of misconception, misrepresentation, and ridicule; but we shall use every instrumentality within our power to effect our object. We shall employ agents, circulate tracts, petition the State and National legislatures, and endeavor to enlist the pulpit and the press in our behalf. We hope this Convention will be followed by a series of Conventions embracing every part of the country.

The Declaration of Sentiments was then explained and amplified by Lucretia Mott, Thomas and Mary Ann McClintock, Amy Post, Frederick Douglass, Ansel Bascom, and others. Ansel Bascom, who had been a member of the New York State Constitutional

Convention and whose sympathies Elizabeth had enlisted when she first came to Seneca Falls, told of the new Married Woman's Property Law in New York State, and of the general attitude toward woman's rights in Albany. There was much free and friendly discussion of the whole subject by both men and women and no objections to the movement were forthcoming—even when asked for.

On the second day the Declaration of Sentiments was passed unanimously and the resolutions were proposed one by one, discussed, and unanimously adopted until Elizabeth, fully aware of the consternation she was causing, stood up with shining eyes and burning cheeks and offered her resolution: "RESOLVED, That it is the duty of the women of this country to secure to themselves their sacred right to the elective franchise." She spoke for it with fervor, surprised at her own eloquence, and Frederick Douglass, pleading for it, moved the audience as he always did his antislavery friends. But there was a decided feeling against the resolution, not against its principle, but against its expediency—a fear that it was so radical that it would make the whole movement ridiculous and close the door to more rational reforms.

The debate over it was long, serious, and occasionally heated. That Elizabeth should have proposed it, after being advised and warned against it, caused no little annoyance among her coworkers. When finally it was put to a vote, it was carried by a small majority. Thus the first formal public demand for woman suffrage in the United States was made through the vision, courage, and determination of Elizabeth Cady Stanton.

Little did she realize then in her enthusiasm and in her conviction of the rightness of her demand, that it would take seventy-two long years of almost continuous effort and pleading by women before a woman suffrage amendment was written into the Constitution of the United States. Little did her disapproving coworkers think that it would be the demand for woman suffrage which would draw the women of the country together into powerful organizations and be the banner under which they would crusade for freedom.

When the convention ended, one hundred men and women signed the Declaration of Sentiments, and Elizabeth, Lucretia, Jane, Mary, and Martha, gratified that their first venture had been so well received, began planning a more pretentious convention to be held two weeks later in Rochester.

Their groping gesture for freedom in an obscure village might never have caused a ripple in the thoughts of the nation had it not been for a hostile press. But the newspapers discovered Seneca Falls and the first Woman's Rights Convention and could not leave it alone, treating it either as a huge joke or a menacing gesture. Nothing like this had ever happened before. It had been bad enough to have a few women presume to form female antislavery societies; but these ventures had the redeeming feature of being guided and encouraged by sympathetic men and were mild in comparison. A woman's rights convention was dangerously independent and boded ill. Editors commented with their most biting sarcasm, and clergymen preached sermons on woman's sphere. The ridicule and pressure brought to bear on the signers of the Declaration of Sentiments was so great that one by one they asked to have their names removed.

Even so, on August 2, before the consternation over the Seneca Falls Convention had died down, another Woman's Rights Convention assembled in the Unitarian church in Rochester, New York. Amy Post, an Abolitionist and Quaker, who had charge of the arrangements for this second convention, urged that Abigail Bush be made president, and that she preside over all the meetings. Elizabeth, Lucretia Mott, and Mary Ann McClintock strongly opposed this, feeling that no woman was yet sufficiently at home on the platform or trained in parliamentary procedure to undertake the task. They wanted this meeting, which would reach a much wider circle, to be perfect in every way. But Amy Post was insistent, and as the majority voted in favor of Abigail Bush, she took the chair. She was calm and efficient, and Elizabeth was ashamed that she had doubted her ability.

The meetings had been widely advertised and the Unitarian church was well filled with a curious, yet sympathetic audience.

With more ease and assurance than she had felt at the Seneca Falls Convention, Elizabeth read the Declaration of Sentiments, asking all those who did not agree to state their objections and freely discuss them. Several men volunteered their views, championing the women, but there were others, who were skeptical about granting women too much freedom, some who disapproved of their occupying the pulpit, and some who felt that without man's headship marriage would go on the rocks. The women answered their arguments firmly and intelligently, and Elizabeth, alert to every objection, was surprised at the number of times she rose to speak.

Reports were given, showing what meager opportunities women had for earning a living, how tradition and prejudice had kept them for the most part in one low-paid occupation, that of seamstress with wages ranging from thirty-one cents to thirty-eight cents a day. But the response was encouraging. The convention was overwhelmingly in favor of opening new fields for women and demanding equal pay for equal work. Elizabeth called attention to the inadequate salaries paid household servants and suggested that women begin their reforms in their own homes.

There was a dramatic moment at one of the sessions when a handsome young woman, Rebecca Sanford, whom none of them knew, asked to say a few words. She was a young bride on her way to the West. Hearing of the convention, she had delayed her departure so that she could attend. Escorted to the platform by her proud and approving husband, she spoke for twenty minutes with eloquence and feeling. The spontaneity of this act made Elizabeth and her coworkers feel that women throughout the country were joining hands.

The Seneca Falls resolutions were proposed one by one and passed, none causing so much discussion and opposition as Elizabeth's suffrage resolution. Frederick Douglass again came to its defense, appealing for the complete equality of woman, and it was passed. People were getting used to that astonishing demand. It did not seem quite so radical and ill-advised as at Seneca Falls.

The Rochester Convention itself caused little newspaper comment. It was the Declaration of Sentiments associated with the

Seneca Falls Convention and Elizabeth's suffrage resolution which attracted attention. Papers throughout the country continued to comment facetiously and insultingly upon these serious, noble efforts of women to better their condition. They flaunted headlines, such as these, "Insurrection Among Women," "The Reign of Petticoats," "Bolting Among the Ladies," "Petticoats vs. Boots." They described the sponsors of the conventions as a rebellious group of aged spinsters, crossed in love, trying to avenge themselves and make others more miserable than themselves. They accused them of neglecting their home duties, of wishing to wear men's clothes, of aiming to put men in the kitchen while they swaggered about the world. The *Philadelphia Public Ledger* fed its public with this sentimental claptrap:

> A woman is nobody. A wife is everything. A pretty girl is equal to ten thousand men, and a mother is, next to God, all powerful.... The ladies of Philadelphia, therefore, under the influence of the most serious sober second thoughts are resolved to maintain their rights as Wives, Belles, Virgins, and Mothers, and not as Women.

Horace Greeley's *New York Tribune* was the one influential newspaper that treated the question of woman's rights with any seriousness or respect. His editorial warmed Elizabeth's heart. He wrote:

> It is easy to be smart, to be droll, to be facetious in opposition to the demands of these Female Reformers; and in decrying assumptions so novel and opposed to established habits and usages, a little wit will go a great way. But when a sincere republican is asked to say in sober earnest what adequate reason he can give for refusing the demand of women to an equal participation with men in political rights, he must answer, None at all. True, he may say that he believes it unwise in them to make the demand—he may say the great majority desire no such thing; that they prefer to devote their time to the discharge of home duties, etc.... However unwise and mistaken the demand, it is but the assertion of a natural right and as such must be conceded.

Encouraged by Horace Greeley's attitude, Elizabeth began writing letters to the *Tribune* stating her position on this vital subject. To her great joy they were published. She sent letters to other papers, correcting misstatements and spreading her message. To

George G. Cooper, Editor of the *National Reformer,* Rochester, New York, she wrote:

> If God has assigned a sphere to man and one to woman, we claim the right ourselves to judge of His design in reference to us, and we accord to man the same privilege. We think that a man has quite enough to do to find out his own individual calling, without being taxed to find out also where every woman belongs.... There is no such thing as sphere for sex. Every man has a different sphere in which he may or may not shine, and it is the same with every woman, and the same woman may have a different sphere at different times.

She and Lucretia Mott corresponded more frequently than before, sending each other clippings and planning future conventions. Commenting on the sarcastic *New York Herald* editorial by James Gordon Bennett, she wrote Lucretia:

> I learn from the editorial that Bennett published in extenso, in a previous issue, our "Declaration." That is just what I wanted. Imagine the publicity given to our ideas by thus appearing in a widely circulated sheet like the *Herald.* It will start women thinking, and men too; and when men and women think about a new question, the first step in progress is taken. The great fault of mankind is that it will not think....I fully agree with Mr. Bennett's closing lines, even if you may not. Here they are: "We are much mistaken if Lucretia would not make a better President than some of those who have lately tenanted the White House." Of course you would.

She read eagerly every comment on the conventions, amazed at the stir they had created, and pasted clippings in a small red-backed scrapbook,[2] sensing even then that the records of the first Woman's Rights Convention would some day be valuable.

She felt as if she had joined forces with that larger crusade for freedom which was sweeping the world. That liberalizing ferment working in France, Italy, and Germany, questioning the divine right of kings and religious dogma and urging the rights of individuals, had made itself felt in her own land in Jacksonian democracy. New lands were being opened. Men were seeking wider horizons. Science and invention were breaking down barriers.

---

[2] Congressional Library—in collection given by Harriet Stanton Blatch.

Democracy was being strengthened, and she and a small group of women looked forward to a full share in democracy.

In the years that followed, when this first Woman's Rights Convention was heralded as one of the outstanding events of the woman's movement, Lucretia Mott was frequently given the credit for initiating it, but Lucretia, who was fairness itself, knew that she did not deserve this honor and often said so. She wrote Elizabeth in 1854:

> Remember the first Convention originated with thee. When we were walking the streets of Boston together in 1841, to find Elizabeth Moore's daughter, thou asked if we could not have a convention for Woman's Rights. Then when James and self were attending the yearly meeting at Waterloo in forty-eight ... thou again proposed the Convention which was afterward held at Seneca Falls. I have never liked the undeserved praise in the Reports of that Meeting's proceedings, of being "the moving spirit of that occasion," when to thyself belongs the honor, aided so efficiently by the McClintocks.

The facts have been blurred through telling and retelling, through prejudice, and through preference for this or that heroine, but historical records make it plain that the first Woman's Rights Convention was the idea and the dream of Elizabeth Cady Stanton, that she assumed the responsibility in her own town of making it a success, and that, by having the vision and the courage to present and plead for her suffrage resolution, she lighted a torch which led women to enfranchisement and which is still pointing the way to full and equal citizenship rights.

VI

AMELIA BLOOMER AND THE "LILY"

E LIZABETH began at once to do what she could to rouse the women in her own village. She knew that women needed to think more on world subjects and discuss them with men, and so, with the help of some of her friends, she started a conversation club of men and women, patterned after the conversations which Margaret Fuller had held some years before in Boston.

There was much of interest for the club to debate in 1849 and in the years that followed. The country was in a state of unrest. The discovery of gold in California had started a tremendous westward movement and the importance of building railroads to open up the West was being realized. Immigrants were pouring into the country from famine-racked Ireland and central Europe, and Americans were beginning to wonder what effect such numbers of foreigners would have upon republican institutions. The slavery question had become acute. Both the North and the South threatened secession. The contest over the territories was bitter—whether they should be admitted into the Union as slave or free states. The admission of California as a free state, the abolition of slavery in the District of Columbia, the passage of the Fugitive Slave Law provoked strong feeling everywhere. The Seneca Falls Conversation Club kept both men and women alert and informed on these subjects.

Elizabeth continued to write for the newspapers, answering the many bitter attacks which were still being made against those who took part in the woman's rights conventions. She had to read a great deal to be sure of her facts, studying canon law, civil law, and history, and turning to the Bible to refute the arguments of the clergy. Now and then she delivered a lecture in a near-by town.

She was happier than she had ever been. Her husband was helpful and sympathetic, and this overshadowed the disapproval of her father. Judge Cady's conservative nature recoiled from the unpleasant publicity which followed the Seneca Falls and Rochester conventions. He hoped this would teach his daughter a lesson. But when he saw that she continued to stir up unfavorable comment by writing and speaking, he wondered if her mind were affected and hurried to Seneca Falls to find out for himself.

He arrived the night before she was to lecture at Junius and began at once to raise objections and put obstacles in the way. She saw that there was going to be a contest between them. She had defied him once when she married Henry and she would oppose him again. It was a matter of conscience, of principle. It had to be done.

They thrashed it out in the parlor that night. Judge Cady used all the pressure of a father and a skilled lawyer to win his point, pleading to save his daughter, as he thought. But Elizabeth, unconvinced, made it very plain that she must fulfill her engagement, adding with pride that she expected to receive ten dollars for it. It was her first lecture for pay.

Annoyed at her defiance, her father delivered his ultimatum, implying that he would disinherit her if she persisted. Then seizing his candle, he stalked out of the room by one door while she with her candle indignantly marched through the other.

She delivered her lecture in Junius.

About this time, a woman began to serve as deputy postmaster of Seneca Falls—Amelia Bloomer, whose husband was postmaster. Many people regarded such a position entirely out of woman's sphere, and made caustic comments, but Amelia Bloomer was determined to prove that if women had the capacity, they had the right to enter any occupation. As this was in line with Elizabeth's ideas, the two women soon put their heads together.

Amelia Bloomer was small in stature, with auburn hair and a friendly smile. She fairly seethed with independent ideas and a capacity for work. In addition to her duties in the post office, she began publishing for her woman's temperance society a monthly paper, called the *Lily*. The first number appeared in January 1849. It was to have been issued by a committee of ladies, but as they lost courage one by one, the work all fell upon her. Her husband, who was editor of the *Seneca Falls County Courier* as well as postmaster, advised against the venture, but she was determined to carry it through, for she did not want people to say that it was just like women to give up. So she wrote for the paper, contracted for the printing, read proof, prepared the paper for mailing, and sent out circulars for subscribers. She fitted up a neat little room adjoining the post office where women of the town could meet to exchange ideas and read the papers and magazines that came to her as editor of the *Lily*. Elizabeth stopped in frequently for a good talk and was soon writing articles for the *Lily* under the signature, Sun Flower.

The *Lily* was a modest little six-page paper, with a purpose noble and pure enough to satisfy the severest critic. "Like the beautiful flower from which it derives its name," declared Amelia in the first issue, "we shall strive to make the *Lily* the emblem of 'sweetness and purity'; and may heaven smile upon our attempt to advocate the great cause of Temperance reform!"

Amelia's great interest was temperance, Elizabeth's, woman's rights. It was inevitable with Elizabeth writing for the *Lily* that sooner or later the subject of woman's rights would creep into the paper. While Amelia Bloomer had liberal and decided ideas about woman's status, she was not like Elizabeth an out-and-out feminist. She was more cautious, less ready to antagonize, more eager to compromise. She had attended the Seneca Falls Convention, but had taken no part, not even signing the Declaration of Sentiments. But she was genuinely dissatisfied with the inferior position of women, and even before Elizabeth exerted her influence on the paper, wrote editorials dealing with the unjust discriminations against women in the law.

The pseudonym Sun Flower, so characteristic of the vitality and color that Elizabeth was to impart to the quiet, modest *Lily,* now dotted the pages of that little paper. At night, after the children were in bed and all was quiet, she sat before the living-room fire, writing. Her first contribution was on the subject of temperance— a series of conversations betwen mother and son, called "Henry Niel and His Mother." In her first woman's rights article, "Woman," published January 1, 1850, she discussed the inferior position of women in all countries. Then followed a series, examining and refuting man's claim to mental and physical superiority. A bill making drunkenness a ground for divorce was introduced in the legislature. The idea appealed to her and she began to champion it.

She grew bolder, dropped the pseudonym, and signed her initials, E.C.S. She wrote on all sorts of subjects from "Why Must Women Vote" to "Housekeeping," "Sewing," and "Free Schools," and always made them interesting and different. Readers began to look for her initials and prepare to be startled and stimulated.

Her highly original ideas on sewing caused considerable consternation, for sewing had become an accepted part of every woman's life. She called sewing a worthless and unhealthy employment, a dead loss to the one who does it. She wrote:

> As an amusement it is contemptible; as an educator of head or heart, worthless; as a developer of muscle, of no avail; as a support, the most miserable of trades. It is a continued drain on sight and strength, on health and life, and it should be the study of every woman to do as little of it as possible.

She acknowledged that some sewing must be done, but she made war on all the frills and furbelows with which women burdened themselves, thus shutting out of their lives opportunities for mental and physical development:

> What use is all the flummering, puffing, and mysterious folding we see in ladies' dresses? What use in ruffles on round pillow cases, night caps, and children's clothes? What use in making shirts for our lords in the wonderful manner we now do, with all those tiny plaits, and rows of stitching down before, and round the collars and wrist bands? Why, all these things are done, to make the men, children, women, chairs, sofas, and tables look pretty.... If the women for the last fifty years had spent all the time they have wasted in furbelowing their rags, in riding, walking, or playing on the lawn with their children, the whole race would look ten times as well as they do now!

But some sewing must be done, and she recommended that each man and woman do his or her own, or leave it to that class especially fitted for it, those idle men who lounge about stores and on street corners whittling and talking away the hours. She continued:

JAMES AND LUCRETIA MOTT ABOUT 1842
(From *James and Lucretia Mott,* by Anna Davis Hallowell. Courtesy of Houghton Mifflin Company)

ELIZABETH CADY STANTON IN HER BLOOMER COSTUME

We must see that boys are early taught to sew. Seriously, I see no reason why boys should be left to roam the streets, day and night, wholly unemployed, a nuisance to everybody, and a curse to themselves, whilst their sisters are over-taxed at home to make and mend their clothes. It will be a glorious day for the emancipation of those of our sex who have long been slaves to the needle, when men and boys make their own clothes, and women make theirs in the plainest possible manner.

She had many novel ideas, advocating, for example, that young women pay for their own amusements instead of expecting their escorts to shoulder the burden. The present custom, she maintained, was degrading to women and an unnecessary financial drain on young men.

Who but Elizabeth Cady Stanton would be bold enough to publish such heretical doctrine! She had begun her lifelong campaign against women's foibles and false traditions.

Much to her joy she found that the seed planted at the Seneca Falls Convention was bearing fruit. Word came from Ohio in the spring of 1850 that women in the town of Salem were to hold a woman's rights convention, prior to the revision of the state constitution. She sent a letter of encouragement and urged them to ask for the ballot. All this was noted in the *Lily*.

Then Paulina Wright Davis wrote that she and Lucy Stone were planning a national woman's rights convention in Worcester, Massachusetts, in October, and wanted her name on the call. Elizabeth had admired both of these women from afar and was proud to be regarded as their colleague. She had heard of Lucy Stone through her antislavery friends who were enthusiastic about her eloquence on the lecture platform. Graduated from Oberlin College just three years before, she was drawing large audiences throughout the country and infusing more and more of woman's rights in her pleadings for the Negro.

She had revered Mrs. Davis ever since she had heard how courageously she circulated petitions for the woman's property bill in New York, and how in spite of bitter criticism she had lectured to women on anatomy and physiology, hoping to dispel their pitiful ignorance regarding their physical structure. She recalled the stories she had been told of the first of these lectures, illustrated with a mannequin imported from Paris; how women, when the mannequin was unveiled, fainted, covered their eyes, or left the class in dismay and moral indignation.

How women had progressed! They were now ready for a national convention on woman's rights.

She was unable to attend but sent a letter to be read at the convention. This letter was printed in the *Lily*. Thus the *Lily,* founded to promote temperance, gradually became the medium—the only one in the whole country—for spreading among women accurate news of the ever-growing woman's rights movement.

Elizabeth read the reports of convention with the greatest eagerness, gratified to find among the resolutions one demanding suffrage for women. It had been worth-while battling alone for her suffrage resolution at Seneca Falls. The idea had now become an important part of every convention.

The newspapers still ridiculed to be sure, and this last noble effort was scornfully labeled the "Hen Convention," but a dignified report of it found its way through the columns of the weekly *New York Tribune* to England to Harriet Taylor, later Mrs. John Stuart Mill, and inspired her to write for the *Westminster Review* a most helpful essay, "Enfranchisement of Women." Elizabeth was jubilant when some months later she read this able defense of the demands of American women. She recalled the attitude toward women at the London Convention ten years before and realized that because of the efforts of American feminists, an Englishwoman could now proclaim in an important periodical woman's right to the elective franchise.

Appointed by the Worcester Convention to take charge of circulating woman suffrage petitions in western New York, she began at once getting signatures, and sent the petitions on to Henry to be presented to the New York Senate. He had been elected to the Senate in the fall of 1849 as a Free Soil Democrat. Because his ability and his eloquence as an orator were soon recognized and highly respected, he could present these petitions without loss of prestige, and he minded not at all the ridicule and the jibes which invariably followed the mention of that subject.

His law practice, political activities, and the sessions of the legislature kept him away from home a great deal, and he and Elizabeth spent far too little time together. He was in Albany in February 1851 when their fourth son, Theodore, was born. Elizabeth had wanted a daughter so much, a daughter whom she could bring up to be a new woman, but her disappointment was soon forgotten, for she loved Theodore dearly.

She had her theories about childbirth: that it should be painless and easy if women lived more naturally and normally, exercising and wearing loose clothing, and she did her best to live up to her theories, much to the dismay of her family and friends.

She wrote her Cousin Libby, who had married Charles Dudley Miller and was bringing up a family of her own:

> Laugh in your turn. I have actually got my fourth son! Yes, Theodore Stanton bounded upon the stage of life with great ease—comparatively!! He weighs ten and one-half pounds. I was sick but a few hours, and did not lie down until half an hour before he was born, but worked round as hard as I could all night to do up the last things. At seven o'clock Sunday morning, he was born. This morning, (Monday) I got up, bathed myself in cold water, and have sat by the table writing several letters.

To Henry in Albany, she wrote:

> I am regarded as a perfect wonder. Many people are actually impatient, waiting for me to die in order to make their theories good. But I am getting better and stronger every day.

She might have felt rather forlorn with Henry away so much during some of the most trying experiences of her life had it not been that she had found a most unusual housekeeper, a young Quaker, Amelia Willard. With three mischievous boys and a baby to look after, Amelia was a godsend to her. Efficient, neat, and intelligent, she was always ready to help her in any way, to do the heavy housework if necessary, or to cook, to look after the children, or sew. She was as fond of the children as if they had been her own, and in full sympathy with Elizabeth's ideas about woman's rights, very proud of all she did.

It was Amelia who made it possible for her to find time to continue writing for the *Lily,* and as she wrote, she not only developed her own ability but added decidedly to the interest of the paper. Its circulation increased from its initial three hundred to several thousand. It became a clearinghouse for women's ideas and aspirations. Women were now ready to read stern, provocative facts about themselves and were delighted to see in print thoughts which they had secretly cherished but had not dared to utter.

Then suddenly the *Lily* stepped into the limelight, quite innocently and unintentionally, and of course Elizabeth Cady Stanton had a hand in it.

VII

THE BLOOMER COSTUME

During the winter of 1851, Elizabeth Smith Miller came to Seneca Falls to visit her old playmate, Elizabeth Cady Stanton, and she appeared in a new and startling costume. Instead of being swathed in long skirts held out like a bell by five or six heavy, starched petticoats and laced in at the waist by a tight, well-boned corset, as was the fashion, she wore a loose costume with long, full Turkish trousers of black broadcloth, a short skirt and Spanish cloak of the same material, dark furs, and a beaver hat trimmed with feathers. For a woman in those days to let the public know that she possessed legs was the height of indiscretion. Therefore her short skirt showing legs from the knee to the ankle, swathed in Turkish trousers, was daring indeed.

Ideas of dress reform had been instilled in her by her father, Gerrit Smith, who maintained that as long as women wore clothes which crippled and handicapped them physically, they would remain in a state of slavery. She had been brought up to romp and play like a boy. Now that she was a married woman with children to care for, she realized more than ever the inconvenience and debilitating effect of the fashionable dress, and designed for herself a costume similar to one worn in sanitariums by women recuperating from the effects of tight lacing and lack of physical exercise. Her husband, Charles Dudley Miller, stood by her staunchly in this reform.

Elizabeth Cady Stanton was delighted with the costume. Always physically active and with much housework to do for her family, she grew more and more enthusiastic about its possibilities. Seeing her cousin walk upstairs with ease carrying a baby and a candle, while she floundered up in long billowing skirts, made her decide to wear a similar outfit. Soon, much to the consternation of the townspeople, they both walked the streets of Seneca Falls in the new costume. It was a joy now to go for a brisk walk in any kind of weather, with no heavy skirts trailing in the mud or slush. They exulted in their freedom. Amelia Bloomer immediately saw the advantage of the new costume, adopted it, and began advocating it in the *Lily*. Thus Seneca Falls again became the nucleus of a daring reform movement.

The introduction of the new costume caused even more furor than the first Woman's Rights Convention. The *New York Tribune,* commenting upon it, spread the news throughout the country, and newspapers at once began their campaign of ridicule. Because Mrs. Bloomer as editor of the *Lily* was sponsoring the new costume in her paper, the press began flaunting such terms as Bloomerism, Bloomerites, Bloomers, and Bloomer Costume. The name, Bloomer Costume, appealed to the public, and therefore Elizabeth Smith Miller's innovation was labeled for all time with the name of Mrs. Bloomer.

The Bloomer costume at once increased the circulation of the *Lily*. Hundreds of letters poured in from women all over the country asking for patterns. Mrs. Bloomer described it and its variations fully in her magazine, publishing in one number photographs of herself and Elizabeth Cady Stanton clad in their adaptation of the costume. The interest in and approval of the costume among women was astounding. Gymnasts and skaters adopted it. It was worn in sanitariums. Farmers' wives delighted in the freedom it gave them to do their heavy work. In one of the mills in Lowell, Massachusetts, all girls who before July Fourth would adopt the costume were promised a bountiful dinner. One by one the feminists wore it, Paulina Wright Davis, Lucy Stone, Sarah Grimké, and Angelina Grimké Weld being among the first. Yet to wear it took supreme courage, for the public in general was up in arms.

The clergy began preaching sermons against this instrument of the devil, quoting Scripture to prove that the wearing of trousers by women was contrary to the will of God. When a prominent clergyman, denouncing the Bloomer costume, quoted Deuteronomy XXII : 5 : "A woman shall not wear that which pertaineth unto a man, neither shall a man put on a woman's garment; for whosoever doeth these things is an abomination unto Jehovah, thy God," Amelia Bloomer with keen wit and satire quoted Scripture to refute him. Laws of fashion in dress, she said, were older than Moses. There is nothing in the Bible to show that Adam's fig leaf was bifurcated and Eve's was not, nor is there any mention of difference in style of coats of skins which clothed men and women. She called his reasoning a presumption and insult which women everywhere should resent. She said:

> Common sense teaches us that the dress which is the most convenient, and the best adapted to our needs, is the proper dress for both men and women to wear. There is no reason why woman should burden herself with clothes to the detriment of her health, comfort, and life, while man adopts a style that gives freedom of limb and motion.... We do not advocate the same style of dress, altogether for both sexes, and should be sorry to see women dress just like men; yet we should like to see a radical reform in woman's costume so that she might be the free, healthy being God made her instead of the corseted, crippled, dragged-down creature slavery to her clothes has made her.

The *Carpet Bag* of Boston, a humorous publication of the day, was one of the few papers friendly to this reform. In spite of its quips, it published authentic cuts and descriptions of the costume and commented as follows:

> We commend the ladies who have become pioneers in the movement and wish them success in what they have so courageously undertaken!...Superiority of the new costume over the old must, we think, establish itself in the minds of all people of taste.

An able defense of the Bloomer costume by Elizabeth Cady Stanton appeared in the *Carpet Bag* of July 5, 1851. In a foreword she was introduced as the wife of Senator Stanton of New York and daughter of Judge Cady of the Supreme Court of that state. In her usual vivid style she wrote:

> I have seen galleries of beautiful paintings and statuary, in the old world, but nowhere is the ideal female form to be found in a huge whaleboned bodice and bedraggled skirt. If the graceful is what you aim at, study the old painters and sculptors, and not Godey's Book of Fashion. But for us, commonplace, everyday, working characters, who wash and iron, bake and brew, carry water and fat babies up-

stairs and down, bring potatoes, apples, and pans of milk from the cellar, run our own errands, through mud or snow; shovel paths, and work in the garden, why "the drapery" is quite too much—one might as well work with a ball and chain. Is being born a woman so criminal an offense, that we must be doomed to this everlasting bondage?

In spite of the obvious comfort of the Bloomer costume, the public would not be won over. They ridiculed and laughed it out of countenance. Little boys followed its wearers about, throwing snowballs at them and shouting such verses as:

> Gibbery, gibbery gab
> The women had a confab
> And demanded the rights
> To wear the tights
> Gibbery, gibbery gab.

Some women were less tolerant than men. They shunned their Bloomer sisters and clung to their chains with all self-righteousness.

Henry made no objections to Elizabeth's new costume; nor did she have to coax him to be seen with her in public. He accompanied her bravely anywhere. He was amused and good-natured about it and would have his jokes. Hearing about Elizabeth Smith Miller's debut in the reform dress, he wrote his wife from Albany:

How does Lib Miller look in her new Turkish dress? The worst thing about it would be, I should think, sitting down. Then ladies will expose their legs somewhat above the knees, to the delight of those gentlemen who are curious to know whether their lady friends have round and plump legs, or lean and scrawny ones.

But the rest of Elizabeth's family were highly indignant and chagrined. Judge Cady wrote that no woman of good sense and delicacy would make such a guy of herself and he hoped she would not come to Johnstown. Tryphena wept when she heard of Elizabeth's latest escapade. Harriet would not write her sister, and Daniel Eaton sent her a letter of merciless disapproval.

Even her boys, Daniel and Henry, who were at the progressive school conducted by Theodore and Angelina Grimké Weld wrote that they did not want her to visit them in the "short dress."

In reply she wrote to Daniel:

You do not wish me to visit you in a short dress! Why, my dear child, I have no other. Now suppose you and I were taking a long walk in the fields and I had on three long petticoats. Then suppose a bull should take after us. Why, you, with your arms and legs free, could run like a shot, but I, alas! should fall a victim to my graceful flowing drapery.... My petticoats would be caught by the stumps and the briars, and what could I do at the fences? Then you in your agony, when you saw the bull gaining on me, would say, "Oh! how I wish mother could use her legs as I can!" Now why do you wish me to wear what is uncomfortable, inconvenient, and many times dangerous? I'll tell you why. You want me to be like other people. You do not like to have me laughed at. You must learn not to care for what foolish people say. Such good men as Cousin Gerrit and Mr. Weld will tell you that a short dress is the right kind. So no matter if ignorant silly persons do laugh.

Her courage was good in her letters, but it was not always so easy to face the sneers and jibes of the public. Her decision to wear the Bloomer costume was made doubly difficult at this time because of Henry's re-election campaign. During Henry's second year in the Senate the Whigs introduced a bill appropriating millions to enlarge the Erie Canal. In order to prevent its passage in the Senate it was necessary that twelve Democratic Senators resign. Henry B. Stanton was one of the twelve. When the election to fill the vacancies was ordered, Henry campaigned for re-election. It was a close and bitter contest. Gerrit Smith who had always worked in harmony with him, now marshaled the forces against him, even coming to Seneca Falls to make a campaign speech. Of the six Senators who resigned and whose constituencies were in the canal regions, only one, Henry B. Stanton, was re-elected and by a majority of five votes. During the campaign Elizabeth paid the penalty of unconventionality. Her Bloomer costume made good election propaganda. She wrote Elizabeth Smith Miller all about it:

I have just received a letter from your father rejoicing over the supposed defeat of my husband last week Tuesday. We have had a crowing letter from Papa also. But he and Cousin Gerrit have "gone off" too soon. The first reached me whilst the guns are firing, crackers popping and bonfires burning in honor of Henry's triumph over the foul lies and cruel machinations of his Whig enemies. I rejoice in the victory with my whole soul, for in spite of all my seeming liberality towards his opposers, I would sooner see every relative and friend I have on the face of the earth blown into thin air, and that old ditch running from Buffalo to Albany filled with mud, than have Henry mortified by defeat in this election.

The severest trial of my life, dear Lizzie, I have just passed through. Your father's tour through this district turned out a more bitter pill for me than for the one for whom it was intended. My going to hear Cousin Gerrit speak and walking out with him flew like wildfire, and all the Whigs had it that Mr. Stanton's family and friends were against him, even his wife disapproving his course. My name was hawked about the streets and in all the public meetings. Two men had a fight in one meeting about my hat. My dress was a subject of the severest animadversions. Some good Democrats said they would not vote for a man whose wife wore the Bloomers. Then the Whigs and pro-canal Democrats—you know the party was not united on the question—got up all kinds of stories about me. Some said I was bribed by Cousin Gerrit to go against Henry. The truth is I felt no interest whatever in the canal question per se, but desired Henry's re-election. But as no one seemed satisfied with my neutral position, after posting myself on the subject, and the Constitution's bearing thereon, I came out an unterrified Democrat, defending resignation and abhorring debt. This seemed to increase the activity of the street urchins, who hissed and sung and screamed "breeches" with the greatest vim throughout the whole campaign. The night after the election...when it was reported that Henry was defeated, they shouted in chorus all through the streets:

> Heigh! ho! the carrion crow
> Mrs. Stanton's all the go:
> Twenty tailors take the stitches,
> Mrs. Stanton wears the breeches.

But tonight no dog dares wag his jaw....

So you see, dear Lizzie, I have had my battle to fight here, whilst you outraged the metropolitans. When I heard of the cold looks you had to encounter, my bruised heart did pity you. Well, we have lived through it—I through this campaign and you through this New York visit—and are stronger for the trial. But had I counted the cost of the short dress, I would never have put it on; however, I'll never take it off, for now it involves a principle of freedom.

Gradually the animosity toward the Bloomer costume began to die down, and there were times when Elizabeth dared hope that a complete revolution in women's fashions might take place. In such a mood she wrote Amelia Opie in London:

I learn that at a ball at Akron, Ohio, on August 4th., over sixty young ladies were dressed in the full Bloomer costume. Henry says however that it may have been with the intention of making fun of it! However, from Cleveland, in the same State, it is reported that two hundred ladies have come out in the new costume. The *Leroy Gazette* in this State—New York—reports that "it has become quite common to see the new costume worn in the streets." But it is in our western States that the reform seems to be making the most advance. One paper in those regions announces "a large and elegant party" in Toledo where "nearly everybody present, some 60 or 70, as we learn, had the good taste to come out in the new costume." Again we are informed that "at Battle Creek, Michigan, 31 young ladies, in Oriental costume, took part in the celebration of the Fourth."

When she attended the Antislavery Festival at Glen Haven, New York, she found ten women there in the Bloomer costume. It was the chief topic of conversation and was highly praised. So delighted was she to meet approval and not denunciation that she wrote in high spirits to her Cousin Libby:

> Theodosia Gilbert's get-up pleased me very much. She was dressed in a short green tunic not reaching to the knee, and white linen drilling trousers made a la masculine. They all wore white trousers with dresses of various colors....

However, the way was not all smooth even on that day, for as they were returning home, crowds gathered to have a good look at women in the much talked of "shorts." There was no disturbance but it was a trying and anxious time. Aside from the unpleasantness of being on exhibit, there was always danger that one of the curious crowd would rouse the mob spirit and they would be jeered or pelted with rotten eggs.

In a white Bloomer costume with a loose waist which she thought the most glorious part of the reform, she went to a ball some weeks later. "Henry and I danced till four o'clock," she wrote Libby. "Everybody said I looked well and I thought I did."

The bitter opposition of her family finally wore off and they no longer considered her utterly mad and incorrigible. Her mother and sister Margaret, visiting her that fall, lost their dislike for the Bloomer costume. And her father, seeing her move about with such ease in her home, confided to his wife that he would never have noticed the "shorts" if he had not heard so much about them and he thought them "well enough." He had expected to find his daughter dressed just like a man.

Even her brother-in-law, Daniel C. Eaton, who had given his ultimatum some months before, now invited Elizabeth and Elizabeth Smith Miller to pay his family a visit in New York. He wrote:

> You and Mrs. Miller can keep each other in countenance whenever you wish to promenade Broadway in "shorts." The novelty of seeing a Bloomer in New York is so effectually worn off that I hear of no more insult or annoyance being offered to such as choose to wear the costume. So please pack up your coats and trousers and come along.

Thereupon Elizabeth and Elizabeth Smith Miller with the enthusiasm of young reformers swept down upon the fashionable, conservative Eatons in their provocative costumes. They both had done their best to make them attractive, using the best materials and softening them with touches of lace. Elizabeth wrote Amelia Bloomer about her visit:

> I have been in the metropolis several days, have walked the streets, rode in the omnibus, etc. and have met nothing in any way unpleasant. The people look at us, to be sure, but that is nothing. We went over to New Jersey on Saturday. The Ferry Boats and Depots were crowded; but not one disrespectful word was said. We have been taken for Hungarians. We all went to church yesterday, and were treated with marked politeness. The talk about it being dangerous to walk the streets in the new costume is, as I told you, all humbug!

This was encouraging. But the women who wore the Bloomer dress were still a mere handful. How long could they stand being branded as cranks, laughed at, snubbed, and stared at? Their one hope was converting their sisters. Could it be done? The new costume lacked beauty of line but they dared not reveal woman's form to a greater degree. The skirt to the knees with bloomers protruding was an effort to be comfortable yet modest. It was far from artistic. Fashion as decreed by *Godey's Lady's Book* demanded long full skirts touching the ground. The cuts were alluring and graceful. Could a few intrepid reformers with health and comfort on their side hope to compete with the lure of this journal of fashion which reached every part of the country? It was well-nigh impossible. Yet Elizabeth still hoped, and bravely wore and championed the Bloomer.

VIII

SUSAN B. ANTHONY

THAT momentous year 1851, which gave Elizabeth Cady Stanton the physical freedom and mental burden of the Bloomer costume, also brought Susan B. Anthony into her life, and the friendship which developed between these two young women had a most remarkable influence on the progress of American feminism.

When Elizabeth and her friends had called the first Woman's Rights Convention in Seneca Falls in 1848, Susan Brownell Anthony was teaching school in the little village of Canajoharie, New York. She was twenty-eight, rather tired of schoolteaching, and not quite sure in which direction her lifework lay. Reading about the convention, she was amused rather than impressed, but when she went home to Rochester on her vacation, she found that her mother, father, and sister Mary had not only attended the Rochester Woman's Rights Convention but had signed the Declaration of Sentiments and the Resolutions, and that her cousin, Sarah Anthony Burtis, had acted as secretary of the convention. They were so enthusiastic over the meetings and over woman's rights; they talked so much about Mrs. Stanton with her black curls and ruddy cheeks, about Mrs. Mott with her Quaker cap and kerchief of finest muslin, both "speaking so grandly and looking magnificent," that Susan was anxious to meet these two women and learn more about their ideas.

She read with great interest in the *New York Tribune* reports of the Woman's Rights Convention held in Worcester in October 1850. She believed heartily in equal rights and had long chafed at the unfair differences in the salaries of men and women teachers. She had observed the injustice wrought by married women's legal disabilities. Yet she was not convinced that suffrage should be included in women's demands. Brought up as a Quaker, she had not the respect for the ballot that others had. Her father, Daniel

Anthony, like other Quakers, did not vote because he felt it wrong to support a government that believed in war.

Staying at home and managing the farm on the outskirts of Rochester while her father looked after his insurance business in Syracuse during 1850 and 1851, Susan became acquainted with an inspiring group of Rochester liberals, who often on Sundays came out to the Anthony homestead to visit with her father and mother. They were all interested in the cause of woman's rights. They were all Garrisonian Abolitionists, bitterly opposed to the Fugitive Slave Law, which had just been passed. Most of them had a part in the operation of the underground railroad. Through them her interests were widened and her zeal for the antislavery cause grew. She thought seriously of becoming an active worker in this movement, feeling it to be the burning issue of the hour.

In May 1851, she came to Seneca Falls to visit Amelia Bloomer and to attend the antislavery meetings led by William Lloyd Garrison and the English Abolitionist, George Thompson. Her friendship with Amelia Bloomer had grown out of their common interest in the temperance cause. Amelia of course was eager to have Susan meet her stimulating coworker Elizabeth, and Susan was even more anxious to meet the heroine of the Rochester Convention who had been so highly praised by her family.

They met on the street corner after one of the meetings, both Elizabeth and Amelia Bloomer in their novel reform costume, and Susan dressed neatly and properly in gray delaine with pale blue ribbons. They liked each other at once, but Elizabeth was so preoccupied with the responsibility of entertaining William Lloyd Garrison and George Thompson that she neglected to invite Susan and Amelia to dinner, much to their disappointment. Susan and Amelia, however, called on her later, and had such a satisfying talk on the antislavery movement, on temperance, and woman's rights, that when Susan left Seneca Falls, Elizabeth felt she had made a most worth-while friend.

Interest in causes, in widening woman's sphere, was a bond that cemented women's friendships in those years. After a few moments' sympathetic conversation about woman's rights and advancement, women previously unknown to each other felt like lifelong friends. Women who had never seen each other exchanged ideas by letter on this all-absorbing subject. In this way Elizabeth was building up a host of good friends. She was becoming widely known through her articles in the *Lily,* in the *New York Tribune,* and other papers and by the spirited letters she sent to the conventions which she was unable to attend. Women were eager to meet her and talk things over with her. Paulina Wright Davis wrote her: "I am glad you like me for I have long liked you. Years ago, when I used to hear of your speaking out so boldly for the rights of women, I got up a most devout reverence for you and resolved that at some time I would know you." And Elizabeth Oakes Smith, winning fame as a lecturer and author, tried hard to arrange to meet her on a trip to the West, writing her, "Your fervor is delightful to me."

Susan B. Anthony was likewise attracted by this fervor, while Elizabeth felt drawn to Susan by her good, earnest face and genial smile, by her open mind, and by the underlying strength of character which she sensed at once.

In the summer of 1851, Susan again came to Seneca Falls, this time to a meeting of those interested in founding the People's College, and she was entertained by Elizabeth as were Lucy Stone and Horace Greeley. They made their plea for a coeducational institution which unfortunately never materialized. However, it was a rare treat for Lucy, Susan, and Elizabeth to be together and to talk over the needs of women and how to meet them; Lucy, soft-voiced and small, with the eagerness of a girl just out of college, Susan, quiet and serious, and Elizabeth, jolly, with a twinkle in her eyes, and yet with the ardor and driving power of a veteran reformer. Both Lucy and Elizabeth were much farther committed to the cause of woman than was Susan. Both since childhood had keenly sensed the discriminations against women, and both had combated them courageously. When Elizabeth was ready for college in 1830, no college would open its doors to women. Brought up in a well-to-do family with social traditions, she had no thought of teaching school or earning her living in any of the ways then open to women. Lucy, one of a large family, living on a farm in western Massachusetts, where work was hard and life frugal, resolved to study all she could and become a teacher, thus winning financial independence and bettering her position as a woman. She taught a few years and saved, and then studied till her savings were gone. By 1843 she had saved enough to enter Oberlin College, and all through college she put up a determined fight whenever she saw that women were not receiving their education on the same terms as men. Then after college, entering the lecture field for the antislavery cause, she defied tradition and demanded for women the right to speak in public. Her work for the abolition of slavery went hand in hand with her work for the emancipation of women. Elizabeth was married and bringing up a family when Lucy entered Oberlin, but she had not forgotten her resolve to better woman's status, and she made the most of every opportunity that presented itself.

Susan, brought up in a liberal Quaker family, had not been made to feel sex distinctions and discriminations as had Elizabeth and Lucy. Her father, broadminded and sympathetic, encouraged her in every way to improve herself and widen her sphere. But she now saw what other women had to combat, and embryo reformer that she was, she prepared to battle for them.

She began at once working among women for the Daughters of Temperance, for temperance at the time was her particular interest. This movement had been entirely in the hands of men, but since the repeal of the license law women had grown militant and their secret societies, the Daughters of Temperance, came out into the open eager to work with the Sons of Temperance. But the Sons of Temperance were not yet ready to welcome them except as silent members, for when Susan, invited to their convention in Rochester in 1852, rose to speak, she was told by the chairman that "the sisters were not invited there to speak but to listen and to learn."

Such treatment only made her more zealous in building up the strength and importance of the Daughters of Temperance, and

she called a Woman's State Temperance Convention to be held in
Rochester several months later.

By this time she had enlisted Elizabeth's aid. The temperance
movement to Elizabeth was but a steppingstone to woman's rights.
While she believed heartily in temperance, realizing the degrading
influence of drink and how women suffered when they and their
children were at the mercy of drunken husbands, she saw clearly
that women could make but little headway to curb the drink evil
until they had the ballot. Women suffered not so much from the
drunkenness of their husbands as from the fact that the law made
them utterly subservient to and dependent on those husbands.
What was important first and foremost was to improve the legal
status of women. The rest would follow.

But she was biding her time. She was ready to do her part in
women's temperance organizations, for they in themselves were
an expression of woman's growing independence. She could keep
their meetings from being too womanly and conservative by injecting her woman's rights ideas. Her radical statements always
caused a flurry and made women think on subjects they had previously avoided. In the women's temperance movement she sensed
a very conservative element and she warned Susan:

> I think you are doing up the temperance business just right. But
> do not let the conservative element control. For instance you must
> take Mrs. Bloomer's suggestions with great caution, for she has not
> the spirit of the true reformer. At the first Woman's Rights Conven-
> tion, but four years ago, she stood aloof and laughed at us. It was
> only with great effort and patience that she has been brought up to
> her present position. In her paper she will not speak against the
> Fugitive Slave Law, nor in her work to put down intemperance
> will she criticize the equivocal position of the Church. She trusts to
> numbers to build up a cause rather than to principles, to the truth
> and the right. Fatal error! ... All this I say to you and to no one
> else, and you will understand why. I would not speak aught to injure
> Mrs. Bloomer. Yes, I repeat, beware of her conservative suggestions.

Although Susan was showing her executive ability in a marked
degree, she was still very reluctant about making speeches, and
turned more and more to Elizabeth for encouragement and guidance. Elizabeth, she felt, was an experienced worker. She respected

her judgment; she was inspired by her devotion to the cause of woman and stimulated by her radical ideas. Elizabeth gave freely of her time and ability to this young Quaker girl, five years her junior, whom she had come to love dearly, and whose consecration to her beloved cause she dimly foresaw. She now called her Susan, but Susan all her life addressed her formally and yet playfully as Mrs. Stanton.

When Susan wrote Elizabeth of her qualms about speaking, she replied:

> In reference to "thinking on one's feet," I have no doubt that a little practice will render you an admirable lecturer. But you must dress loosely, take a great deal of exercise, be particular about your diet, and sleep enough.... If you are attacked in your meetings, be good natured and keep cool; and if you are simple and truth-loving, no sophistry can confound you.

All this wisdom she had learned from observing her orator husband and using her own good common sense. She was still pleading for loose dress and exercise for women, but she had not yet been able to convert Susan to the Bloomer costume.

In spite of all the encouragement that she gave Susan and the help she gave her in planning and writing her speeches, she was impatient that she herself could not do more. In despair she wrote her:

> O Susan! Susan! You must manage to spend a week with me before the Rochester Convention, for I am afraid that I cannot attend it; I have so much care with all these boys on my hands. But I will write a letter. How much I do long to be free from housekeeping and children, so as to have some time to read, and think, and write. But it may be well for me to understand all the trials of woman's lot, that I may more eloquently proclaim them when the time comes.

But when the first Woman's State Temperance Convention met in Corinthian Hall, Rochester, on April 20, 1852, Elizabeth was there as the presiding officer. She, who four years before had felt that women were too inexperienced to preside at such meetings, now stood before a gathering of five hundred women, as their chairman. She had poise and presence of mind. She spoke easily and loudly enough to be heard throughout the hall. Weak voices were a problem at these early conventions. She held her audience. Yet inwardly she felt very timid and inexperienced, and it was only her firm conviction that she must do all in her power for the advancement of women that gave her the courage to do the work that lay before her.

"How my heart throbs," she said in her opening speech, "to see women assembling together in convention, to inquire what part they have to take in the great moral struggles of humanity."

She then told them what they could do for the cause of temperance and made the startling suggestion that women should divorce confirmed drunkards. She said: "Let no wife remain in the relation of wife with a confirmed drunkard. Let no drunkard be the father of thy children. Let us petition our State government so to modify the laws affecting marriage and the custody of children that a drunkard shall have no claims on either wife or child."

To understand her advocacy of such a drastic step at a time when divorce was a real disgrace for a woman, it is necessary to realize the great amount of suffering among women because of the drunkenness of their husbands. An appalling amount of liquor was consumed by men and boys as a matter of course, and drunkenness was not looked upon in a too unfavorable light.

She was satisfied with no halfway measures, but if this program was too drastic for some of her audience, she had milder temperance work for them. She urged them not to use liquor in any way in the home not even in cooking, and to spread the message of temperance by lectures, tracts, and efficient organizations. But she could not end on such a mild note, and so she concluded her speech with pertinent but ultra-radical remarks aimed at the church, which to most people was an institution that must not be criticized or questioned. She said:

Inasmuch as charity begins at home, let us withdraw our mite from all associations for sending the Gospel across the ocean, for the education of young men for the ministry, for the building up of a theological aristocracy and gorgeous temples to the unknown God, and devote ourselves to the poor and needy around us. Let us feed and clothe the hungry and naked, gather children into schools and provide reading rooms and decent homes for young men and women thrown alone upon the world. Good schools and homes, where the young could ever be surrounded by an atmosphere of purity and virtue, would do much more to prevent immorality and crime in our cities than all the churches in the land could ever possibly do toward the regeneration of the multitude sunk in poverty, ignorance, and vice.

In spite of this, she was elected president of the newly formed Woman's State Temperance Society, with Susan, Amelia Bloomer, and Mary C. Vaughn as secretaries. The society aimed to do more than talk, to do something practical, and voted to employ six women agents at $25 a month to travel through the state to hold meetings and to secure memberships and signatures to pledges and petitions. Susan was one of the agents.

Although the women felt they had held a very successful inspiring convention, the press was incensed especially at Elizabeth Cady Stanton. The *Troy Journal* gave a column and a half to condemning the presumption of the ladies for calling a meeting and doing the talking themselves. It would have been excusable had they called upon men to instruct them. Elizabeth was bitterly censored for her remarks on the church.

Another paper maligned her thus:

> Mrs. Stanton's bearing at this Convention was dogmatic and egotistic in the extreme. And she is described by an eye witness, as resembling a man in her dress, having on boots like a man, pants like a man, dickey like a man, vest like a man....

She of course had worn her Bloomer costume when she was presiding, and this as well as her radical remarks drew fire from the conservatives. The *Lily* thought it well to reply to this attack, giving the impressions of another eye witness:

> Mrs. Stanton's bearing at the Convention was modest, dignified, and unpretending. She was habited in a rich black satin dress, a plain waist after the prevailing style of ladies' dresses, full skirt falling six or eight inches below the knee, plain wide trousers of the same material about her ankles. Neither her "boots," "pants," or "dickey" were "like a man," and she wore no vest—not having adopted as yet the latest Parisian style for ladies. Her hair is cut short, but in that she is not singular at home—many of our ladies of the first respecta-

bility, both married and unmarried, having taken a notion to enjoy the luxury of short hair. And this is not confined to the wearing of the short dress, as some may suppose—the majority of those thus shorn still adhering to the draggling skirts.

All this hostile criticism in no way curbed Elizabeth. The first Woman's Rights Convention had taught her what to expect when she spoke out freely and frankly.

It was a year of conventions. The National Woman's Rights Convention, now held annually, convened in Syracuse in September. Elizabeth could not attend because a baby was coming very soon, but she sent a vigorous letter and resolutions to be read by Susan. At home, waiting for her baby, caring for the children, and mending their clothes, she eagerly awaited Susan's letters.

It was Susan's first Woman's Rights Convention and thoroughly won her over to the demand for suffrage. Here she met the outstanding women of the feminist movement. She renewed her acquaintance with Lucy Stone. She met Antoinette Brown who had attended Oberlin College with Lucy and was now the first woman ordained as a minister. She met the capable Paulina Wright Davis, who had successfully managed and presided over the conventions of 1850 and 1851, but who was so eager to prove that not all woman's righters were "horrid old frights with beards and mustaches" that she overdressed, at least in Susan's opinion. There were others of great interest to her: Elizabeth Oakes Smith, a fashionable literary woman of Boston; Ernestine L. Rose, the brilliant Jewess, ultraliberal, who had fled from Poland to escape religious persecution and was now lecturing throughout the country on "The Science of Government"; Dr. Harriot K. Hunt of Massachusetts, who now for some years had protested against taxation without representation; and Matilda Joslyn Gage, also at her first meeting, the youngest member of the convention. Gerrit Smith was there, making his first appearance at a woman's rights gathering, and with him his daughter, Elizabeth Smith Miller; and James Mott and Lucretia, who to Susan's delight was made president. Susan was elected secretary. There were letters of advice, approval, and encouragement from Angelina Grimké Weld, Wil-

liam Lloyd Garrison, William Henry Channing, and Horace
Greeley.

Elizabeth, eagerly reading the newspapers, was pleased to find a
few flattering reports of the convention among the many bitter
attacks. The *Syracuse Standard* praised Lucretia Mott:

> It was a singular spectacle to see this Quaker matron presiding
> over a convention with an ease, grace, and dignity that might be
> envied by the most experienced legislator in the country.

But the *Syracuse Star* wrote:

> The poor creatures who take part in the silly rant of "brawling
> women" and Aunt Nancy men are most of them "ismizers" of the
> rankest stamp, Abolitionists of the most frantic and contemptible
> kind....

James Gordon Bennett in his most withering style expressed his
views in an editorial in the *New York Herald,* which read in part:

> How did women first become subject to man, as she now is all
> over the world? By her nature, her sex, just as the Negro is and
> always will be to the end of time, inferior to the white race and,
> therefore, doomed to subjection; but she is happier than she would
> be in any other condition, just because it is the law of nature....What
> do the leaders of the woman's rights convention want? They want
> to vote and to hustle with the rowdies at the polls. They want to be
> members of Congress....They want to fill all other posts which men
> are ambitious to occupy, to be lawyers, doctors, captains of vessels
> and generals in the field. How funny it would sound in the news-
> papers that Lucy Stone, pleading a cause, took suddenly ill in the
> pains of parturition and perhaps gave birth to a bouncing boy in
> court!...A similar event might happen on the floor of Congress, in a
> storm at sea or in the raging tempest of battle, and then what is to
> become of the women legislators?

Such reasoning as this always made Elizabeth's blood boil and
she, expecting her baby very soon, was more determined than ever
that childbirth should be natural and easy and should not in-
capacitate woman. Doctors as yet knew next to nothing about
obstetrics and the care of babies. It was woman's duty, she felt,
to free herself through more knowledge. It was the duty of the few
women doctors to help women annul the Biblical curse, "In
sorrow thou shalt bring forth children." Because she wanted women

to know more about their own bodies, she sponsored in Seneca Falls a course of lectures given by a woman who understood the subject thoroughly. But she and her committee could only get fifty women out of a population of three thousand to attend. She was discouraged and impatient with their lack of interest in a subject of such importance to themselves, and saw ahead years of work to rouse them from their apathy. But at least she would prove what women could do.

Her fifth child was born late in October and to her great joy was a girl. She wrote Elizabeth Smith Miller:

The fact of my having a daughter you already know; but the particulars I must give you. Well, on Tuesday night I walked nearly three miles, shopped and made five calls. Then I came home, slept well all the night and on Wednesday morning at six awoke with a little pain which I well understood. Thereupon I jumped up, bathed and dressed myself, hurried the breakfast, eating none myself of course, and got the house and all things in order, working bravely between the pains. I neither sat down nor lay down until half past nine when I gave up all my vocations and avocations, secular and domestic, and devoted myself wholly to the one matter then brought more especially before my mind. At ten o'clock the whole work was completed, the nurse and Amelia alone officiating. I had no doctor and Henry was in Syracuse. When the baby was twenty-four hours old, I got up, bathed, taking a sponge and sitz bath, put on the wet bandage, dressed, ate my breakfast, walked on the piazza, and, the day being beautiful, I took a ride of three miles on the plank road; then I came home, rested an hour or so, read the newspapers and wrote a long letter to mama. The short dress I wore until the last. It is grand for such occasions and I love it more than ever. And finally let me say that everything with me and the baby is as it should be. My joy in being the mother of a precious little girl is more than I can tell you. The baby is very large and plump, and her head is covered with black curly hair. Oh! how I do rejoice in her. And now what shall I call her? What is the most beautiful name ever given to woman? I shall not name her after any one, for friendships are such passing, changing things in the present undeveloped state of the race....

After due deliberation over a name beautiful enough for this first daughter, she chose Margaret.

She wrote exultantly to Lucretia Mott about her experience, and Lucretia, duly impressed, replied:

We feared to hear from thee again, after such an account of thy-
self, only the third day after giving birth to such a child.... What a
woman!... We who live after the older school methods cannot tell
what the hardy reformers can bear. I rode out in less than a week
after the birth of one of my children and was classed among the
Indians for so rash an act. I was persuaded then that the close
month's confinement was an injury to mothers and I have encouraged my children to be moderately venturesome.

Elizabeth continued to prosper physically and suffered no ill
effects from her venturesomeness. But as the winter went on, she
was appalled by her household duties. She so much wanted to have
a share in the woman's movement, but with four lively boys, and
a small baby to look after, and two inefficient Irish servant girls
to direct, she had, even with Amelia Willard's help, little time or
energy left for the work she so dearly loved. Henry was still away
a great deal, but had decided not to try for re-election to the legislature as he felt it necessary to devote himself whole-heartedly to
his law practice to provide for his growing family. Alone at home
so much with the children and the servants, she longed for stimulating companionship.

She could not, however, stay discouraged long. Life was too interesting. If there was not time to do all she wanted to do during
the day, she stayed up reading and writing before the grate fire
long after everyone else was in bed. She read *Uncle Tom's Cabin,*
and urged Cousin Libby to read it at once, adding: "It is the most
affecting book I ever read. That book will tell against slavery. Of
that you may be sure." She enjoyed Mrs. Child's sketch of Madame
de Stael, and commented to Libby: "What a magnificent creature
that mortal was! How I do love that woman!"

She was elated over Cousin Gerrit Smith's election to Congress.
And Susan came to visit and finally put on the Bloomer costume.
This was triumph indeed. Elizabeth had been urging it for over
a year. Susan was now completely converted.

IX

BEFORE THE NEW YORK LEGISLATURE

S USAN's conversion to woman suffrage and the Bloomer costume
did not, however, send her directly into the woman's rights
movement. She continued her work for temperance until she was
forced to take the next step ahead.

Elizabeth, marking time, gave what help she could as president
of the State Temperance Society, always emphasizing woman's
rights, always indignant at the treatment women delegates received at the larger temperance conventions.

In June 1853, when the Woman's State Temperance Society met
in Rochester, there were rumblings of discontent over the independent policies Elizabeth and Susan had inaugurated. They were
accused of talking too much about woman's rights, divorce, and
the Church, and not enough about temperance. A scheme was on
foot to swing the balance of power to the more conservative group.

When the society was organized, men had been included as members, ineligible for office but with the privilege of speaking at
meetings. The purpose of this was to make it truly a woman's
organization and to force women to do the active work, to preside
and think out its policies. Men were so used to taking charge and
most women were so ready to let them, that Elizabeth, Susan, and
a few other capable women provided constitutional safeguards.

Now some of the women proposed that men be given equal
rights and they pleaded so eloquently that the constitution was
amended at this meeting. Immediately it became evident that Elizabeth's and Susan's fears had been well-grounded. The men did most
of the speaking; they insisted that the name of the society be
changed to the People's League, that it deal only with temperance
and have nothing whatever to do with woman's rights. They organized the conservative women against Mrs. Stanton and defeated
her for the presidency. When she was elected vice-president, she

refused to serve, realizing it would be impossible for her to work with such a reactionary group. Miss Anthony also refused to act as secretary, saying, that since the vote of the society had shown they would not accept the principle of woman's rights, she could not act as an officer of the society. They both withdrew from the organization, which continued in a desultory way for a few years and then disbanded.

When Elizabeth returned home and thought over this experience, she was convinced that their work no longer lay in the direction of temperance, but definitely with woman's rights. In answer to a downhearted letter from Susan, she wrote:

> You ask me if I am not plunged in grief at my defeat at the recent convention for the presidency of our society. Not at all, I am only too happy in the relief I feel from this additional care. I accomplished at Rochester all I desired by having the divorce question brought up and so eloquently supported by dear little Lucy Stone. How proud I felt of her that night! We have no woman who compares with her. Now, Susan, I do beg of you to let the past be past, and to waste no more powder on the Woman's State Temperance Society. We have other and bigger fish to fry.

Susan saw the wisdom of this and devoted herself more and more to the cause of woman's rights. While she was traveling from place to place, organizing woman's rights societies, raising money, sending out letters, attending woman's rights and teachers conventions and spreading consternation because she, a woman, wished to express her opinions publicly, Elizabeth at home rescued her lively boys from dangerous pranks, supervised the housework, struggled to train inefficient servants, preserved the fruit for the family, and took all the care of her precious baby, Margaret. Somehow she found time late at night to write an article or a speech or woman's rights tract for Susan.

But there were times when Susan had to buoy her up, when she was so harassed by her many household cares and her children that she felt it impossible to do any more work for woman's rights until her children were grown. Her children were a real responsibility to her and she felt she owed them the very best up-bringing she could possibly give them. When Susan saw signs of this mood, she hurried to Seneca Falls, took on her shoulders some of the housework, told Elizabeth of the humiliating encounters she had had in her organizing work because she was a woman, or repeated to her an insufferable remark of a pompous male, and Elizabeth again was ready for the fray.

Susan now visited her frequently. At night after the children were in bed, they sat for hours before the open fire, thrashing out their opinions on education, marriage, divorce, or the next step to be taken in the woman's rights movement. The next morning Susan would take full charge of the household and the children, while Elizabeth, secluded in the most quiet spot in the house, would write a speech, an appeal, or resolutions in her best style.

It was a godsend to Elizabeth to have such a friend, one who cared enough for her and the cause to be a real helpmate and inspiration. The friendship was equally a blessing to Susan, who, brimming over with ideas, was still a little uncertain how to express them and found it a hardship to write out a speech. She could always depend on Elizabeth for a ringing speech and virile resolutions. She could always be sure when she came to Elizabeth, incensed by the intolerance of men and discouraged by the apathy of women, that she would give her new courage to continue the fight. She admired Elizabeth's clear-cut reasoning and the daring way in which she dissected venerable traditions and institutions.

To both of them the Bloomer costume was still a problem. Elizabeth had now worn it for two years—years of physical comfort and freedom, but filled as well with many trying situations, with bitter criticism, ridicule, endless publicity, unpleasant notoriety, and the knowledge that she caused her friends constant embarrassment. Susan was humiliated again and again by the impertinent remarks of men and boys and the scorn of women, as she traveled about the country arranging woman's rights meetings. Lucy Stone was having similar troubles. Elizabeth Smith Miller, in Washington during her father's term as Congressman, wore the Bloomer costume everywhere. She was snubbed and stared at and often tried almost beyond endurance. They all exchanged experiences, comforted, and cheered each other. They were willing to suffer as long as they felt their dress-reform movement was making headway, but now they began to doubt.

Elizabeth gradually came to the conclusion that the physical freedom the Bloomer gave her was not worth the price and that it often prejudiced people against woman's rights. The men who were the most ardent supporters of the woman's rights cause, Garrison, Phillips, and Channing did everything they could to get her, Susan, and Lucy to give up the Bloomer. Gerrit Smith alone pleaded for it. She was soon experimenting with the costume, trying to make it less conspicuous. She wrote her cousin Libby:

> I have a pair of morocco boots about four inches higher than an ordinary gaiter, laced up in front. My dress comes about one inch below the top of the gaiter. Everybody says the costume is far prettier than the Bloomer. In fact I have now three dresses within one inch of my boot tops. They are not so convenient as the Bloomer, but I shall wear the new style when I travel as it attracts but little attention.

By the end of the year, she had given up wearing the Bloomer dress except in her own home. Her decision once made, she felt happier and freer mentally than she had in years. She had not realized what a mental defense she had had to build up. Now she urged Susan to give it up with as much vehemence as she had urged her to wear it; and Susan found it as hard to give up as to put on, for she felt guilty about deviating from her principles. Susan and Lucy wrote each other long letters about it, and Susan read Lucy's letters to Elizabeth. Lucy needed the convenience of the short dress as she traveled about the country in all kinds of weather on her lecture tours. She also felt that present fashions made it almost impossible for women to engage in business and consequently kept them from financial independence, the very basis of their freedom and development. Yet she suffered so much from the attention she attracted and the embarrassment she caused her friends that even she began to think of making herself one long dress. Then Susan wrote her:

> Mrs. Stanton has had a most bitter experience in the short dress, and says she now feels a mental freedom among her friends that she has not known for two years past. If Lucy Stone, with all her power of eloquence, her loveliness of character, who wins all that

hear the sound of her voice, can not bear the martyrdom of the dress, who can?

Elizabeth added this postscript:

I have but a moment to say, for your own sake, lay aside the shorts. I know what you suffer among fashionable people. Not for the sake of the cause, nor for any sake but your own, take it off. We put the dress on for greater freedom, but what is physical freedom compared with mental bondage? By all means have the new dress made long.

A little later Elizabeth again pleaded with Susan, writing:

I hope, Susan, you have let down a dress and petticoat. The cup of ridicule is greater than you can bear. It is not wise, Susan, to use up so much energy and feeling in that way. You can put them to better use. I speak from experience.

Before long both Susan and Lucy capitulated, and from then on the feminists dressed in the fashion of the day and were distinguishable from other women only through the independence of their ideas.

Susan now planned a big piece of work for Elizabeth. She would call a State Woman's Rights Convention in Albany in February 1854 and have her deliver an address on the legal disabilities of women before the joint judiciary committees of the legislature.

Traveling through southern New York trying to raise money for her work, Susan had realized as never before how utterly enslaved women were and how little financial aid they could give the cause, while their husbands controlled their earnings. She determined to get action from the legislature and started in at once circulating petitions asking that married women be entitled to their earnings and to the equal guardianship of their children. A hearing before the legislature with an address by Elizabeth Cady Stanton should awaken the people to the need for these reforms. She had found an enthusiastic ally in William Henry Channing, pastor of the Unitarian church in Rochester, and he agreed to help her put through these ambitious plans.

The next thing was to get Elizabeth's consent. She was honored but appalled by the request, and although she felt very inadequate, finally consented. She wrote Susan:

> Can you get any acute lawyer—perhaps Judge Hay is the man—sufficiently interested in our movement to look up just eight laws concerning us—the very worst in all the code? I can generalize and philosophize easily enough of myself; but the details of the particular laws I need, I have not time to look up. You see, while I am about the house, surrounded by my children, washing dishes, baking, sewing, etc., I can think up many points, but I cannot search books, for my hands as well as my brains would be necessary for that work. If I can, I shall go to Rochester as soon as I have finished my Address and submit it—and the Appeal too for that matter—to Channing's criticism. But prepare yourself to be disappointed in its merits, for I seldom have one hour undisturbed in which to sit down and write. Men who can, when they wish to write a document, shut themselves up for days with their thoughts and their books, know little of what difficulties a woman must surmount to get off a tolerable production.

Judge Hay was willing to prepare notes on the laws unjust to women but wrote Susan:

> The person who arranges and condenses our suggestions into an address should, from every consideration be Mrs. Stanton, because her style is admirably suited to such a subject.

And William Henry Channing wrote Elizabeth:

> Let me add my word of earnest request to that of Judge Hay that you will draft the Address to the Legislature on the Legal Disabilities of Women. On all accounts you are the person to do it, at once from your sex, talent, knowledge of the subject and influence. There is not a man of us, who could tell the story of woman's wrongs as strongly, clearly, tersely, eloquently as yourself. Some woman too ought to be the voice of her sisterhood—at once to prove woman's sagacity, justice, and power to right herself, and because men will listen to a woman's claim on her own behalf as they will not to any words of men.

This was high praise indeed, and Elizabeth set to work with real consecration to make her address come up to their expectations. She worked under difficulties however. The children continually demanded her attention. The nurse was ill. One of the boys shot an arrow into the baby's eye, frightening Elizabeth so that she hated to let the precious baby out of her sight. A month before the convention she wrote Susan:

> My address is not nearly finished; but if I sit up nights, it shall be done in time. I fear, however, it may not suit the Committee, for it does not suit me.

Then Susan came to Seneca Falls to stay with the children while Elizabeth went to Rochester to read her address to William Henry Channing. He was delighted with it, suggesting only that she add more legal references. She did this at once and then read it to Henry who was at home for a few days. He thought it excellent. This gave her confidence. Every day now she stole up to the garret to rehearse, to train her voice so that it would reach every part of the Senate Chamber. She was frightened but determined.

Judge Cady, reading in the *Albany Evening Journal* that his daughter was to address the legislature, was extremely nervous about it, and hoping to dissuade her, urged her to stop en route. She consented, bringing with her Theodore, Margaret, and two nurses.

Soon after she arrived, he handed her the *Albany Evening Journal,* and pointing to the announcement that Elizabeth Cady Stanton, daughter of Judge Daniel Cady, the distinguished jurist, would address the legislature, asked her sternly if this were true.

"Yes, it is true," she confessed.

"Have you ever spoken before such an assemblage of men?" he demanded, as if he were questioning a witness.

"No."

"Then how do you know you can?"

"I have carefully prepared my speech," she explained. "I have memorized it, and it has been pronounced good by several men."

"After tea this evening," the Judge ordered, "I want you to come to my office and read it to me."

She dreaded above everything the pending interview with her father. She wanted his approval so much, as she had ever since she was a child. And always their views clashed. What seemed to her progress and noble work for humanity, he regarded as folly.

Her connection with the woman's rights movement hurt and humiliated him.

They went to his office together that night, and sat before the open fire as they had in her childhood. He begged her not to deliver the speech, not to disgrace him in his old age by making a public appearance in Albany. He offered her the deed to her Seneca Falls house if she would only desist, but she refused without the slightest hesitation, although she had been asking him for that house for years. Then he threatened once more to disinherit her, but even this made no impression. Instead she reminded him that she was only acting on the advice he had given her years ago in that same room when he told her that the only way she could do away with the laws which made the farm women cry, was to go to Albany, when she was older, to persuade the legislators to change them.

Seeing that she would not yield, he asked her to read her speech. She began with misgivings, but looking up from her papers to gauge the impression she was making, she saw tears in his eyes. When she had finished, she waited anxiously for his comments. He was silent for a long time, and then said in a voice tense with emotion: "Surely you have had a happy comfortable life, with all your wants and needs supplied; and yet that speech fills me with self-reproach; for one might naturally ask, how can a young woman, tenderly brought up, who has had no bitter personal experience, feel so keenly the wrongs of her sex? Where did you learn this lesson?"

"I learned it here," she replied, "in your office, when a child, listening to the complaints women made to you."

"You have made your points clear and strong," he continued, "but I think I can find you even more cruel laws than those you have quoted."

Then together they looked up the laws, made some changes in her speech, and at one o'clock kissed each other good night. She never knew just how her father felt. She knew he disapproved of her course of action and was hurt by her defiance, yet secretly perhaps he was proud of her determination and ability. At any rate, if she must make speeches, he would see that she was properly prepared.

When the New York State Woman's Rights Convention met in Association Hall, Albany, February 14, 1854, Elizabeth Cady Stanton, as president, delivered the address which a few days later was destined for the legislature. It was a speech to be proud of, and so enthusiastic was Susan that she had 50,000 copies printed, a copy placed on the desk of every legislator, and many circulated throughout the state. The convention was planned for two days, but the interest was so great that evening meetings were held for two weeks with Ernestine Rose, Antoinette Brown, Wendell Phillips, and William Henry Channing as the principal speakers.

The event of the convention, however, was Elizabeth's eloquent appeal to the legislature. The Senate Chamber was crowded when she was ushered in by the chairman. Many prominent Albany citizens were there, as the Cadys and the Stantons were well known in the capital. There was great curiosity for few had heard a woman speak in public.

As Elizabeth sat on the platform, looking down into the sea of faces, waiting for the chairman to introduce her, she suddenly came to the full realization of what she was doing. She was terrified and yet exultant. Her mind flashed back to the day long ago when she had planned to cut out of her father's books all the laws which made women suffer, and she knew that all her life she had been consciously and unconsciously working toward this moment.

Then suddenly the chairman's voice broke her reverie. He was introducing her. As she arose, the applause sounded through the Senate Chamber. Tastefully dressed in black silk, with lace at her throat and wrists, she would have honored any drawing room. In the prime of life, at 39, wholesome and intelligent, she contradicted all the characteristics attributed to bold women who presumed to speak in public.

She opened her speech with a flare of oratory and soon forgot her fears. She pictured vividly woman's status under the law:

It is not enough for us, that by your laws we are permitted to live and breathe, to claim the necessaries of life from our legal protectors—to pay the penalty of our crimes; we demand the full recognition of all our rights as citizens, property holders, taxpayers; yet we are denied the exercise of our right to the elective franchise. We support ourselves, and, in part, your schools, colleges, churches, your poor houses, jails, prisons, the army, the navy, the whole machinery of government, and yet we have no voice in your councils. We have every qualification required by the Constitution, necessary to the legal voter, but the one of sex. We are moral, virtuous, intelligent, and in all respects quite equal to the proud white man himself, and yet by your laws we are classed with idiots, lunatics, and Negroes.... Now, gentlemen, we would fain know by what authority you have disfranchised one-half the people of this State? You who have so boldly taken possession of the bulwarks of this republic, show us your credentials; and thus prove your exclusive right to govern, not only yourselves, but us.

She cited case after case of woman's humiliating and tragic legal status as a wife, mother, and widow:

The wife who inherits no property holds about the same legal position that does the slave on the Southern plantation. She can own nothing and sell nothing. She has no right even to the wages she earns; her person, her time, her services are the property of another. She cannot testify in many cases against her husband. She can get no redress for wrongs in her own name in any court of justice. She can neither sue nor be sued. She is not held responsible for any crime committed in the presence of her husband, so completely is her very existence supposed by the law to be merged in that of another.... By the common law of England, the spirit of which has been but too faithfully incorporated into our statute law, a husband has the right to whip his wife with a rod not larger than his thumb, to shut her up in a room, and administer whatever moderate chastisement he may deem necessary to insure obedience to his wishes, and for her healthful moral development! He can forbid all persons harboring or trusting her on his account. He can deprive her of all social intercourse with her nearest and dearest friends. If by great economy she accumulates a small sum, which for future need she deposits little by little, in a savings bank, the husband has a right to draw it out, at his option, to use as he may see fit.

As she recited these grievances, she grew more and more impassioned. She told the tragic story of mothers, how the law allowed fathers to apprentice sons to gamesters and rum sellers, to bind their daughters to owners of brothels, how it allowed the father about to die to bind out all his children and will away the guardianship from the mother, how in the case of separation, the law gave the children to the father whatever his character or condition. She told of widows deprived by the state of all but one-third of their husbands' property if their husbands died without a will. She demanded a new code of laws in line with justice. She demanded for women in criminal cases "that most sacred of all rights," trial by a jury of her peers. She continued:

> Would to God you could know the burning indignation that fills woman's soul when she turns over the pages of your statute books, and sees there how like feudal barons you free-men hold your women. Would you could know the humiliation she feels for her sex, when she thinks of all the beardless boys in your law offices, learning these ideas of one-sided justice—taking their first lessons in contempt for all womankind—being indoctrinated into the incapacities of their mothers, and the lordly, absolute rights of man over all women, children, and property....
>
> In conclusion, then let us say, in behalf of the women of this State, we ask for all that you have asked for yourselves in the progress of your development, since the Mayflower cast anchor beside Plymouth Rock; and simply on the ground that the rights of every human being are the same and identical.

Her audience had listened intently to every word. Now their applause thundered through the Senate Chamber. Susan was radiant. Friends of her husband and father came up to congratulate her. It was a triumph she knew, but best of all was the fact that she had not disgraced her father. No words of praise were sweeter than those of Judge Page when he said: "You did your father credit. You tell him that I say he should be very proud of such a daughter."

But neither her eloquence nor the justice of her pleas, nor the intelligent persuasive speeches of Ernestine Rose, Susan B. Anthony, and Antoinette Brown at other hearings influenced the legislators in the least to change the laws. Petitions with thousands of signatures of men and women were presented by friendly legislators, but availed nothing. The only tangible evidence of progress was that women were listened to with greater interest and respect, and were gaining advocates among the legislators. There was less ridicule and there were more friendly newspapers, although the majority still flaunted devastating criticisms, such as this in the *Albany Register*:

> While the feminine propagandists of woman's rights confined them-
> selves to the exhibition of short petticoats and long-legged boots,
> and to the holding of conventions and speech-making in concert
> rooms, the people were disposed to be amused by them, as they are
> by the wit of the clown in the circus, or the performances of Punch
> and Judy on fair days, or the minstrelsy of gentlemen with black-
> ened faces, on banjos, the tambourine, and bones. But the joke is
> becoming stale. People are getting cloyed with these performances,
> and are looking for some healthier and more intellectual amusement.
> People are beginning to inquire how far public opinion should sanc-
> tion or tolerate these unsexed women, who would step out from the
> true sphere of the mother, the wife, and the daughter, and taking
> upon themselves the duties and the business of men, stalk into the
> public gaze, and by engaging in the politics, the rough controversies,
> and trafficking of the world, upheave existing institutions, and over-
> turn all the social relations of life.

When she read this, Elizabeth wondered what it was that could make people so distort her actions and her purpose. It was disturbing, but no longer important. The letters of praise which came from old and newly made friends overshadowed all criticism. She treasured these lines written to her by the Reverend A. D. Mayo, Universalist clergyman of Albany:

> It is the first time I have listened to you; and you will not accuse
> me of flattery when I say that the hearing has confirmed my previous
> "suspicion" that you are the head and front of this offence against
> the oppressions of woman. I only trust that you will again appear
> before the Legislature, and never rest till your side prevails.

X

SEVEN CHILDREN

SINCE Elizabeth's and Susan's great effort to win the support of the legislature had been unavailing, there was but one thing to do—to roll up more petitions, to call more conventions, and to send out more appeals to the women of New York State. Petitions, ineffectual as they seemed, were the only means a disenfranchised class had of presenting its grievances and its demands to the governing bodies of the state and nation.

Susan who was agent of the state woman's rights organization at once planned another campaign, and it was because she was so invincible, so ready to continue the fight that William Henry Channing called her the Napoleon of the movement. She had no funds to start with, but had she waited to have the necessary money in hand, the work would never have been done. Often she spent her own savings. Sometimes a generous sympathizer like Wendell Phillips would start her off with his personal check for $50. Canvassing the state was difficult, especially in winter. She traveled by stage, wagon, and sleigh in all kinds of weather, from door to door on foot in large towns and small. She held meetings and made speeches which she and Elizabeth had drawn up; she circulated tracts which Elizabeth had written; she obtained signatures for her petitions. In the country, crowds came to her meetings, curious to hear their first woman speaker. They treated her respectfully, but had little sympathy for her message. It was desperately hard, lonely work. It might have been bearable had the women responded. Some few of course were eager to help her, some were ready but timid, afraid of the censure of their husbands and their friends, but the majority slammed the door in her face, exclaiming angrily that they had all the rights they wanted.

How Elizabeth longed to help Susan, to be with her on her difficult campaign trips! She wrote her:

I wish I were as free as you and I would stump the State in a twinkling. But I am not, and what is more, I passed through a terrible scourging when last at my father's. I cannot tell you how deep the iron entered my soul. I never felt more keenly the degradation of my sex. To think that all in me of which my father would have felt a proper pride had I been a man, is deeply mortifying to him because I am a woman. That thought has stung me to a fierce decision—to speak as soon as I can do myself credit. But the pressure on me now is too great. Henry sides with my friends, who oppose me in all that is dearest to my heart. They are not willing that I should write even on the woman question. But I will both write and speak. I wish you to consider this letter strictly confidential. Sometimes, Susan, I struggle in deep waters.... However, a good time is coming and my future is always bright and beautiful.

Henry, while really not at heart opposed to Elizabeth's interest in the woman's movement, was sometimes influenced by the strong opposition of her family. She had five children to look after and he felt that was all she could handle to advantage. When things did not run smoothly or the money did not go as far as he thought it might, it was only natural for him occasionally to blame it on her outside interests. He was away from home so much and she did not write him often enough. He wrote three and four times to her one. If she were not writing so many articles and tracts, he might hear from her oftener. He liked Susan but sometimes resented her visits, for they meant renewed interest for Elizabeth in the woman's rights movement. But this opposition and dissatisfaction were only temporary. He was proud of Elizabeth's ability; he respected her independence; and he was still very much in love with her.

In spite of all opposition she continued her much-loved work. She lectured before the Teachers' Association for a fee of ten dollars for she was vitally interested in improving public school education. She lectured in Rochester and Waterloo. Her father heard of it and threatened again to disinherit her. This time he was in earnest and made the necessary changes in his will.

She was writing more and more for the *New York Tribune*. It often meant staying up till two o'clock at night. At first she sent her articles to Henry for correction, but he was far too critical and

she decided henceforth to send them direct to Horace Greeley. She
wrote Susan:

> I have rewritten my "Indian" and given it into the hands of
> Oliver Johnson, who has promised to see it safely in the *Tribune*.
> I have sent him another article on the "Widow's Teaspoons," and
> I have mailed you one of mine which appeared in the *Buffalo
> Democracy*. I have sent six articles to the *Tribune* and three have
> already appeared.

She had also become a regular contributor to a new woman's
magazine, the *Una,* published and edited by Paulina Wright Davis.
This refined little monthly with its elaborate title and corner decora-
tions was first issued in February 1853, at a dollar a year.

Mrs. Davis hoped to interest women in a paper which would be
of a higher caliber than the ladies' magazines and miscellanies
with their emphasis on fashions and woman's moral influence, with
their sweet, ineffectual poems and sentimental stories. She expected
to reach a wider audience than the *Lily* and make the *Una* a real
power in the regeneration of women. She called to her aid a corps
of able writers as regular contributors, among them Elizabeth
Oakes Smith, Frances D. Gage, Elizabeth Preston Peabody, Fannie
Fern, and Elizabeth Cady Stanton.

There was great need for a magazine that would tell women
honestly of the progress of the woman's rights movement and urge
them to support it, for *Godey's Lady's Book,* which was molding
the opinion of women throughout the country, spoke out against
women suffrage. Sarah Josepha Hale, of *Godey's Lady's Book,* in
spite of her interest in higher education for women and the re-
moval of some of their legal disabilities, kept assuring them that
their indirect influence was far more valuable than the ballot
and more ladylike.

Elizabeth's original, refreshing articles in the *Una* were a much-
needed antidote. She struck out fearlessly against the smugness
of women with a sarcastic and devastating article, "I Have All the
Rights I Want."

She had scathing words for society matrons who criticized
feminists for their boldness and lack of modesty:

You women who with bare arms and neck join in the midnight revels with men whose tongues and brains are thick with wine and excess, talk not of want of delicacy in those who assemble in woman's conventions to talk with sober men, to talk on great questions of Human Rights.

She urged financial independence for women, emphasizing the fact that the right over a person's subsistence was a power over all his thoughts and actions. She wrote:

Woman will always be dependent until she holds a purse of her own. I would therefore have every girl of sixteen begin this day some profitable business.... Encourage our young girls, therefore, to enter all honest and profitable employment, and you will have struck a blow at vice and licentiousness, stronger and more effectual than any that has yet been dealt.

Unfortunately, however, Elizabeth could not direct the editorial policy of the *Una,* and it drifted into paths too ladylike and ineffectual. Offering nothing new nor sensational, it could not compete with the well-established *Godey's Lady's Book,* and after three years ceased publication.

In spite of her outside interests, Elizabeth was devoted to her home and children. She put her ideas for the improvement of humanity to work in her own family circle. All in all she was an exceptional housekeeper. Her house was neat and artistic, the childrens' lives were well-regulated, their clothes were mended and clean, their food was good and appetizing. She could do anything herself, if the occasion demanded it, from baking cakes or pies, or preserving, to the hardest menial tasks, and she always looked neat and unruffled when at work, in a clean gingham dress and white apron. She made it a point to look her best for her family. Realizing only too well how easily women were swamped by the humdrum details of housekeeping to the detriment of their intellectual development, she was determined that this should not happen to her —for her own sake and her children's. Her children, she vowed, would have more than a household drudge to mother them.

With their father away so much, the burden of upbringing was upon her shoulders, and she assumed the full responsibility, never referring the children to him for discipline, nor threatening to tell him of their disobedience when he came home. As a result they never dreaded his return and it was a treat for all of them to have him at home. He loved romping with the children and telling them stories. He loved working in the garden, raising fruit and vegetables, planting trees and watching them grow. Every night they played games and Elizabeth played her guitar or the piano.

Puritanical discipline, fear, and gloomy beliefs did not cloud her children's days. She was careful to keep them free from the orthodox dogmas that haunted her childhood and taught them that God was all that was beautiful, noble, and good, like sunshine, flowers, and affection. They went to church regularly, the boys choosing where they would go, and this most often was the Episcopal church where the clergyman, the boys insisted, wore "a nightgown and mantilla."

The boys were lively and hard to manage. They got into mischief so continually that she never knew where she would find them—on the ridgepole of the house or floating the baby on corks in the cold water of the brook. As Daniel, Henry, and Gerrit grew older they learned to swear with gusto and nothing she could do would break them of the habit. She talked the matter over with Susan and Lucretia Mott, who were visiting her, and Lucretia suggested that at the next meal they swear to see if that would shame the boys. Elizabeth had trained them to wait on the table when she had company, for she entertained frequently, wanted her meals served properly, and servants were inefficient. The boys were paid for serving, and, dressed in their white suits, took great pride in doing it well.

At the next meal the three accomplices were all ready to try their experiment. The boys were serving in their best style when suddenly Lucretia Mott, trim and proper in her white Quaker cap and kerchief, said to Elizabeth, "May I give thee some of this damned chicken?"

The boys fairly gasped in astonishment, thinking at first that they had not heard correctly, but as the meal progressed and all three women swore at every opportunity, they were perplexed. This continued for three meals, and at the fourth Senator Seward and Gerrit Smith were present. They had been told of the plan, and whenever Lucretia, Susan, or Elizabeth uttered a profane word, the two men looked horrified, but said nothing.

That night as soon as the boys could get their mother alone, they exclaimed with tears in their eyes, "What will the Senator and Cousin Gerrit think of you, swearing like that!"

"Well," she replied, "you boys all do it, and so we thought we would. Don't you like to hear us?"

"Oh no, Mother!" they cried in a chorus, with distress written on their faces.

"Very well then," she said, putting her arms around two of the boys, while the third sat on a stool at her feet, "if you boys stop swearing, I will also."

They did. Lucretia's plan had worked.

Elizabeth was convinced that boys, if interested in healthy sports and games, would not be tempted to find undesirable companions and amusements. So she had all sorts of swings, bars, and ladders put up on the grounds, and had the barn equipped as a gymnasium for rainy days. She bought a billiard table for the older boys so that they could bring their friends home to play, instead of gathering in the village around a billiard table where they might be tempted to drink, smoke, or gamble. She organized a dancing school for the young people of Seneca Falls. She was one of the prime movers in the establishment of a boy's gymnasium in the village with a German instructor in charge. Because she thought that girls' amusements were sadly neglected and because she wanted girls to grow up strong, well-developed, and free, she used to go regularly to the Academy after school and march a number of girls to the gymnasium, where they were given the same exercises as the boys.

All this gave the villagers, who wished to be critical, opportunity to say that she was too busy minding other people's affairs, that she had too many newfangled notions, that she might better look after her own family. But the people who knew her appreciated her even if they did not understand all of her ideas. Her poor Irish neighbors knew that they could count on her for help in any emergency. And her children were never neglected.

Sometimes the children suffered because their mother was a reformer. Sometimes their playmates shouted derisively, "Your
mother believes in woman's rights!" They had hooted at the
Bloomer costume. But these disturbing experiences were soon explained away. Her children were proud of her and resented every
disparaging remark. They were taught not to mind what people
said.

While she was busy with her babies and her writing and Susan
was finishing up her tour of New York State and planning conventions, Lucy Stone was married on May 1, 1855, to Henry B.
Blackwell, Abolitionist and stanch friend of the feminists. Susan
was truly discouraged, not because she disapproved of matrimony,
nor of Lucy's husband, but because she feared that one of the best
orators and workers of the feminist movement would now be
handicapped as Elizabeth was. She was not even comforted by
Lucy's independence in keeping her own name and in drawing
up with Henry Blackwell a protest against the present laws of
marriage and the legal disabilities they inflicted upon women.

Elizabeth was delighted when she heard that Lucy was to keep
her own name and was one of the first to express her approval. She
wrote Lucy:

> Nothing has been done in the woman's rights movement for some
> time that so rejoiced my heart as the announcement by you of a
> woman's right to her name....It may do for the slave to be Cuffee
> Brooks or Cuffee Douglass, just whose Cuffee he may chance to be;
> but for us who have grown up into the full stature of womanhood,
> demanding all our social, civil, and religious rights, and diligently
> fitting ourselves to maintain them, too, it does seem to me a proper
> self-respect demands that every woman may have some name by which
> she may be known from the cradle to the grave.

A little later when Antoinette Brown was married, Susan was
completely out of patience. Whom could she get to speak at conventions? They had all deserted her. She could never carry on
alone. All this she poured out to Elizabeth, and Elizabeth wrote
her:

> Let Lucy and Antoinette rest awhile in peace and quietness and
> think great thoughts for the future. It is not well to be in the excite-

ment of public life all the time; do not keep stirring them up or mourning over their repose. You need rest too, Susan. Let the world alone awhile. We cannot bring about a moral revolution in a day or a year.... It is not in vain that in myself I have experienced all the wearisome cares to which woman in her best estate is subject.

Then again late in January 1856, she wrote Susan about the birth of another daughter:

Well, another female child is born into the world! Last Sunday afternoon [January 20, 1856] Harriot Eaton Stanton—oh! the little heretic thus to desecrate that holy holiday—opened her soft blue eyes on this mundane sphere. Maggie's joy over her little sister is unbounded. I am very happy that the terrible ordeal is past and that the result is another daughter. But I feel disappointed and sad at the same time at this grievous interruption of my plans. I might have been born an orator before spring, you acting as midwife. However, I feel that it will not be in vain that I am held back. My latent fires shall sometime burst forth.... I sent off another article to the *Tribune.*

When Harriot was four months old, Susan appealed to Elizabeth in desperation, begging her to write a speech for her. She had been asked by the State Teachers' Association to read a paper on "Coeducation" at their meeting in Troy in August. This was an opportunity not to be lost, but she felt utterly incompetent. To make a short impromptu speech or offer a resolution as she had so often done in teachers' meetings of late was quite a different matter. This must be a pretentious speech, a long speech packed with well-arranged facts which would command attention. She had pleaded so often in teachers' meetings that women's ability be recognized. She must not fail now that she had an opportunity to prove it.

By June, with the date of the meeting just two months away and only a few scattered ideas on coeducation in her mind, she worked herself into a frenzy and sent this letter off to Elizabeth:

Not a word written on that Address for Teachers' Convention ... and the Mercy only knows when I can get a moment, and what is *worse,* as the Lord *knows full well,* is, that if I *get all the time* the *world has—I can't get up a decent document.* So for the love of me and for the saving of the *reputation* of *womankind,* I beg you with one baby on your knee and another at your feet and four boys whistling, buzzing, hullooing *Ma Ma* set yourself about the work—it is of but small moment *who writes* the Address, but of *vast moment* that it be *well done.* I promise you to work hard, oh, how hard, and *pay you whatever you say* for your *time* and *brains*—but ah Mrs. Stanton *don't* say *no,* nor *don't delay* it a moment, for I must have it all done and *almost commit* it to memory.

Now let me tell you, Do you write all you think of ready to copy, and then you come out here, or I will come to you and copy.

The Teachers' Convention comes the 5th and 6th of August. The Saratoga Woman's Rights Convention, the 13th and 14th, and probably the Newport [Convention] the 20th and 21st.

During *July* I want to speak certainly twice at Avon, Clifton and Sharon and Ballston Springs and Lake George—Now will *you load my gun,* leaving me only to pull the trigger and let fly the powder and ball— Don't delay one mail to tell me what you *will do*—for I *must not* and *will not* allow those *school masters* to say—*see* these *women can't* or *won't* do anything when we do give them a chance— No they shan't say that, even if I have to get a *man* to write it— but *no man can* write from *my stand point,* nor no woman but *you*— for *all all* would base their *strongest* argument on the *un*likeness of the *sexes.* Nettie [Antoinette Brown] wrote me that she should, were she to make the Address—and more than any other place does the *difference* of sex, if there is any, need to be *forgotten* in the school room.... Will give you every thought I have *scared up* on another slip—Now do I pray you give heed my prayer—those of you who have the *talent* to do honor to poor, oh how poor womanhood, have all given yourselves over to *baby* making, and left poor brainless me to battle alone— It is a shame, such a lady as *I might* be *spared* to *rock cradles,* but it is a *crime* for *you* and *Lucy* and *Nettie*—I have just engaged to attend a Progressive Meeting in Erie County the 1st of September just because there is *no other woman* to be had, not because I feel in the least competent—oh dear, dear. If the *spirits* would only just make me a *trance medium* and put the *rights* into my mouth—you can't think how earnestly I have prayed to be made a speaking medium for a whole week— If they would only come to me thus, I'd give them a hearty welcome....

Do get all on fire and be as cross as you please. You remember Mr. Stanton told how cross you always get over a speech.

Elizabeth of course came to the rescue, inviting Susan to Seneca Falls. Together they thrashed out the subject of coeducation, one of their favorites, and made an outline of their points. Then while Susan looked after baby Harriot and made the puddings, Elizabeth wrote the speech in her best style. And she helped Susan with speeches for all her summer meetings.

The lecture on "Coeducation" was delivered by Susan before a large audience in Troy and highly praised. Together Elizabeth and Susan had once more made a mark for women, and together they laughed at the cautiously qualified commendation of the president of the Association. "I could not have asked for a single thing different either in matter or manner," he said, "but I would rather have followed my wife or daughter to Greenwood cemetery than to have her stand here before this promiscuous audience and deliver that address."

A year later at the State Teachers' Convention in Binghamton Susan, egged on by Elizabeth, proposed a resolution calling upon all schools, colleges, and universities to open their doors to women. It was a very bold thing in those days for a woman to advocate coeducation. She was supported by a few broad-minded men and women, but the conservative element headed by Professor Charles Davies of West Point were in a frenzy, pleading for the preservation of woman's delicacy and the sanctity of marriage which they knew coeducation would undermine. The women present could have carried the resolution, for they were in the majority, but they failed Susan.

Elizabeth, eagerly searching the newspapers for reports of the convention, found much to rouse her indignation and much to make her proud of Susan. She wrote Susan:

> I did indeed see by the papers that you had once more stirred that pool of intellectual stagnation, the educational convention.... The *Times* was really quite complimentary. Henry amused me very much. He brought every notice he could see about you. "Well, my dear," he would say, "another notice of Susan. You stir up Susan and she stirs the world!" I glory in your perseverance. Oh! Susan, I will do anything to help you on. If I do nothing else this fall I am bound to help you get up an antislavery address. I will write a letter to the Convention of course.... You must come here a week or two and we will do wonders. Courage, Susan, this is my last baby and she will be two years old in January. Two years more and—time will tell what! You and I have the prospect of a good long life. We shall not be in our prime before fifty, and after that we shall be good for twenty years at least. If we do not make old Davies shake in his boots or turn in his grave, I am mistaken.

The year 1857 was the only year, until the Civil War, in which Susan was unable to call a woman's rights convention. All of her workers were kept at home by family cares. Lucy Stone's baby was born in September. Susan was very impatient with Lucy for failing her and the cause of woman, and kept after her so much that a strained feeling began to grow between them. This troubled Elizabeth and she wrote Susan:

> I was glad to hear of Lucy Stone. I think a vast deal of her and Antoinette Brown. I regret so much that you and Lucy should have had even the slightest interruption to your friendship.

She found she often had to calm and comfort Susan, who, discouraged by the lack of woman's rights workers, had thrown herself into antislavery work with such zeal that she was utterly worn out. Susan wrote her:

> How I do long to be with you this very minute—to have one look into your very soul and one sound of your soul-stirring voice.... Mrs. Stanton, I have *very weak moments*—and long to lay my weary head somewhere and nestle my full soul close to that of another in full sympathy. I sometimes fear that, *I too*, shall faint by the wayside—and drop out of the ranks of the faithful few.... Oh Mrs. Stanton, how my soul longs to see you in the great Battlefield. When will the time come? You say in two or three years. God and the Angels keep you safe from all hindrance.... If you come not to the rescue, who shall! Mrs. Stanton do write me a good long letter.... Don't fail to write me. It always does me so much good to hear from you.

Then Elizabeth herself suffered one of her keenest disappointments, all on account of a baby—that impediment which Susan said was always stalking between women and their efforts for emancipation. The Theodore Parker Fraternity were planning a series of lectures in Tremont Temple, Boston, and to show that they recognized woman's equality with man on the lecture platform invited Elizabeth Cady Stanton to take her place in the series along with Theodore Parker, Wendell Phillips, George William Curtis, Ralph Waldo Emerson, and Bayard Taylor, for a lecture fee of $50. To be asked to take part with such men as these was an honor indeed, and she appreciated deeply this recognition of her ability as a speaker. But more than that she appreciated the wonderful opportunity to spread her message.

She was, however, carrying her seventh child. Harriot had not been her last baby, after all. For the first time she was experiencing great physical discomfort in pregnancy, and it was utterly impossible for her to think of attempting the lecture. As it had always been her theory that women need not be incapacitated by childbirth, she was ashamed to give her real reason for not filling the engagement. So she gave no adequate reason—merely refused. No one understood and she received urgent requests to reconsider. This of course she was unable to do. Finally, Mrs. Caroline Severance was persuaded to take her place, and thus the day was saved for women.

Four months later, in March 1859, her last child, Robert, was born. As soon as she was able, she wrote Susan:

> I have a great boy, now three weeks old. He weighed at his birth without a particle of clothing 12¼ pounds. I never suffered so much. I was sick all the time before he was born, and I have been very weak ever since. He seemed to take up every particle of my vitality, soul and body. Thank Heaven! I am through the siege once more. But oh! Susan, what have I not suffered for the past year? It seems to me like a painful dream.

It took her a long time to regain her strength. By June, however, she was ready for work, eager to help Susan plan an intensive campaign in New York State. "I am full of fresh thoughts and courage," she wrote Susan, "and feel all enthusiasm about our work."

For the first time there was money in hand to start the campaign. In the fall of 1858 Francis Jackson of Boston had given $5000 to Wendell Phillips, Lucy Stone, and Susan to be used to win the ballot for women. Wendell Phillips was willing that Susan have $1500 for the New York campaign and for once she started out on her speaking tour free from financial worries. She took with her a corps of able women speakers.

By the will of Charles F. Hovey of Boston a $50,000 trust fund was established, in 1859, to promote various causes, among them woman's rights. It now looked as if the way were opening for effective work to be done for women's enfranchisement and as if victory might be in sight.

XI

THAT DANGEROUS SUBJECT, DIVORCE

W AR clouds loomed on the horizon just as Elizabeth and
Susan were at last equipped for a successful woman's
rights campaign. For some time they had been watching with grave
concern the trend in national affairs—the growing arrogance of
the slave states, the selfishness of Northern business interests, the
widening breach between the North and the South, and the apparent impossibility of settling the slavery issue.

Whenever possible they discussed these matters as well as woman's
rights with Lucretia Mott when she visited her sister, Martha
Wright, in Auburn, and with Mrs. William H. Seward and her
sister, Mrs. Worden. Martha Wright had been Elizabeth's co-
conspirator in the Convention of 1848. Mrs. Seward and Mrs.
Worden were new recruits to the woman's cause.

All of these women were Abolitionists. All had been indignant
over the passage of the Kansas-Nebraska Bill repealing the Missouri
Compromise and providing that each territory make its own decision on the question of slavery. All knew men who had settled
in Kansas to take their stand against slavery. Susan's brother, Mer-
ritt, was there, with John Brown. All were interested in the new
Republican party. Senator Seward, Republican leader of New York
State, was being looked upon as a Presidential possibility. Henry
Stanton, once more in politics, an enthusiastic Republican, had campaigned for "Frémont and Freedom." Naturally, Mrs. Seward, Mrs.
Worden, and Elizabeth took an increased interest in the burning
questions of the hour. To them the Republican party offered the
solution.

Susan, Lucretia, and Martha, while watching the progress of
the Republican party with interest, were at heart Garrisonian Abolitionists. To them political action was futile. A party might start
with the highest of principles, but soon it was bound to compromise.

To Garrisonians there was only one principle, only one issue, the immediate abolition of slavery. There could be no compromise. Because the Constitution of the United States compromised with slavery, Garrison had publically burned it, denouncing it as "a covenant with death and an agreement with hell." Thomas Wentworth Higginson, Wendell Phillips, and other Abolitionists called a Disunion Convention in Massachusetts (1857) demanding that the free states secede. Susan, as agent for the Garrisonians in New York was arranging meetings and tacking up posters, bearing that provocative slogan, "No Union with Slaveholders." Elizabeth sympathized with the uncompromising stand of these out-and-out Abolitionists. Yet her way must be the more practical one of political action.

Then came the Dred Scott decision with its ruling that Congress could not constitutionally abolish slavery in the territories. It blasted the hopes of confident young Republicans, the principal plank of whose platform was freedom in the territories. There was much to ponder over, much to talk over, and these six women could discuss these questions without quarreling over methods.

Elizabeth's thoughts now often turned to Gerrit Smith, whose ideals she so admired. He was so close to these questions, constantly in touch with antislavery leaders. She longed to talk with him. He had always stood for political action. She had hoped for much from him in Congress, but his health could stand the strain of only one term. She wrote her Cousin Libby:

> What does Cousin Gerrit think of the present course of the government? My own opinion is that the "staving off" policy has been fairly tried, and I am becoming more and more convinced that we shall be in the midst of violence, blood, and civil war before we look for it. Our fair republic must be the victim of the monster, slavery, unless we speedily rise in our might and boldly shout freedom. I am sure Cousin Gerrit holds this view. I know old John Brown does, for a letter from him passed through my hands the other day. Perhaps I may see him after all, for he is expected at Rochester next month on a visit to Frederick Douglass.

She was leaning more and more to the side of the Garrisonians. Then John Brown stirred the nation by his raid on Harper's

Ferry, and his trial and execution roused bitter feelings everywhere. This tragedy bore down upon Elizabeth with double force as she saw the havoc it wrought in the life of her beloved cousin, Gerrit Smith. Like other Abolitionists who had befriended John Brown he was suspected as an accomplice. The shock and anxiety were more than he could bear, and he suffered a nervous collapse.

In the midst of this Judge Cady, who a few years before had resigned as judge of the Supreme Court of New York, died at the age of eighty. The rebellious, unmanageable daughter who loved him dearly, grieved for him, her longing to make him understand unsatisfied. But Judge Cady's impatience with her ideas had been somewhat appeased. Shortly before he died, he decided not to disinherit her.

Elizabeth begged Susan to come to her at this time. She wrote:

> Where are you? I have looked for you every day....It would do me such great good to see some reformers just now. The death of my father, the worse than death of my dear Cousin Gerrit, the martyrdom of that grand and glorious John Brown—all this conspires to make me regret more than ever my dwarfed womanhood. In times like these everyone should do the work of a full-grown man. When I pass the gate of the celestial city and good Peter asks me where I would sit, I shall say, "Anywhere, so that I am neither a Negro nor a woman. Confer on me, good angel, the glory of white manhood so that henceforth...I may enjoy the most unlimited freedom."

But the opportunity soon came for her to do the work of a full-grown man and to strike a telling blow for women.

During the winter of 1860 an amendment to the Property Law of 1848, greatly improving women's legal status, passed the Senate. The chairman of the judiciary committee urged Susan, who was lobbying in Albany, to get Mrs. Stanton to address the legislature on behalf of the amendment.

Knowing how busy Elizabeth was with her seven children, Susan feared a great deal of persuasion might be necessary to induce her to undertake this difficult task. But to her great relief Elizabeth replied promptly, "If Napoleon says cross the Alps, they are crossed."

A speech before the legislature meant days of careful preparation, and Susan went to Seneca Falls to give her suggestions and to relieve Elizabeth of the care of the children.

On March 19, 1860, Elizabeth Cady Stanton made her second appearance before the New York Legislature. Six years before she had addressed the joint judiciary committees in the Senate Chamber. Today from the speaker's desk she faced a joint session of the legislature. The galleries were packed. In a clear, compelling voice she pleaded for the rights of women—for the repeal of unjust laws and for women's enfranchisement.

She called attention to the similarity between woman's legal status and that of the Negro slave. She demanded for woman the rights of a citizen:

> But, say you, we would not have woman exposed to the grossness and vulgarity of public life, or encounter what she must at the polls. When you talk, gentlemen, of sheltering woman from the rough minds and revolting scenes of real life, you must be either talking for effect, or be wholly ignorant of what the facts of life are. The man, whatever he is, is known to the woman. She is the companion not only of the statesman, the orator, and the scholar, but the vile, vulgar, brutal man has his mother, his wife, his sister, his daughter . . . and if man shows out what he is anywhere, it is at his own hearthstone. There are over 40,000 drunkards in this State. All these are bound by the ties of family to some woman. . . . Gentlemen, such scenes as woman has witnessed at her own fireside, where no eye save Omnipotence could pity, no strong arm could help, can never be realized at the polls. . . .

She spoke for over an hour and her audience listened intently. The general opinion was that her eloquence could not have been surpassed by any man in the United States.

The important thing to Elizabeth, however, was that the next day the bill passed the legislature and was signed by Governor Morgan. Now throughout New York State a married woman could hold property, could collect her wages and invest them without the legal interference of her husband; she could make contracts with her husband's consent, and without it if he were a drunkard, insane, or a convict, or had deserted her; she could sue and be sued; she was now the joint guardian of her children; and at her husband's death would have the same property rights as he would have at her death. The ballot had not been won, but this legal burden removed from woman's shoulders was a great victory. Both Elizabeth and Susan found great encouragement in the fact that some of the most able men in the legislature were now their allies.

At the tenth national Woman's Rights Convention in Cooper Institute, New York, May 10, 1860, Elizabeth repeated by request the speech which she had delivered before the legislature. It was a notable gathering. All the eloquent speakers of the movement were there, Wendell Phillips, William Lloyd Garrison, Antoinette Brown Blackwell, and Ernestine Rose. The proceedings were unusually harmonious until the second day, when Elizabeth offered resolutions advocating more liberal divorce laws and defended them ably.

The subject of marriage and divorce occupied her mind a great deal. There were few women who had as liberal ideas on marriage as she, and the few who did were hesitant about expressing them especially in connection with woman's rights, thinking that woman suffrage and an improved legal status should be won before these subjects were brought up.

Her own marriage was happy and no personal bitterness influenced her or distorted her views, but she was sufficiently sympathetic and sensitive to feel keenly the sufferings of others, and her analytical mind always probed the root of the matter. Her sense of justice and independence could not tolerate the prevailing dictum that a woman was disgraced if she left her husband, no matter how cruel or unprincipled he might be.

The tragic experience of a girlhood friend, her own love for Edward Bayard, and his unsatisfactory marriage with Tryphena made her realize how easily the most well-intentioned might make the wrong choice. Seeing drunken fathers abuse wives and children among the poor families of Seneca Falls, seeing the tragedy of unwelcome motherhood, all this made her want to do something about it. If marriage and divorce were carefully and fearlessly considered, a more intelligent and just attitude would prevail, and where could these discussions take place if not at Woman's Rights Conventions? She talked the matter over often and freely with Susan. Lucy Stone and she wrote each other long letters about it.

The question of marriage had seemed an unanswerable, unsurmountable one to Lucy, and only the persistent, kind reasoning of Henry Blackwell and their real love for each other had been able to convince her that the relation might work out happily when the legal status of the sexes was so unequal. During the first years of her married life Lucy felt as did Elizabeth that the questions of marriage and divorce should be discussed at the Woman's Rights Conventions. She had written Elizabeth:

> All that you consider legitimate for our convention, I do too. I not only think that so much is proper to be discussed, but ought to be.... It is a great, serious subject that only a few intuitive souls dimly understand, while a thousand aching and uncompanied hearts and minds, *wedded* only in name, wait for the first ray of light to lead out of their abyss of sorrow. I wish I could see you. I want so much to talk with someone who has thought this matter over and who dares to speak. I am not one bit afraid of the censure which a discussion of this question will bring. If I were only sure what was the right, I can stand by it through fire and flood. I very much wish that a wife's right to her own body should be pushed at our next convention. It does seem to me that you are the one to do it. Can't you come? I will help all I can. The subject is too broad for a letter and needs to be heard on both sides.

They continued their letters on the question intermittently, and Lucy, as she thought over the matter and talked it over with Henry Blackwell and others, came to the conclusion that although the subject should be thoroughly discussed, it should be brought up at a convention called expressly for that purpose. She wrote Elizabeth:

> It seems to me that all that pertains intrinsically to marriage is an entirely *distinct* question from ours; but one to which this leads, just as naturally, as rivers run to the ocean. Its magnitude is too immeasurable. And there ought to be a convention especially to consider that subject—but it ought not to be mixed with ours, it seems to me. Not that it is not just as imperative and sacred, but because they do not belong together, just as temperance is not a part of a distinct movement.

Two months before the 1860 Convention, Lucy again wrote Elizabeth:

I wish you would call a convention to discuss divorce, marriage, infanticide, and their kindred subjects.

But Elizabeth intended to discuss the matter, right where she thought it belonged, in the coming Woman's Rights Convention. To her it was intrinsically a part of the program of equal rights. She wrote Lucy of her intention and asked her to sustain her if any controversy arose. Lucy replied that she could not prepare a speech for the convention, but might speak in the discussion, and added:

I am glad you will speak on the divorce question, provided you are yourself *clear* on the subject. It is a great grave topic that one shudders to grapple, but its hour is coming—and will have fully come when we are ready. God touch your lips if you speak on it.

In the meantime Indiana had passed a liberal divorce law, sponsored by Robert Dale Owen, and one patterned after it was introduced in the New York Legislature. Horace Greeley came out strongly against it in his *New York Tribune* while Robert Dale Owen defended it with vigor. This newspaper controversy soon made the pros and cons of divorce the topic of discussion at many a fireside. Horace Greeley, then still a popular idol, swayed the sentiments of thousands, and they liked to believe that his sentimental, theoretical statements were true. Robert Dale Owen was a dangerous radical! Doctrines such as his, they feared, led to free love.

Elizabeth had no patience with Horace Greeley's smug opinions on marriage and divorce. Her clear-cut thinking slashed right and left through his choicest arguments. She followed the Greeley-Owen battle with the keenest interest, and it aroused in her a determination to make women discuss this problem, to make them think about it, because they, bound hand and foot by the law, were most often the sufferers in unhappy marriages.

And so in that harmonious Woman's Rights Convention of 1860, she fired her bombshell—her well-thought-out, liberal resolutions on divorce. As she read them, the atmosphere of the convention changed. People were not used to hearing a cultured, refined woman make such a statement as this:

That any constitution, compact, or covenant between human beings, that failed to produce or promote human happiness, could not
in the nature of things, be of any force or authority; and it would
be not only a right, but a duty to abolish it.

This was only one of ten startling points.

She knew that she must defend her resolutions to the very best
of her ability. She felt more confident, more able than she had in
1848, when to the dismay of that first convention, she had presented her suffrage resolution. She had traveled a long way since
then in experience and wisdom, but she had lost none of her
daring. She said:

> For years there have been before the Legislature of this State a
> variety of bills, asking for divorce in cases of drunkenness, insanity,
> desertion, cruel and brutal treatment, endangering life.... I have ever
> felt the deepest interest in all that has been written and said upon
> the subject, and the most profound respect and loving sympathy for
> those heroic women, who, in the face of law and public sentiment,
> have dared to sunder the unholy ties of a joyless, loveless union.

Then she pictured marriage as it was, a human institution, subject to all the frailties and mistakes of human nature. It might
approach the divine when two people were drawn together by
love and understanding, but unfortunately this was rarely the
case. She cited examples of tragic marriages and asked her audience if they believed these marriages were made in heaven, if they
believed that these sad, miserable husbands and wives were bound
together by God.

She had her fling at Horace Greeley:

> I know Horace Greeley has been most eloquent for weeks past
> on the holy sacrament of ill-assorted marriages; but let us hope that
> all wisdom does not live, and will not die with Horace Greeley.
> I think if he had been married to the *New York Herald,* instead
> of the Republican Party, he would have found out some Scriptural
> arguments against life-long unions, where great incompatibility of
> temper existed between the parties.

Laughter and applause rang out, and the tenseness was somewhat broken. She continued:

> Horace Greeley, in his recent discussion with Robert Dale Owen,
> said that this whole question has been tried in all its varieties and

conditions from indissoluble monogamic marriage down to free love; that the ground has all been gone over and explored. Let me assure him that but just one half of the ground has been surveyed, and that half but by one of the parties, and that party certainly not the most interested in the matter. Moreover, there is one kind of marriage that has not been tried, and that is a contract made by equal parties to lead an equal life, with equal restraints and privileges on either side. Thus far, we have had the man marriage, and nothing more. From the beginning man has had the sole and whole regulation of the matter. He has spoken in Scripture, he has spoken in law. As an individual, he has decided the time and cause for putting away a wife, and as a judge and legislator, he still holds the entire control.... The right of woman to put away a husband, be he ever so impure, is never hinted at in sacred history.... We cannot take our gauge of womanhood from the past, but from the solemn convictions of our own souls, in the higher development of the race.

When she had finished there was loud applause, for although her ideas were not fully approved, her eloquence and her courage demanded respect and recognition. As soon as the applause died down, the Reverend Antoinette Brown Blackwell was on her feet, offering another set of resolutions utterly opposed to Elizabeth's. To Mrs. Blackwell the marriage obligation was such that it could not be dissolved during the lifetime of the contracting parties and all divorce was naturally and morally impossible.

Elizabeth was not surprised at Antoinette's views. They frequently disagreed. Antoinette liked to keep woman on a pedestal, different from man. Elizabeth always insisted that intrinsically man and woman were alike, that their differences were due to training. Antoinette saw life as she thought it should be, Elizabeth saw life as it was. How she wanted to get up again to demolish Antoinette's arguments!

But someone was doing this for her. Ernestine Rose, so calm, confident, and clear, was meeting Antoinette's arguments point by point. Surely after this intelligent rebuttal, there could be no opposition. As she listened, she admired Ernestine Rose more than ever, remembering the warning which Wendell Phillips and George William Curtis had given Susan, that such a woman—an atheist they called her—would harm their cause. She and Susan had always championed Ernestine Rose, and once more Elizabeth was convinced that she was a great woman, head and shoulders above the men who challenged her.

Now Wendell Phillips was speaking:

> I object to entering these resolutions upon the journal of this Convention. I would move to lay them on the table; but my conviction that they are out of order is so emphatic that I wish to go further than that, and move that they do not appear on the journals of this Convention.

This convention, he contended, was no marriage convention. It assembled to discuss laws that rested unequally upon women, and had nothing to do with marriage, a question which affected men and women equally. There were many who agreed with Wendell Phillips and supported his motion. He was a man so respected and so magnetic, that he easily made up people's minds for them, if they were in doubt on any issue.

William Lloyd Garrison then stated he felt the subject was inappropriate for the convention, that they had not come together to settle the question of marriage. He did not think, however, that the resolutions should be expunged from the records.

Elizabeth was aghast at the opposition she had aroused. She had not expected everyone to agree with her, but she was unprepared for the strong feeling against what seemed to her so just and right. She respected Wendell Phillips so much and wanted his approval. As the debate proceeded, she grew more and more uncomfortable, and Samuel Longfellow, sitting next to her, whispered to her comfortingly, "Nevertheless you are right, and the Convention will sustain you."

Now Susan B. Anthony came to her rescue and asked Wendell Phillips to withdraw his motion. She added:

> As to the point that this question does not belong to this platform, from that I totally dissent. Marriage has ever been a onesided matter, resting most unequally upon the sexes. By it man gains all; woman loses all; tyrant law and lust reign supreme with him; meek submission and ready obedience alone befit her. Woman has never been consulted; her wish has never been taken into consideration as regards the terms of the marriage compact. By law, public sentiment, and religion—from the time of Moses down to the

present day—woman has never been thought of other than a piece of property, to be disposed of at the will and pleasure of man....She must accept marriage as man proffers it, or not at all.

Although the convention did not expunge the divorce resolution from its records, Elizabeth found herself the target of criticism and abuse. Only the more radical feminists stood by her. Even Lucy Stone now sided with Wendell Phillips. The newspapers took the matter up. Horace Greeley, commenting on the convention, maintained with Wendell Phillips that the laws on marriage and divorce were equal for men and women. In a letter to the *New York Tribune,* Elizabeth answered them both, citing laws to prove her points. But this did not put an end to the matter. Editors made the most of such an opportunity. She was accused of advocating free love, of proposing that men change their wives every Christmas, of undermining the whole social order. Letters poured in asking all sorts of absurd questions. But there were a few letters which cheered her. Mrs. Seward and Mrs. Worden wrote that they considered the subject an appropriate one for the convention as there could be no such thing as equal rights under existing conditions of marriage and divorce. Lucretia Mott sent these words of comfort:

> I have the fullest confidence in the united judgment of Elizabeth Stanton and Susan Anthony and I am glad they are so vigorous in the work.

From Lydia Mott, James Mott's sister, came this encouraging letter:

> I hope neither Susan nor yourself will be turned aside by Phillips' course whatever it may be. I am sure he will be no barrier to the truth. It seems to me that he has been used in this matter by those who are not very high on the ladder of reform as regards woman. One good thing you have done, if nothing more, that is driven the *New York Tribune* to that very absurd position that divorce is wrong in *any case.*

Elizabeth and Susan, however, both felt very badly to be censured so severely by Wendell Phillips. He had been their ideal of liberality, justice, and helpfulness. They had always been able to count on him and had fully expected his support and Garrison's in this important venture. Elizabeth wrote Susan:

> With all his excellence and nobility Wendell Phillips is a man. His words, tone, and manner came down on me like a clap of thunder. We are right, however. My reason, my experience, my soul proclaim it. Woman's degradation is in man's idea of his sexual rights. Our religion, laws, customs are all founded on the belief that woman was made for man. One word of thanks from a suffering woman outweighs with me the howls of all Christendom. How this marriage question grows on me! It lies at the very foundation of all progress. I never read a thing on this subject until I had arrived at my present opinion. My own life, observation, thought, feeling, reason brought me to the conclusion. So fear not that I shall falter. I shall not grow conservative with age. I feel a growing indifference to the praise and blame of my race, and an increasing interest in their weal and woe.

XII

WAR TURNS BACK THE CLOCK

THE affairs of the nation every day looked more menacing. The Republicans had won the Presidential election and Southern states were threatening secession if Abraham Lincoln were inaugurated. But secession did not trouble the Abolitionists so much as the fear that in desperation some compromise might be made with slavery to fasten it more firmly on the nation. The Republicans' pledge that slavery would not spread to the territories did not satisfy them. They demanded immediate and unconditional emancipation of the slaves. And the once-Republican Elizabeth now stood with the Abolitionists.

Because she felt with the Abolitionists that every effort should be made at this critical time to impress the public with the seriousness of the situation and the need of pressing for immediate emancipation, she joined Susan, the Rev. Samuel J. May, Stephen S. Foster, and other Abolitionists in a lecture tour of New York State. They began their meetings in Buffalo but were greeted with such hissing, hooting, and stamping that their speeches could not be heard. Their reception was the same all the way from Buffalo to Albany. People were not going to let the radical, fiery words of the Abolitionists make them face the real issue. They preferred to cry peace where there could be no peace. They were in no mood for anti-slavery meetings. But Susan would not let her speakers give up.

Henry in Washington on law business, combining with it the more exciting work of correspondent for the *New York Tribune*, read about the mob at the Rochester meeting and felt anxious for Elizabeth. He wrote her it was folly to hold antislavery meetings in large cities at this time, for the mobs could not be controlled. Chaos reigned in Washington, he added, and all slave states would secede before Lincoln came in.

After a few days of respite on the Anthony farm with Susan's mother and father who always looked forward to Elizabeth's visits, Susan and Elizabeth set out again to join their fellow workers and faced mob after mob. In Albany the Democratic Mayor, George H. Thacher, in spite of the protests of prominent citizens, allowed the Abolitionists to hold their convention and made it a point of honor to protect them in their right of free speech. He escorted Susan and Elizabeth to and from their hotel, put an extra force of policemen on duty in the hall, and sat on the platform with a revolver across his knees, maintaining order.

Susan and Elizabeth not only had the threats of the mob to worry them at this time; they were involved in a conspiracy in which they were defying the law. Yet so convinced were they that justice was on their side, that they could not be persuaded to alter their course.

Shortly before they started out on their antislavery speaking tour, Susan in Albany with Lydia Mott had been sought out by a cultured, educated woman, who begged for help, saying that her husband, Dr. Charles Abner Phelps, a member of the Massachusetts Senate, had committed her to an insane asylum, because she, discovering his unfaithfulness, threatened to expose him. After a year, her brothers, one a United States Senator and the other a prominent lawyer, secured her release on a writ of habeas corpus and took her to their home. She was so lonely for her children that her husband consented to let them visit her for a few weeks. She could not bear to give them up, but by law they belonged to the father, and she was told impatiently by her brothers that it was her place to submit. Determined that she would not give up her thirteen-year-old daughter, she fled with her to the home of a Quaker family, and then, fearing that her hiding place had been discovered, came in desperation to Susan.

Susan, indignant at the treatment Mrs. Phelps had received and convinced that she was sane, took her and her daughter to New York and there in the city crowds found a safe place for her.

She was soon suspected of aiding Mrs. Phelps, and not only was she implored to reveal her hiding place, but threatened when she failed to do so. But she remained silent and Elizabeth was her stanch ally. They both felt it was as imperative to help this woman, a victim of unjust laws, as to smuggle fugitive slaves to Canada. Mrs. Phelps's brothers threatened to arrest Susan during some of her meetings because she had broken the law by abducting a man's child. Dr. Phelps, a man of influence, had enlisted William Lloyd Garrison and Wendell Phillips in his behalf, and they now urged Susan not to involve the cause unnecessarily, and to realize that she had broken the law. When at the antislavery convention in Albany, Garrison again pleaded with her saying, "Don't you know the law of Massachusetts gives the father the entire guardianship and control of the children?" she replied: "Yes, I know it, and does not the law of the United States give the slaveholder the ownership of the slave? And don't you break it every time you help a slave to Canada?"

It was very disillusioning to Elizabeth and Susan to find Garrison and Phillips taking the side of the father in this matter—very surprising that they could feel so keenly the wrongs of the Negro slave and be so oblivious of the wrongs of women. "Only to think," said Susan, "that in this great trial I should be hounded by the two men I adore and reverence above all others." This was the second time that these noble, idealistic men had failed women. They had been unable to see that the laws of marriage did not apply equally to men and women. They had been unable to see in this last instance that a fugitive woman needed as much help as a fugitive slave. Susan and Elizabeth were beginning to wonder if even the noblest, most liberal men could really understand woman's problem.

Elizabeth, at home again, away from the threats and confusion of mobs, still found the atmosphere charged with unrest and uncertainty. Letters from Henry in Washington made her feel war was inevitable. She was almost eager to hurry it on, so sure was she that it was the only means of settling the slavery issue. Her boys talked of war. Neil was nineteen, Henry, seventeen, and Gerrit, sixteen. They drilled with the youth of Seneca Falls.

As the states seceded and the call for volunteers continued,

Elizabeth watched her son, Henry, anxiously. He was eager to enlist. She sent a letter to her old friend, William H. Seward, who was now Secretary of State, asking him for a West Point recommendation for Henry. Like all proud mothers she wrote:

> The boy has the essential elements of a hero and as all his proclivities are to the army, I desire that he should have a scientific military education, for I feel that our present struggle for liberty is to be a long one.

Henry did not receive his appointment, and he finally ran away to join the army but was overtaken and brought home.

Elizabeth had also written Secretary Seward:

> This war is music in my ears. It is a simultaneous chorus for freedom; for every nation that has ever fought for liberty on her own soil is now represented in our army.

Susan could not feel that way. A Quaker and a nonresistant Abolitionist, she abhorred war. One by one she saw her fellow Abolitionists come out for war, but she could not believe that the end justified the means. She was puzzled and sad. She tried hard to arrange for the usual national Woman's Rights Convention in New York, but made no headway. No one would co-operate. The war filled people's minds. When she saw that even the Abolitionists would not hold their annual convention, she gave up. But she knew it was a mistake. The work for women should go on, war or no war. Even Elizabeth did not see eye to eye with her in this, blinded as she was by the war spirit. Like the others, Elizabeth thought women should do all they could to save the Union and free the slaves, should prove how valuable their services could be, and after the war be rewarded with the ballot.

While women had their eyes on the war, the Legislature of New York in 1862 amended the hard-won Women's Property Law of 1860, taking away from women the right to equal guardianship of their children and their right to their husbands' property at his death. Thinking of all the hard work, of the 20,000 petitions rolled up to pass the bill of 1860, Susan was heartsick. She wrote Lydia Mott:

All our reformers seem suddenly to have grown politic. All alike say, "Have no conventions at this crisis!" Garrison, Phillips, Mrs. Mott, Mrs. Wright, Mrs. Stanton, etc., say, "Wait until the war excitement abates...." I am sick at heart, but I can not carry the world against the wish and the will of our best friends.

Later Elizabeth saw her mistake.

Meanwhile Henry had received an appointment in the Custom House Office in New York. This meant a steady salary to support his large family and would help solve his financial problems. Elizabeth now looked forward to moving the family to New York. The thought of living in the heart of things was pleasant. The boys could go to college there. The family could all live together again. In the spring of 1862 Susan came to Seneca Falls to help Elizabeth with the moving. She went on ahead to New York with the four boys and looked after them until Elizabeth arrived with the rest of the family. For a year the Stantons lived in Brooklyn and then moved to 75 West Forty-fifth Street, New York. Henry soon went back to his law practice. He also became a valuable, dependable editorial writer for the *New York Tribune.*

After the turmoil of moving and settling was over, Elizabeth was eager to do something vital to help win the war, to make it a war for freedom. The Abolitionists were impatiently waiting for the freeing of the slaves. They distrusted Lincoln and doubted his ability. The military victories were all on the side of the South. Henry Stanton was utterly discouraged, but Elizabeth was hopeful, watching events with the keenest interest and mulling them over in her mind.

She wrote Elizabeth Smith Miller:

It takes great faith to be calm now in this sea of trouble. Henry fears we are going to flinders; but it does not seem so to me. Out of this struggle we must come with higher ideas of liberty, the masses quickened with thought, and a rotten aristocracy crushed forever. I have no misgivings as to the result. But I do hope the rebels will sack Washington, take Lincoln, Seward, and McClellan and keep them safe in some southern fort until we man the ship of state with those who know whither they are going and for what purpose....
The war spirit has a certain indirect, perhaps direct, influence on my domestic system just now. While my boys are growing in grace,

they are all drilling every evening in the gymnasium. I believe in the religious influence of exercise, especially at this time. I place the gymnasium above the "meeting house" for boys on the threshold of manhood. The girls skate, dance, and play much of the time in the open air. . . . Like your Charles, I have great respect for saints with good strong bodies.

There was great rejoicing when in January 1863, Lincoln issued his Emancipation Proclamation, freeing the slaves in the rebel states, but all realized this was but a futile gesture unless it were confirmed by Congress. Legislation must be passed to end slavery forever throughout the length and breadth of the United States.

Henry went to Washington soon after and wrote Susan:

> Since I arrived here I have been more gloomy than ever. The country is rapidly going to destruction. The army is almost in a state of mutiny for want of its pay and lack of a leader. Nothing can carry through but the Southern Negroes, and nobody can marshall them into the struggle except the Abolitionists. The country was never so badly off as at this moment. Such men as Lovejoy, Hale, and the like have pretty much given up the struggle in despair. You have no idea how dark the cloud is which hangs over us. . . . We must not lay the flattering unction to our souls that the proclamation will be of any use if we are beaten and have a dissolution of the Union. Here then is work for you. Susan, put on your armor and go forth.

Susan and Elizabeth put their armor on and began planning the formation of the Women's National Loyal League. Feeling as they both did that the war was a conflict between freedom and slavery, they wanted this issue clearly stated. They did not want the war fought in vain. They saw the futility of providing the army with bandages and supplies when the war was not being conducted on a sound policy. Women were flocking into organizations to relieve suffering, to provide bandages and clothing, to aid the families of soldiers, and were holding fairs and theatricals to raise money. But they must do more than this. They must work for an idea. They must influence public opinion to demand that this be a war for freedom. The rebellion must be suppressed and to accomplish this the slaves must serve as soldiers on the side of the Union. Too many Copperheads were spreading their insidious propaganda. There was too much grumbling and dissatisfaction.

Given an ideal to fight for, people's patriotism would be aroused. They conferred with Horace Greeley, William Lloyd Garrison, and Robert Dale Owen and won their approval. Then they called a meeting of women in the Church of the Puritans, New York, sending their notices out over the entire country. The call read in part:

> What is woman's legitimate work and how she may best accomplish it, is worthy of our earnest counsel one with another. We have heard many complaints of the lack of enthusiasm among Northern women; but when a mother lays her son on the altar of her country, she asks an object equal to her sacrifice. In nursing the sick and wounded, knitting socks, scraping lint, and making jellies the bravest and best may weary if the thoughts mount not in faith to something beyond and above it all. Work is worship only when a noble purpose fills the soul. Woman is equally interested and responsible with man in the final settlement of this problem of self-government; therefore let none stand idle spectators now.

The phraseology was definitely Elizabeth's, though the ideas were Susan's as well. These two women had a most salutary effect upon each other. They roused ideas in each other and stimulated each other to action. Action for Elizabeth meant writing and speaking; for Susan, it meant organizing, doing all of that humdrum but most necessary detailed work of canvassing, advertising, hiring halls, sending out literature, making one dollar do the work of two, and often adding to all that a brief speech straight from the heart.

On May 14, 1863, the Church of the Puritans was crowded with women from many states. Susan called the meeting to order and nominated Lucy Stone for president. Elizabeth made the opening address, summing up the reasons for calling the meeting. Susan urged women to recognize the real cause of the war. "There is great fear expressed on all sides," she said, "lest this war shall be a war for the Negro. I am willing that it shall be....Shame on us if we do not make it a war to establish the Negro in freedom...." She offered resolutions, the first heartily approving that part of the President's proclamation which decreed freedom to the slaves of rebel masters and urging him to devise measures for emancipating all slaves throughout the country; another, "Resolved, There never can be a true peace in this Republic until the civil and political rights of all citizens of African descent and all women are practically established," roused spirited discussion. Some women declared angrily that they had not come to the meeting to hear antislavery or woman's rights speeches.

Ernestine Rose with her usual alertness at once answered them. "It is a painful fact," she said, "that woman under the law has been in the same category with the slave. Of late years she has had some small privileges conceded to her. Now mind, I say conceded; for publicly it has not yet been recognized by the laws of the land that she has a right to an equality with man. In that resolution it simply states a fact that in a republic based on freedom, woman, as well as the Negro, should be recognized as an equal with the whole human race."

Then Angelina Grimké Weld, roused from her retirement by this meeting, added her plea for the resolution: "I rejoice exceedingly that the resolution should combine us with the Negro. I feel that we have been with him; that the iron has entered our souls....I want to be identified with the Negro; until he gets his rights, we shall never have ours."

Still a few women objected that nothing so obnoxious to a portion of the people as woman's rights should be dragged into the meeting, but Lucy Stone and Lucy Coleman came to the defense of the resolution and it was carried.

At the business meeting Elizabeth was elected president of the Women's Loyal League, and Susan, secretary, and the following resolution was passed and signed by nearly all of the women present: "We loyal women of the Nation, assembled in convention this 14th day of May, 1863, hereby pledge ourselves one to another in a Loyal League to give support to the government in so far as it makes a war for freedom."

The evening meeting at Cooper Institute was a great success. Elizabeth presided. Susan read the masterful address to President Lincoln which Elizabeth had written, thanking him for the Emancipation Proclamation and pledging women's support to a war for freedom. It was adopted and sent to the President. There were stirring speeches by Ernestine Rose and Antoinette Blackwell.

When all this was over, there was much hard work to be done. The immediate business at hand was circulating petitions demanding that Congress pass an amendment abolishing slavery. Republicans, under the leadership of Charles Sumner, were urging Congressional action and petitions pouring in would convince Congressmen of what the people wanted. A million names on the petitions was the goal Elizabeth and Susan aimed at.

They opened an office for the Women's Loyal League at Cooper Institute. Susan took full charge and lived with Elizabeth. She received $12 a week for the work from the Hovey trust fund, but the expenses were heavy for office rent, printing, and postage. They asked all who signed the petitions to give one cent, and in this way collected $3000. They held a lecture course at Cooper Institute to raise money and spread their message. The ever-faithful Gerrit Smith gave a contribution. Henry Ward Beecher took up a collection of $200 for them in Plymouth Church. Susan begged other contributions. There was much clerical work to be done, addressing envelopes, sending out letters and petitions. Many volunteer workers came to their aid, and Elizabeth put her sons to work rolling up the petitions from each state separately, and noting on the outside the number of signers. She tried to interest other children in the work, offering a badge to any boy or girl who would get one hundred names. In addition, there were hours spent in the Stanton dining room at the big table, scraping lint for wounded soldiers.

This work was interrupted during the summer of 1863 by draft riots. It had been necessary to draft men for the army, but a man might hire a substitute for $300. For four days the mob held sway in New York. Abolitionists and Negroes were singled out for attack. The Negro orphan asylum, a block from the Stantons was burned, and so threatening and destructive was the mob, that Elizabeth hurried her children off to Johnstown and Susan went to her cousins.

Safe in Johnstown, Elizabeth wrote her Cousin Nancy about her harrowing experiences:

Last Thursday I escaped from the horrors of the most brutal mob I ever witnessed, and brought my children here for safety. The riot raged in our neighborhood through the first two days of the struggle largely because the colored orphan asylum on Fifth Avenue was only two blocks away from us. I saw all those little children marched off two by two. A double portion of martyrdom has been meted out to our poor blacks, and I am led to ask if there is no justice in heaven or on earth that this should be permitted through the centuries. But it was not only the Negroes who feared for their lives. Greeley was at Doctor Bayard's a day and night for safety, and we all stayed there also a night, thinking that, as Henry, Susan, and I were so identified with reforms and reformers, we might at any moment be subjects of vengeance. We were led to take this precaution because as Neil was standing in front of our house a gang of rioters seized him, shouting: "Here's one of those three-hundred-dollar fellows!" I expected he would be torn limb from limb. But with great presence of mind he said to the leaders as they passed a saloon: "Let's go in, fellows, and take a drink." So he treated the whole band. They then demanded that he join in three cheers for "Jeff Davis," which he led with apparent enthusiasm. "Oh," they said, "he seems to be a good fellow; let him go." Thus he undoubtedly saved his life by deception, though it would have been far nobler to have died in defiance of the tyranny of mob law. You may imagine what I suffered in seeing him dragged off. I was alone with the children, expecting every moment to hear the wretches thundering at the front door. What did I do? I sent the servants and the children to the fourth story, opened the skylight and told them, in case of attack, to run out on the roof into some neighboring house. I then prepared a speech, determined, if necessary, to go down at once, open the door and make an appeal to them as Americans and citizens of a republic. But a squad of police and two companies of soldiers soon came up and a bloody fray took place near us which quieted the neighborhood.

When peace reigned in New York once more, she returned and set to work again on the petitions. The first installment of Women's Loyal League petitions were presented by Senator Sumner in February 1864. They represented 100,000 signers and made an impressive showing as they were carried into the Senate by two stalwart Negroes. More installments followed as the year went on and by August, 400,000 signatures had been obtained. By this time the Senate had acted, and it looked as if the House were ready to concur, but the necessary majority for the Thirteenth Amendment was not obtained until after Lincoln's re-election.

Elizabeth took a great interest in the Presidential campaign of 1864. She distrusted Lincoln and thought him utterly incompetent. Once more she championed her hero, Frémont, around whom many dissatisfied Abolitionists were rallying. Susan did not agree with her in this although she too was impatient with Lincoln.

With her characteristic impulsiveness Elizabeth wrote her friends urging them to support Frémont. To Garrison she wrote:

> Can this nation survive another four years under such a dynasty? Is the two-term principle in harmony with the genius of our institutions.... Oh! no, let us change the despot, the wire pullers, and long line of retainers.... Put on your armor once more. Put the name of Frémont at the head of your *Liberator*. Sound again that old cry for freedom.... Help to send Abraham to the shacks of Springfield, that his vulgar jokes (like Nero's fiddling in Rome) may no longer hang heavy in a mourning nation's ears.

Many felt as she did about Lincoln, especially the Abolitionists. Wendell Phillips wrote her:

> I would cut off both hands before doing anything to aid Abraham Lincoln's election. I wholly distrust his fitness to settle this thing and indeed his purpose.

The re-election of Abraham Lincoln, however, was not as disastrous as Elizabeth had anticipated. The Thirteenth Amendment was passed on his recommendation. The North did not go down in defeat, but was victorious in April 1865, a little more than a month after he began his second term. And even she was saddened by his assassination.

Although her impulsiveness and her fervor might sometimes lead her into errors of judgment, she was always ready to acknowledge her mistakes when she saw them. As the years went by, she realized how blinded and how prejudiced she had been about Lincoln. Late in life on Lincoln's birthday, she wrote in her diary:

> I see now the wisdom of his course, leading public opinion slowly but surely up to the final blow for freedom.... My conscience pricks me now when I recall how I worked and prayed in 1864 for the de-

feat of Lincoln's re-election, and now I perceive what a grave misfortune it was that he was not left to reconstruct the South according to what would surely have been a better and wiser plan than that pushed through by the Radicals with whom I then stood. So when his birthday comes around each year I celebrate it somewhat in sackcloth and ashes.

XIII

THE NEGRO'S HOUR

EARLY in 1865 Susan made the long journey to Kansas to visit her brother, Daniel. Besides helping her brother edit his newspaper, she directed the work of caring for the Negro refugees who now were flocking into the state. There was so much constructive work to be done that she often wondered whether she should settle there. She wrote such glowing accounts that Elizabeth who was always looking for new and wider horizons wondered if it might not be the place for her family. Henry and Gerrit were graduating from Columbia Law School. Might not this new western country give them a better start in life than the East?

But Susan thinking it over carefully wrote her: "No I cannot see a place for you here. It is such isolation from all our workers. If you and I had the means to carry on some reform work in New York or here all would be right."

Elizabeth kept Susan informed of the state of affairs in the East. At the close of the war, differences in policy separated the Abolitionists, Garrison insisting that the work of the Antislavery Society was over, and Phillips insisting with equal firmness that the work must go on until the Negroes were enfranchised. The majority of Abolitionists sustained Phillips at the May meeting of the Society in New York in 1865, and Garrison, still unconvinced, would not accept the presidency. Wendell Phillips was elected to take his place, and from then on his policies dominated the Antislavery Society.

Both Elizabeth and Susan, sad at the break in the antislavery ranks and sorry to differ from their idol, Garrison, agreed heartily with Phillips that the work must go on until the Negroes were full-fledged citizens of the United States.

However, it soon became evident to Elizabeth that she and Wendell Phillips were going to disagree over what was more important to her than the enfranchisement of the Negro—the enfranchisement of woman. To Wendell Phillips the Negro came first, and he was not going to let woman's rights clog his program. He wrote to her, May 10, 1865:

> While I could continue, just as heretofore, arguing for woman's rights, just as I do for temperance every day, still I would not mix the movements. That in my view is where, and the only point where you and I differ, i.e., in a matter of method, of expedient action. I think such mixture would lose for the Negro far more than we should gain for the woman. I am now engaged in abolishing slavery in a land where abolition of slavery means conferring or recognizing citizenship, and where citizenship supposes the ballot for all men. Whenever I begin to labor on suffrage as such, be sure I will never stultify myself by claiming it for only half the race.

And she, with ability to pick a flaw in the most suave argument, replied:

> May I ask in reply to your fallacious letter just one question based on the apparent opposition in which you place the Negro and woman. My question is this: Do you believe the African race is composed entirely of males?

Not only Phillips and the majority of the Abolitionists felt this way; the Republicans as well in their zeal for the Negro overlooked the women. They forgot or ignored all the services of women in the war. Senator Sumner, who before the passage of the Thirteenth Amendment had been lavish in his praise of the Women's Loyal League, urging them to send on petitions, now felt that any consideration of woman suffrage was ill-advised. Forgotten were the services of Anna Ella Carroll, whose influence not only saved Maryland from secession, but whose brilliant mind planned the military campaign which changed the fortunes of the North and for which General Grant was given credit. Forgotten were the services of Dr. Elizabeth Blackwell, who originated the Sanitary Commission; of Dorothea Dix, Superintendent of Women Nurses; of Clara Barton and other brave war nurses; of Dr. Mary Walker, army surgeon; of Josephine Griffing, who inspired and organized the Freedmen's Bureau for the relief of the Negroes; of Anna E. Dickinson, whose brilliant oratory and political campaigning carried the Republicans to victory in critical moments. Ignored were the countless self-sacrificing women who sent their husbands and sons to war and kept their farms and their businesses going, often under great physical hardship in the newly opened West.

It was the Negro's hour. This catch phrase was repeated until people actually believed that it was more important to enfranchise thousands of illiterate Negroes than to confer that inherent right of citizenship upon educated, intelligent women, granddaughters of the founders of the Republic. Even some women began to believe this was true. But not Elizabeth and not Susan. How Elizabeth longed to have Susan at hand to help break the mesmerism of this propaganda! She wrote her a long letter urging her to return, closing it with this personal appeal:

> I hope in a short time to be comfortably located in a new house where we will have a room ready for you when you come East. I long to put my arms around you once more and hear you scold me for my sins and shortcomings. Your abuse is sweeter to me than anybody's else's praise for, in spite of your severity, your faith and confidence shine through all. O, Susan, you are very dear to me. I should miss you more than any other living being from this earth. You are intertwined with much of my happy and eventful past, and all my future plans are based on you as coadjutator. Yes, our work is one, we are one in aim and sympathy and we should be together. Come home.

From Robert Dale Owen, in Washington, who, as chairman of the Freedman's Inquiry Commission, had been invaluable to the Women's Loyal League, Elizabeth was receiving copies of bills being proposed to enfranchise the Negro. With horror she saw the word "male" being written into the Fourteenth Amendment. Congressmen found that the only way they could confer suffrage upon the Negro without also including women was to write "male" into the Constitution. This was a direct affront to the women, and they did not wish blatantly to offend them. Charles Sumner wrote and rewrote bills trying to avoid the word "male," but it could not be done; and good Republicans felt that Negro suffrage was all the strain the party could stand.

Elizabeth was frantic. She tried to influence her political friends. She wrote her Cousin Gerrit Smith:

> Do you see what the sons of the Pilgrims are doing in Congress? Nothing less than trying to get the irresponsible "male citizen" into our immortal Constitution. What a shame it would be to mar that glorious bequest of the Fathers by introducing into it any word that would recognize a privileged order. As our Constitution now exists, there is nothing to prevent women or Negroes from holding the ballot, but state legislation. But if that word "male" be inserted as now proposed...it will take us a century at least to get it out again.... The knights of old thought themselves honored in striking brave blows for women. Shall it be said in this Republic, chivalry has died out, that our noblest and best will not rush unasked to resent this first insult to the mothers of the Republic. Sage of Peterboro, unsheath your sword to the rescue. The United States Constitution has always been one of your pet theories. Save it now from this desecration by the recreant sons of the Fathers.

Lucy Stone plead with Charles Sumner, but with no success. Utterly discouraged, Elizabeth wrote Susan:

> I have argued constantly with Phillips and the whole fraternity, but I fear one and all will favor enfranchising the Negro without us. Woman's cause is in deep water. With the League [Women's Loyal League] disbanded, there is pressing need of our Woman's Rights Convention. Come back and help. There will be room for you. I seem to stand alone.

Elizabeth's letters and newspaper reports of the proposed amendment alarmed Susan, and she made immediate preparations to leave Kansas and get into the battle.

With Susan's return to the East imminent, Elizabeth began to realize what an unfriendly feeling had grown up between Lucy Stone and Susan. Lucy came to her full of antagonism toward Susan, urging her to cut loose from her influence. Elizabeth knew that Susan had too persistently chided Lucy for giving up her work for the cause after her marriage and the birth of her daughter. She had often warned Susan to let Lucy alone. Susan had said sharp, rankling things to Lucy, just as she often said them to her in a moment of impatience, when she had not completed a resolution, a tract, or an address at a stated time or in a certain way. She knew how brusque and biting Susan could be, but she knew too how hard Susan tried to control this impatience with people and things. She tried to explain Susan's character to Lucy, her innate goodness and nobility, her genius as an executive, her willingness to give all for the cause—her savings as well as her strength. She was aghast that Lucy should be suspicious of Susan's handling of the meager finances of the woman's rights organization, when Susan made every effort to use each dollar so carefully and added her own money when there was a deficit. She was determined that these two noble women should not be estranged. She labored with Lucy for hours one afternoon as they walked up and down in front of her house on Forty-fifth Street.

There were others who were dissatisfied with Susan, for a leader who hews straight to the line and does not stop to placate or cajole inspires enmity as well as admiration. Susan heard of it and was troubled, and Elizabeth wrote her:

> Dearly Beloved, Of course your critics take no note of all you have been to me, though I have often told them what a stimulus and inspiration you were through years of domestic cares.... Well, the human family is affording you abundant experience in the degrada-tion of women; their littleness and meanness are the result of their abject dependence, their utter want of self-respect. But this must needs be so until they reach a higher development. Poor things! How can they be frank and magnanimous in view of their education? So let us expect nothing of the present generation of them, and then we shall not be disappointed.... You cannot imagine how much I miss you.

When Susan arrived in New York late in September, the needs of the cause were so pressing that these troubles were forgotten. To-gether she and Elizabeth planned a campaign. While Elizabeth wrote an appeal and a petition asking Congress to confer suffrage on women, and countless letters to politicians and women previ-ously interested in woman's rights, Susan interviewed old friends of the cause, trying to weld them together again.

Elizabeth now saw that Susan had been right when she wanted to continue the woman's rights organization during the war, and she acknowledged that she had been wrong in not standing by her against everyone else. She made up her mind from then on to take Susan's judgment against the world. She realized that when the two of them thrashed out a subject together and agreed, they were indomitable and could not be turned aside from their purpose by ridicule or opposition from any quarter.

They had to begin all over again spurring women on to action. Mrs. Seward and Mrs. Worden were doubtful that anyone would be interested in woman's rights while the difficult problems of reconstruction confronted the nation. Even Martha Wright needed a rousing letter from Elizabeth:

> I have just read your letter and it would have been a wet blanket to Susan and me were we not sure that we are right. With three bills before Congress to exclude us from all hope of representation in the future by so amending the United States Constitution as to limit suffrage to "males," I thank God that *two* women of the nation felt the insult and decided to do their uttermost to rouse the rest to avail themselves of the only right we have in the government—the right of petition. If the petition goes with two names only, ours be the glory, and shame to all the rest. We have had a thousand petitions printed, and when they are filled they will be sent to Democratic members who will present them to the House. But if they come back to us empty, Susan and I will sign every one, so that every Democratic member may have one with which to shame those hypocritical Republicans. Martha, what are you all thinking about that you propose to rest on your oars in such a crisis? I conjure you and Lucretia to be a power at this moment in taking the onward step. There is not the slightest hope of settling the Negro question now. When Andrew Johnson began the work of reconstruction, the Negro's opportunity was lost. Politicians will wrangle over that question for a generation. Our time is now.

They found the Democrats more willing to listen to their demands than the Republicans. They were aware, however, that most of their friends among the Democrats took an interest in woman suffrage not for love of the cause, but for political reasons, to badger the Republicans. Nevertheless they intended to make use of them although it would antagonize some of their old Abolitionist friends. They antagonized someone no matter what they did, and they were determined, as Elizabeth so tersely put it, no longer to boost the Negro over their own heads.

They sent their petition to women in all parts of the country and with the petition went long letters explaining the importance of speedy action. The petitions read: "To the Senate and House of Representatives: The undersigned women of the United States, respectfully ask an amendment to the Constitution that shall prohibit the several states from disfranchising any of their citizens on the ground of sex." It was amplified by several well-stated arguments for woman suffrage.

By the close of the 1865-66 session, petitions with ten thousand signatures had been presented to Congress. This was the first request made by women for Congressional action on woman suffrage, the first demand for an amendment to the Constitution conferring suffrage on women, and it was made through the joint efforts of Elizabeth Cady Stanton and Susan B. Anthony. So closely was their work interwoven, so similar were their reactions regarding the needs of women that it is impossible to say which was the originator of the idea. Both should receive the credit.

There was considerable discussion of woman suffrage in Congress when the petitions were presented. Democratic Congressmen admirably supported the petitions, while Senator Sumner, Republican, presented under protest and "as most inopportune" a petition from Massachusetts headed by Lydia Maria Child, his valiant supporter in antislavery work. In a spirited debate Senator Cowan of Pennsylvania warned his colleagues that Mrs. Elizabeth Cady Stanton, Mrs. Frances D. Gage, and Susan B. Anthony were on their heels. "They have their banner flung out to the winds," he said. "They are after you; and their cry is for justice, and you cannot deny it."

The Republican press was facetious about the whole matter, emphasizing the vileness of politics and the purity of women, offering as a panacea for all the imagined wrongs of women "a wicker-work cradle and a dimple-cheeked baby." Even Horace Greeley, whom the feminists had always counted as their friend, said the time had not come for the enfranchisement of women.

Susan and Elizabeth found Henry Ward Beecher and Theodore Tilton sympathetic toward their point of view. They were glad to have the backing of a man so influential as Henry Ward Beecher. Theodore Tilton, the popular young orator and editor of the *Independent,* could also be of great service to them. He printed in the *Independent* a strong editorial for woman suffrage which delighted Elizabeth. He had a plan to combine the Antislavery Society and the woman's rights organization and to form a national Equal Rights Association, demanding suffrage for Negroes and women. For president he suggested Wendell Phillips, and the *Antislavery Standard* as the Association's official organ.

It is hard to tell whether Theodore Tilton was sincere in his effort to help women when he suggested the formation of the Equal Rights Association, or whether he felt that in such an association men would have control, and if woman suffrage did not seem expedient to them, they could defer action. At any rate there was a marked feeling among the Abolitionists that an Equal Rights Association would be a desirable thing, but they failed to take the necessary steps in their own organization.

Susan and Elizabeth, however, called a Woman's Rights Convention at the Church of the Puritans in New York—the first since 1860, and at this convention, on May 10, 1866, the American Equal Rights Association was formed. Elizabeth presided. Most of the faithful workers were there, and it was a happy gathering with the usual good speeches, but Susan and Elizabeth, listening carefully to the remarks of Wendell Phillips, Theodore Tilton, and Henry Ward Beecher, were troubled over the way they avoided the real issue, the immediate enfranchisement of women; and they were soon to find out that men in the Equal Rights Association were not supporting them whole-heartedly.

A New York State Constitutional Convention had been announced for 1867, and Elizabeth and Susan, seeing it as the great opportunity for women of New York to win the right of suffrage, prepared to make the most of it.

They went to the office of the *Antislavery Standard* to discuss their plans with Wendell Phillips and Theodore Tilton a few weeks after the organization of the American Equal Rights Association. Wendell Phillips emphatically stated his position at once, that the time had come to strike the word "white" out of the New York constitution but not to strike out the word "male." Disappointed but not surprised, they waited to hear Theodore Tilton remonstrate with him; but instead he agreed heartily and recommended that women circulate petitions throughout the state praying for the enfranchisement of the Negro, and postpone their own demands until the next revision of the constitution. Both women were dumfounded. It was incredible that trusted coworkers like Wendell Phillips and Theodore Tilton would make such a recommendation. Highly indignant, Susan declared that she would rather cut off her right hand than ask for the ballot for the black man and not for woman. Growing more and more infuriated by the suavity and sophistry of these two men who should have been champions of women, she gave them a ruthless verbal lashing. Elizabeth, just as indignant, but astonished at Susan's display of temper, tried to avert a complete break. She still hoped to convert Theodore Tilton to her way of thinking. To Susan who had to hurry away to keep an appointment, Elizabeth's efforts for conciliation seemed almost like treason. She did not see her again until night, and then to her great relief found that she was equally dismayed and insulted by the attitude of the two men. As they talked the matter over, they were thoroughly roused and more determined than ever to continue their demand for woman suffrage at this time, even if it estranged them from all their friends.

Fortunately Elizabeth was able to throw herself into this campaign almost as freely as Susan. Her children were growing up. Daniel had graduated from college and had been working for several years. Henry and Gerrit were starting the practice of law. Theodore was enrolled at Cornell; Margaret and Harriot were beginning to think of college. Robert her youngest child was eight, but with Amelia Willard her capable housekeeper at the helm and no baby to look after, she felt carefree indeed.

They began at once to hold meetings throughout New York State and to circulate petitions, demanding that the word "male" as well as the word "white" be struck out of the constitution. In this state campaign some of their Abolitionist friends stood by them, Gerrit Smith, George William Curtis, and Henry Ward Beecher. Horace Greeley, however, was adamant. He talked the matter over earnestly with them, his little eyes behind his spectacles imploring them to listen. "This is a critical period for the Republican party and the life of the Nation," he declared as emphatically as his rather squeaky voice would allow. "The word 'white' in our Constitution at this hour has a significance which 'male' has not. It would be wise and magnanimous in you to hold your claims, though just and imperative, I grant, in abeyance until the Negro is safe beyond peradventure, and your turn will come next. I conjure you to remember that this is 'the Negro's hour' and your first duty now is to go through the State and plead his claims."

When they protested, he uttered his ultimatum, "If you persevere in your present plan, you need depend on no further help from me or the *Tribune*."

One more enemy, one whose pen would influence thousands. But they of course continued their work in spite of Horace Greeley.

In the midst of circulating petitions, Elizabeth decided that woman's constitutional right to run for office should be tested. She had found that although women could not vote, they could, if elected, hold office. So to the chagrin of many of her friends and the amusement of the public, she announced her candidacy for Representative in Congress for the Eighth District, New York City, at the November election, 1866. Her platform, she told the voters, was free speech, free press, free men, free trade, and universal suffrage. She was an independent candidate because she could not subscribe to the present policies of either the Democratic or Republican parties. Much discussion was stirred up by this first woman candidate for Congress. The press commented freely but mildly. There was no such furor as when she had offered her suffrage resolution at Seneca Falls in 1848. "A lady of fine presence and accomplishments in the House of Representatives," said the *New York Herald* with irony to be sure, "would wield a wholesome influence over the rough and disorderly elements of that body." The *Antislavery Standard* gave her the endorsement she deserved: "The electors of the Eighth District would honor themselves and do well by the country in giving her a triumphant election." The District, however, did not take her seriously. It gave her only twenty-four votes. But she was not surprised. She had entertained no false hopes. The candidacy had been a gesture for women—publicity for her cause.

In June 1887, Elizabeth and Susan were granted a hearing before the committee of the Constitutional Convention which was to consider the question of woman suffrage. They hurried to Albany by the night boat, made their usual able pleas for the enfranchisement of women, and answered the many questions and objections which were raised. Horace Greeley, chairman of the committee, thought he had a question which would silence them. Making himself as pompous as possible, he droningly announced, "The ballot and the bullet go together." Then, turning to Elizabeth, he asked, "If you vote, are you ready to fight?"

Quick as a flash, she retorted, "Yes, we are ready to fight, sir, just as you did in the late war, by sending our substitutes."

The next day, when Horace Greeley was to give to the Constitutional Convention the recommendation of his committee on woman suffrage, the galleries were crowded with women. Petitions came pouring in, headed by influential citizens, among them Gerrit Smith, Henry Ward Beecher, and Mrs. Daniel Cady of Johnstown. Twenty-eight thousand men and women were asking that the women of New York State be enfranchised.

Elizabeth and Susan, knowing that Horace Greeley would make an adverse report and knowing too that his wife Mary Cheney Greeley had circulated a petition for woman suffrage, arranged with George William Curtis to present her petition last, just before Mr. Greeley made his recommendation to the Convention. Willing to help the women as much as he could in this, he arose just at the crucial moment, and much to Mr. Greeley's embarrassment announced, "Mr. Chairman, I hold in my hand a petition signed by Mrs. Horace Greeley and 300 other women of Westchester asking that the word 'male' be stricken from the constitution."

In the face of this, Horace Greeley, looking more ill at ease than usual, more awkward and shabby, and angered at the amusement of the audience, stubbornly gave his report: "Your Committee does not recommend an extension of the elective franchise to women. However defensible in theory, we are satisfied that public sentiment does not demand and would not sustain an innovation so revolutionary and sweeping, so openly at war with a distribution of duties and functions between the sexes as venerable and pervading as government itself, and involving transformations so radical in social and domestic life."

He never forgave the two whose shrewdness had put him in such an uncomfortable position. They did not see him again until a few weeks later when they met him at one of his favorite haunts, a Sunday night reception at the home of Alice and Phoebe Cary. He made straight for them and they, eager to show him that they harbored him no ill feeling because of his adverse report, extended their hands in greeting. But he would not shake hands. In response to their cordial, "Good evening, Mr. Greeley," he said curtly with bitterness in his voice, "You two ladies are the most maneuvering politicians in the State of New York. You set out to annoy me in the Constitutional Convention, and you did it effectually. I saw in the manner my wife's petition was presented that Mr. Curtis was acting under instructions. I saw the reporters prick up their ears and knew that my report and Mrs. Greeley's petition would come out together, with large headings in the city papers, and probably be called out by the newsboys in the street."

Then turning to Elizabeth, he said, "You are so tenacious about your own name. Why did you not inscribe my wife's maiden name, Mary Cheney Greeley on her petition?"

"Because," replied Elizabeth, "I wanted all the world to know that it was the wife of Horace Greeley who protested against her husband's report."

"Well," he continued, "I understand the animus of that whole proceeding, and now let me tell you what I intend to do. I have given positive instructions that no word of praise shall ever again be awarded you in the *Tribune* and that if your name is ever necessarily mentioned, it shall be as Mrs. Henry B. Stanton."

He kept his word, and the paper which was the first of the

important New York dailies to befriend woman's rights, the paper which had welcomed Elizabeth Cady Stanton's first literary efforts, was henceforth closed to her.

Their prospects for woman suffrage in New York State shattered for the time being, Elizabeth and Susan continued to demand that the Fourteenth Amendment also apply to women; and one by one their old allies deserted them.

The *Antislavery Standard,* financed by the Hovey fund, which was also intended to further woman suffrage, would not carry their message. The men on whom they had always relied, William Lloyd Garrison, Horace Greeley, Thomas Wentworth Higginson, Frederick Douglass, and Gerrit Smith, as well as Wendell Phillips and Theodore Tilton, were now persuading many of the women to step aside for the sake of the Negro. Women, so used to stepping aside, obeyed. Only a few, led by Elizabeth, Susan, Lucretia Mott, Lucy Stone, and Ernestine Rose, remained loyal to the cause. Only four of the old-time Abolitionists stood by them—Samuel J. May, Stephen S. Foster, Parker Pillsbury, and Robert Purvis, the cultured wealthy Negro merchant of Philadelphia, who wrote Susan, "With what grace could I ask the women of this country to labor for my enfranchisement, and at the same time be unwilling to put forth a hand to remove the tyranny, in some respects greater, to which they are subjected?"

Never before had there been such an opportunity to demand the enfranchisement of women. Faced with the problems of reconstruction, the nation was taking stock of the rights of citizens. The Constitution, the rights it conferred, the protection it offered, the power and importance of the ballot, were subjects widely discussed among the people and in political gatherings, state legislatures, and Congress.

Had women solidly backed Elizabeth Cady Stanton and Susan B. Anthony in their almost superhuman efforts, had Abolitionists, politicians, and journalists, who at heart believed in the justice of woman suffrage, given their support and demanded the right of suffrage for all citizens at this time, there is every reason to believe that Negroes and women could have been enfranchised together.

But the men who believed in woman suffrage saw the rights of men as more important than the rights of women. And the rights of men in this instance meant the rights of male Negroes. The excuse given was political expediency. Little did it matter that the Negroes were ignorant and utterly untrained in the principles of government. Little did it matter that educated women were urging their claims. The Negro as a male citizen was of first importance. Women could come along afterward at any time. But not for fifty years did another such opportunity present itself.

As Elizabeth so aptly expressed it:

Would Horace Greeley, Wendell Phillips, Gerrit Smith, or Theodore Tilton be willing to stand aside and trust their individual interests, and the whole welfare of the nation, to the lowest strata of manhood? If not, why ask educated women, who love their country, who desire to mold its institutions on the highest idea of justice and equality, who feel that their enfranchisement is of vital importance to this end, why ask them to stand aside while 2,000,000 ignorant men are ushered into the halls of legislation?

The failure of the finest, most liberal men to understand women's position and humiliation taught Elizabeth and Susan a most valuable lesson—that women could not depend on men for help in this matter—that they would have to fight their own battles.

XIV

A RAY OF HOPE IN KANSAS

Good news had come from Kansas. Amendments were being submitted to the people of the state, which would enfranchise women and Negroes. State Senator Samuel N. Wood urged Miss Anthony to send out her best speakers to campaign for woman suffrage. It was a thrilling prospect. One state in the new West might give women the ballot.

Susan and Elizabeth had not been able to go to Kansas at once because of the New York State Constitutional Convention, but they persuaded Lucy Stone to undertake the campaign, and late in March 1867 she and Henry Blackwell set out for Kansas. As Susan and Lucy had insisted, against the protest of Wendell Phillips, that $1500 of the Jackson fund be turned over to this work, they were able to start without financial worries.

It was the first time since her daughter's birth that Lucy Stone had felt equal to a speaking tour. She feared she had lost her gift of oratory, but she found she had not. Both she and her husband were enthusiastically received. Both sent encouraging letters to Elizabeth and Susan. Henry Blackwell wrote:

> Now, Mrs. Stanton, you and Susan and Fred Douglass must come to this State early next September; you must come prepared to make *sixty speeches* each. You must leave your notes *behind you.* These people won't have written sermons. And you don't want notes. You are a natural orator, and these people will give you inspiration!... This is a glorious country, Mrs. S., and a glorious people. If we succeed here, it will be the State of the Future.

As time went on they were disturbed by the attitude of the eastern Republicans. Good Republican papers like Greeley's *New York Tribune* and Theodore Tilton's *Independent,* which were widely read in Kansas and could have molded public opinion, pleaded only for Negro suffrage. Republican leaders in Kansas consequently were lukewarm or on the fence. Henry Blackwell wrote:

But they dare not oppose us openly, and the Democratic leaders are quite disposed to take us up. If the Republicans come out against us, the Democrats will take us up.

And again he urged:

Do not let anything prevent your being here September 1 for the campaign.... There will be a big fight and a great excitement. After the fight is over Mrs. Stanton will never have *use* for *notes* or written speeches any more.

They came back in May, well-satisfied. They had made many friends for woman suffrage. Only one thing was ammunition for their opponents—Lucy's keeping her own name and calling herself Mrs. Lucy Stone while she traveled with Henry Blackwell. Unreasoning critics called them "free lovers." But suffrage workers were used to epithets.

Olympia Brown went to Kansas in July and persuaded the singing Hutchinson family to join her. Together they drove over the prairies, Olympia Brown speaking day after day, and the Hutchinsons singing suffrage songs as they had once sung antislavery ballads.

Elizabeth and Susan finally boarded the train for Kansas late in August. It had been hard to raise money for the trip. Nothing more was available from the Jackson or Hovey funds. They could not afford to pay all of their own expenses. Susan had already spent everything for suffrage. Elizabeth had her large family to educate. They needed hundreds of tracts to take with them. But nothing could stop Susan. All summer she had trudged up and down Broadway soliciting advertisements for the tracts, and sold enough to warrant the printing of 50,000. A few of the faithful made contributions to finance the trip.

The journey was long and uneventful, and Elizabeth was impatient to be in the thick of the contest. It was her first real campaign with Susan—something she had looked forward to for years. If they could only win in Kansas, what an impetus for woman suffrage!

Her excitement increased as she glimpsed from the car windows the vast undeveloped West that she had read about—prairie that rolled on for miles and miles, crude little towns, houses clustered together like so many wooden boxes, isolated sod shanties—mere dots on that undulating ocean of prairie grass. Something in this new untamed country gripped her, as it did the pioneers, and Kansas was sacred to her because of John Brown, because he and his sons had saved it for freedom.

As soon as they reached the state, Senator Wood started them on a speaking tour of the larger cities and towns. Elizabeth's fame as an orator had preceded her, as had reports of her good looks, her culture, her kindness, and her motherliness. The fact that she was married and had raised a large family endeared her to the people. They felt she was safe and decent. She was a fine-looking woman, now fifty-two, possibly a little too short and plump, with unusually beautiful, soft white hair artistically arranged, blue eyes, and a fresh, rosy complexion. She was always faultlessly gowned in black silk with a lacy white collar and cuffs.

Susan's reputation was not so favorable. She had to overcome the sarcastic jibes of newspapermen, which had reached Kansas, that she was an angular, sour old maid, disgruntled with her lot and determined to ape man. Instead they saw a lithe, middle-aged woman with indomitable nervous energy, with a kind, earnest face and a ruggedness and a hominess that they at once took to their hearts.

As usual Susan was the advance agent, the manager, and Elizabeth the attraction of every meeting. Unselfishly Susan spared herself nothing to make Elizabeth a success. There was stimulation in the efficient arrangement of details. She still avoided speaking when possible, feeling that Elizabeth's ability was so much greater than her own. But she could make a telling speech, clear and simple, without rhetorical flourishes.

Elizabeth delivered the long address which she had prepared for the occasion. It was worthy of any silver-tongued lyceum lecturer, such as Wendell Phillips or Theodore Tilton, and was filled with literary allusions and learning. It pleased the men and women in her audiences, hungry for anything that smacked of culture.

They had not been in Kansas long before they realized that the political situation was a very troubled one. A large Republican mass meeting in Lawrence in September repudiated the woman suffrage amendment, reaffirming Negro suffrage as a party measure. Pressure from the East was responsible, warning Republicans not to endanger the Negro's opportunity by linking him with woman.

But Elizabeth and Susan expected to win the people in spite of party dictates. Still hoping to influence Theodore Tilton and gain the support of the *Independent* for the woman suffrage amendment in Kansas, Elizabeth wrote him a long letter describing their experiences:

> We had a large meeting here [Louisville, Kansas] yesterday in the new Court House, to discuss suffrage for women. The people came in from miles around and seemed deeply interested in the question. I spoke yesterday on the political advantages of the enfranchisement of women. Today being Sunday I am to give the Bible argument for the equality of the sexes. These Kansas women are ready for the new doctrine. "You need not wonder," said one of them to me the other day, "if after all the difficulties and dangers we have encountered, standing sentinels alone at our doors many nights for the last twelve years, that we should come to think that our divinely constituted heads are on our own shoulders. We should have been in a poor fix if they had not been, with our men far away, or killed by Quantrell before our eyes...."
>
> We find the *Tribune* and *Independent* are the papers out here.... We find subscribers are pleased with your liberal theology, as there is not much sectarianism out here.... We find many nice brick school houses going up on all sides, the result of women's voting on that question....
>
> We have had a good opportunity to see the working men of Kansas, as they are generally boarding at the Hotels where we stay, and we have found them a quiet, orderly, sober class of citizens. You may imagine this class about, these days, smoking their pipes on the long piazzas, each one reading a Woman's Rights tract, as Miss Anthony and myself, like faithful missionaries, distribute them wherever we go. We have scattered thousands and sold enough to pay all our expenses traveling through the State. The people are eager to get everything on this question.

As it was important to cover every part of the state, even the remote settlements inaccessible by rail, Elizabeth and Susan decided that they must separate and tour different sections. Charles Robinson, first free-state Governor of Kansas, offered to take Mrs.

Stanton in his carriage and pay all expenses. It was more than an adventure for her. It was real hardship.

Day after day in a low easy carriage drawn by two mules, she and Governor Robinson drove over almost unbroken treeless prairie, following trails dimly outlined in the grass. Often they lost their way and had to drive on for miles in the dark. Prairie nights were blacker than any she had ever seen, in spite of the countless stars which were the one comfort in that vast engulfing darkness. Streams lined with cottonwoods were an oasis in the desert unless they were deep and had to be forded. Sometimes it was so dark when they forded streams that the Governor walked ahead to find the way, taking off his coat so that she could see his white shirt and slowly drive after him. Though outwardly calm and cool, she dreaded these night adventures, and was in constant fear of being upset and rolled into the water.

There was no respite at night, no clean comfortable bed to sink into after a long hard journey. The accommodations were crude. The crudeness would not have mattered, but there was unbelievable dirt; there were insects that made the night torture; the food was unfit to eat, bacon floating in grease, coffee without milk or cream, sweetened with sorghum, bread or biscuits green with soda, and only occasionally canned vegetables or dried fruit. How she longed to teach the tired pioneer women to cook! When they stopped in small towns, they bought crackers, dried herring, gum arabic, and slippery elm, and felt they were dining royally in their carriage. These were trying experiences for a fastidious woman who loved comfort, but she did not complain. She was crusading for the cause dearest to her heart. It gave her an added self-respect that she could endure these hardships with cheerfulness. Her sense of humor saved many a trying situation, and she and the Governor good-naturedly chewed their gum arabic and slippery elm as a substitute for the hearty, well-cooked meal they longed for.

The days were bright with sunshine and filled with the tang of autumn. The wide stretches of prairie cast their spell, so much, in fact, that Elizabeth began to wonder if they might not all move to

Kansas. She would want to if she could vote in Kansas. She wrote Henry:

I have been so far on the outskirts of civilization, that I have had no time or place to write, tables and chairs even being scarce. Last night we arrived here, in the first decent quarters we have had in two weeks. I am still traveling with Governor Robinson. The weather is charming. We have not had one rainy day since I came into the State. Everybody says the woman proposition will be carried but the Negro one will not. The Democrats here go for us strong. This is the country for us to move to. Of all the spots I have seen, I should like to buy a section next to Governor Robinson who lives in a splendid valley and a house on the hill. The Governor has a handsome house. We could build one for $3000. His home is five miles from Lawrence. Ponies are cheap here, so that all our children could ride and breathe, and learn to do big things. I cannot endure the thoughts of living again that contracted eastern existence. Here the boys could rise. Sam Ward offers me his farm for $12,000. Governor Robinson says that would be cheap.... You would feel like a new being here. I have not had a stiff knee or rheumatism since I came into the State. You could be a leader here as there is not a man in the State that can make a really good speech.

Governor Robinson and Mrs. Stanton made their pleas for woman suffrage wherever they could gather a few people together, in log cabins, depots, unfinished schoolhouses, churches, hotels, barns, and in the open air. Elizabeth wrote:

I spoke in a large mill one night. A solitary candle shone over my head like a halo of glory; a few lanterns hung around the outskirts of the audience made the darkness perceptible; but all I could see of my audience was the whites of their eyes in the dim distance.

Speaking so often in such informal gatherings as these, she had no need for a written address, as Henry Blackwell had foretold. She became an easy speaker, sensing at once the caliber of her audience and its needs.

Day by day it became more evident that the unfriendliness of the Republicans was growing and that the Democrats might fall in line. In October a group of influential Republicans, including Phillips and Garrison, realizing what confusion their attitude had caused in Kansas and fearing the effect of this confusion on the vote for Negro suffrage, issued a statement approving woman suffrage. But this tardy recognition of woman's rights had little effect on Kansas Republicans. Their policy had been formulated months before.

To Susan and Elizabeth, deep in the campaign, only one hope remained—to win the Democratic vote. They owed allegiance to no political party. No party had given their cause the slightest consideration. If Democrats would help in this crucial hour, all hail to the Democrats. And a Democrat appeared to champion their cause—the wealthy, eccentric, dramatic George Francis Train. The Woman Suffrage Association of St. Louis sent word that Train would speak in Kansas for two weeks paying all his expenses. Susan accepted his offer, hoping that he would win the Irish vote. She knew little about him except that he was erratic, fabulously wealthy, and interested in the Union Pacific. She was assured that he was eloquent. None of her Kansas colleagues objected to this eleventh hour chance to save the woman suffrage amendment.

His first speech was made in Leavenworth. The hall was packed with Irishmen. They hissed when he mentioned woman suffrage, but when he shook his finger at them and shouted, "Every man in Kansas who throws a vote for the Negro and not for woman, has insulted his mother, his daughter, his sister, and his wife," they cheered him. They continued to cheer him for he was the best entertainment they had had in many a day. He was tall, vigorous, and handsome, with curly brown hair and flashing gray eyes. He was fastidiously and wondrously arrayed in a blue coat with brass buttons, black trousers, patent leather boots and lavender kid gloves. He capered about the platform, enjoying the dramatics of the situation thoroughly. His speech was a rapid-fire succession of pithy statements, epigrams, and jingles.

Nothing gave him more pleasure than to have his fling at the Abolitionists who had deserted the women. "Where is Wendell Phillips, today?" he cried. "Lost caste everywhere. Inconsistent in all things and cowardly in this. Where is Horace Greeley in this Kansas war for liberty? Pitching the woman suffrage idea out of the convention and bailing Jeff Davis. Where is William Lloyd Garrison? Being patted on the shoulders by his employers, our enemies abroad, for his faithful work in trying to destroy our nation. Where is Henry Ward Beecher? Writing a story for Bonner's *Ledger*. Where is Theodore Tilton? He had time to lecture in every place but Kansas. Where is George W. Curtis? I will except him. He did stand by the guns at Albany and Tilton too for he published the speech."

Susan planned a tour for George Francis Train with one of the leading Democrats of the state, but when he failed her, she took charge and put Train through the most strenuous campaigning he ever experienced. When he hesitated because of the hardships and she said she would go on without him, he followed chivalrously. She opened the meetings with a brief clear argument for suffrage for both the Negro and woman. Train followed with his fireworks, his wit, his mimicry, and his bombast. He brought in his own ideas and theories—paying the national debt in greenbacks, freeing Ireland from British oppression, the eight-hour day, and George Francis Train for President. But he was sincere in his advocacy of woman suffrage.

He continued to entertain his audiences, and Susan felt he was getting the labor vote. She grew to respect him more and more during that trying campaign. He did not drink nor smoke and was a gentleman through and through. His life had been one adventure after another—building clipper ships, introducing American goods in Australia, traveling in China, India, and Russia, building the first street railways in England, developing the far West, and starting work on the Union Pacific Railway. His enthusiasm, his energy, and his generosity were irresistible.

The press differed in its estimates of him. "Train certainly has a wonderful power in the West," said the *Fort Scott Monitor*. "His extraordinary life, his great wealth, which may be exaggerated, his magnetism on the masses, and his singular moral record is opening up the eyes of the people to one of the most misunderstood statesmen of our country."

But the *Burlington Sentinel* called him "one of the most wide-awake specimens of the Yankee Doodle, spread-eagle, rip-up-and-tear-to-pieces Young Americans this country has ever produced."

One afternoon near the end of their tour, Mr. Train asked Susan why the equal-rights people did not have a paper to spread their message.

"Not lack of brains, but money," she replied.

"Will not Greeley and Beecher and Phillips and Tilton advance the money?" he questioned.

"No, they say this is the Negro's hour and no time to advocate woman suffrage."

"Well," he continued, "I will give you the money."

She thought no more about it, but that night in Junction City, when greeting his audience, he announced, "When Miss Anthony gets back to New York, she is going to start a woman suffrage paper. Its name is to be the *Revolution;* its motto, 'Men, their rights, and nothing more; women, their rights and nothing less.' This paper is to be a weekly, price $2 per year; its editors, Elizabeth Cady Stanton and Parker Pillsbury; its proprietor, Susan B. Anthony. Let everybody subscribe for it!"

They talked this over again the next day and Mr. Train assured Susan that he would advance the money for the paper. He also offered to pay her expenses and Elizabeth's if they would join him in a lecture tour of the principal cities on their way back to New York.

Elizabeth and Susan met in Leavenworth for election day. The singing Hutchinsons joined them. In open carriages they visited all the polling places. Here they made their last speeches and the Hutchinsons sang once more:

> Who votes for woman suffrage now
> Will add new laurels to his brow;
> His children's children, with holy fire,
> Will chant in praise their patriot sire.
> No warrior's wreath of glory shed
> A brighter lustre o'er the head
> Than he who battles selfish pride,
> And votes with woman side by side.

The result of the election was disappointing. Both amendments were defeated, the Negro Suffrage Amendment receiving 10,843 votes out of a total of 30,000 and the Woman Suffrage Amendment, 9,070. However, many friends had been won for woman suffrage, and the question had for the first time been put to a vote of the people.

George Francis Train was now eager to begin his lecture tour with Susan and Elizabeth. They talked the matter over seriously and decided to accept in spite of the protests of their Kansas friends and in spite of the letters of warning from the East. Their Kansas friends had no use for George Francis Train. They thought him much too erratic, always seeking notoriety for himself. Their eastern friends, the Abolitionists, were horrified at their association with a man whom they considered a Copperhead, a man who hated the Negro. They were ready to blame the defeat of the Negro Suffrage Amendment in Kansas on Train. They resented his criticism of them. They disliked having the cause of woman suffrage linked up with a man who to them was an unbalanced charlatan.

But Elizabeth and Susan had become hardened to criticism. They were used to standing alone. They had listened to their friends during the war and were sorry. Mr. Train offered them an opportunity to campaign for woman suffrage in a well-planned lecture tour. He was willing to finance a paper in which they could freely expound their views on woman's rights. How they had longed for such a paper! He was eccentric to be sure. But their proper friends had forsaken them for the Negro at this crucial moment and would not finance them. They could get nothing from the Hovey fund. It was all going to the *Antislavery Standard,* which would not champion woman suffrage at this time. Here was a wonderful opportunity for publicity. They could not give it up.

They joined George Francis Train in Omaha. They spoke in St. Louis, Chicago, Springfield, Louisville, Cincinnati, Cleveland, Buffalo, Rochester, Syracuse, Albany, Springfield, Massachusetts, Worcester, Boston, and Hartford, and ended with a big meeting at Steinway Hall, New York, December 14, 1867.

Never had they traveled in such luxury. Mr. Train reserved for them the best rooms in the best hotels. Delayed by a railway wreck, he chartered a special train. He arranged for publicity. He scattered handbills, spicy with his epigrams. He had a pamphlet printed with which he was especially pleased, called "The Great Epigram Campaign of Kansas," containing newspaper comments on his Kansas campaign. The title page carried one of his many rimes, one most uncomplimentary to the unfaithful Abolitionist suffragists:

> The Garrisons, Phillipses, Greeleys, and Beechers
> False prophets, false guides, false teachers and
>   preachers,
> Left Mrs. Stanton, Miss Anthony, Brown and Stone
> To fight the Kansas battle alone;
> While your Rosses, Pomeroys, and your Clarkes
> Stood on the fence, or basely fled
> While woman was saved by a Copperhead.

This pamphlet, so characteristic of Train, also glowingly advertised the *Revolution* and listed the woman's rights tracts which could be purchased from Susan B. Anthony, Secretary of the American Equal Rights Association. To discover that the Association was advertised by George Francis Train was more than Elizabeth's and Susan's eastern colleagues could bear. Lucy Stone, hearing of it, first thought it a joke, and then, convinced that it was true, felt obliged to print a notice explaining that the Equal Rights Association was not sponsoring the lecture tour of George Francis Train. They all grew more and more bitter about it, feeling that the cause was being trailed in the dust. They shared their views with suffragists throughout the country; and Elizabeth and Susan found that although they talked before large audiences in all of the cities, few of the old suffrage workers were to be seen. But their message was reaching a new group.

The Republican press abused Train mercilessly. Governor Robinson wrote Mrs. Stanton: "It is very remarkable that Miss Anthony and yourself should be so magnetized by him [Train] when everyone else seems to regard him simply as an egotistic clown."

Still Elizabeth and Susan did not regret their alliance with George Francis Train. Nor were they magnetized by him as their friends supposed. They could overlook his foibles for his generosity to them and their cause. Their insistence on woman suffrage in this, "the Negro's hour," had already made them unpopular with many of their old friends. A little more unpopularity because of Train seemed unimportant compared to the work to be done. None of the criticism, harsh as it was, none of the sincere pleading of good friends could keep them from making plans with George Francis Train for their woman suffrage paper, the *Revolution*.

XV

THE "REVOLUTION"

THE first number of the *Revolution* was issued January 8, 1868, and ten thousand copies were sent to all parts of the country under the frank of the Democratic Congressman, James Brooks of New York. It announced itself as the organ of the National Party of New America, devoted to principle not policy, discussing educated suffrage irrespective of sex or color, equal pay to women for equal work, eight-hour labor, abolition of standing armies and party despotisms. Its slogan was "Down with politicians; up with the people."

The paper was devoted primarily to woman's rights under the excellent editorship of Parker Pillsbury and Elizabeth Cady Stanton. Both were virile writers. Both expressed their ideas freely without fear of the consequences. Parker Pillsbury was an experienced journalist and a reformer at heart. He had severed his connection with the *Antislavery Standard* because he felt it was not doing its duty toward woman suffrage and yet was being financed by the Hovey fund, which had been established to further the cause of woman as well as that of the Negro. He was one of the most loyal friends the feminists ever had.

Susan B. Anthony was the actual business manager. George Francis Train and David M. Mellis, who had agreed to finance the paper until it was self-supporting, expressed their ideas on the last two or three pages of each number, advocating greenbacks, prohibition of foreign manufactures, the open door to immigrants, the Credit Foncier and Credit Mobilier systems, more organized labor, and penny ocean postage. Occasionally there was a poem, an epigrammatic article, or a letter from Mr. Train. Mr. Mellis conducted a racy column of Wall Street gossip.

The *Revolution* was received with horror by the conservatives. The name was impossible, far too inflammatory. The association with Train and Mellis was unpardonable. Garrison, Phillips, Higginson, and Lucy Stone could not forgive Elizabeth and Susan for what they considered treachery to the cause. Gerrit Smith was sorely tried by their affiliation. Susan had established the office of the *Revolution* at 37 Park Row in rooms which had been used as headquarters of the Equal Rights Association, and there were complaints; but as she had always been personally responsible for the rent, she stayed on, and the Equal Rights Association withdrew.

Now persecution began in earnest. Practically all of Susan's old friends deserted her and tried to persuade Elizabeth and Parker Pillsbury to do the same. She was the baneful influence leading them to destruction, determined to have her own way and dominate all her associates. But Elizabeth and Parker Pillsbury were loyal to Susan. Elizabeth had made up her mind to stand with her against the world.

To their good friend Martha Wright, who was being deluged with complaints against them, Elizabeth wrote:

> Mr. Train is a pure, high-toned man, without a vice. He has some extravagances and idiosyncrasies, but he is willing to devote energy and money to our cause when no other man is. It seems to me it would be right and wise to accept aid even from the devil himself, provided he did not tempt us to lower our standard. . . . They might better turn their attention to Wendell Phillips, who by his false philosophy has paralyzed the very elect. To think of Boston women holding an antislavery festival when their own petitions are ignored in the Senate of the United States!

When Thomas Wentworth Higginson expostulated with them because they were aligning themselves with the Democrats, who had the reputation of hating the Negro, she wrote:

> Our "pathway" is straight to the ballot box, with no variableness nor shadow of turning. I know we have shocked our old friends, who were half asleep on the woman question, into new life. Just waking from slumber, they are cross and can't see where we are going. But time will show that Miss Anthony and I are neither idiots nor lunatics. . . . We do care what good men like you *say;* but just now the men who will do something to help us are more important. Garrison, Phillips, and Sumner, in their treatment of our question today, prove that we must not trust any of you. . . . No, my dear

friend, we are right in our present position. We demand in the reconstruction, suffrage for all the citizens of the Republic.

The *Revolution* not only created a stir among Elizabeth's and Susan's friends and coworkers, but it received unusual attention from the press. The *Cincinnati Enquirer* said:

> Mrs. Elizabeth Cady Stanton's *Revolution* grows with each additional number more spicy, readable, and revolutionary. It hits right and left, from the shoulder and overhand at everybody and thing that oppose the granting of suffrage to females as well as males.

From the *Daily Times* of Troy, New York, came these words of praise:

> We are bound in all candor to say that the *Revolution*, Miss Anthony's Woman's Rights paper, is a readable, well-edited and instructive journal. Mrs. Stanton and Mr. Pillsbury are the editors and they are certainly sharp and able writers. Their correspondence too is spicy and interesting. The *Revolution* is a paper of ideas, however impracticable they may be, and its beautiful mechanical execution renders the appearance very attractive.

Both Susan and Elizabeth looked eagerly for some word from Horace Greeley's *Tribune* and Wendell Phillips' *Antislavery Standard,* but they did not even notice that the *Revolution* existed. This was almost harder to bear than criticism.

The *New York Sunday Times* assailed them vigorously in good antisuffrage style for being out of their sphere:

> THE LADIES MILITANT.—It is out at last. If the women as a body have not succeeded in getting up a revolution, Susan B. Anthony, as their representative, has. Her *Revolution* was issued last Thursday as a sort of New Year's gift to what she considered a yearning public, and it is said to be "charged to the muzzle with literary nitro-glycerine." If Mrs. Stanton would attend a little more to her domestic duties and a little less to those of the great public, perhaps she would exalt her sex quite as much as she does by Quixotically fighting windmills in their gratuitous behalf, and she might possibly set a notable example of domestic felicity. No married woman can convert herself into a feminine Knight of the Rueful Visage and ride about the country attempting to redress imaginary wrongs without leaving her own household in a neglected condition that must be an eloquent witness against her. As for spinsters, we have always said that every woman has a natural and inalienable

right to a good husband and a pretty baby. When, by proper "agitation" she has secured this right, she best honors herself and her sex by leaving public affairs behind her, and endeavoring to show how happy she can make the little world of which she has just become the brilliant center.

Elizabeth could never allow to go unchallenged any insinuation that she neglected her family. In the *Revolution* of January 22 she replied to the *Times:*

> We know—what not one woman in ten thousand does know—how to take care of a child, make good bread, and keep a home clean.... Our children ... are healthy, rosy, happy, and well-fed. Pork, salt meat, mackerel, rancid butter, heavy bread, lard, cream of tartar and soda, or any other culinary abominations are never found on our table. Now let every man who wants his wife to know how to do likewise take the *Revolution* in which not only the ballot, but bread and babies will be discussed.

The office of the *Revolution* made a very favorable impression on Nellie Hutchinson of the *Cincinnati Commercial* in contrast to the untidiness and confusion of most newspaper offices. She described it in detail for her readers:

> What editorial bliss is this! Actually a neat carpet on the floor, a substantial round table covered by a pretty cloth, engravings and photographs hung thickly over the clear white walls. Here is Lucretia Mott's saintly face, beautiful with eternal youth; there Mary Wollstonecraft looking into futurity with earnest eyes. In an arched recess are shelves containing books and piles of pamphlets, speeches and essays of Stuart Mill, Wendell Phillips, Higginson, Curtis. Two screens extend across the front of the room, enclosing a little space around the two large windows which give light and air and glimpses of City Hall Park. Glancing around the corner we see editor Pillsbury seated at his desk by the further window.... Ah! Here comes Susan—the determined—the invincible—the Susan who is possibly destined to be Vice-President or Secretary of State some of these days. ... She talks awhile in her kindly incisive way.... She rises. "Come let me introduce you to Mrs. Stanton." And we walk into the inner sanctum, a tiny bit of a room, nicely carpeted, one-windowed and furnished with two desks, two chairs, a little table—and the senior editor, Mrs. Stanton. The short substantial figure, with its handsome black dress and silver crown of curls, is sufficiently interesting. The fresh girlish complexion, the laughing blue eyes and jolly voice are yet more so. Beside her stands her sixteen-year-old daughter, who is as plump, as jolly, as laughing-eyed as her mother. We study Cady

Stanton's handsome face as she talks on rapidly and facetiously. Nothing little or mean in that face; no line of distrust or irony; neither are there wrinkles of care—life has been pleasant to this woman.

Subscriptions for the *Revolution* came in very encouragingly, and Susan, able business manager that she was, did everything she could to increase the circulation and to sell advertising space. She knew that sooner or later the entire financial burden would be on her shoulders, for just as the first copy was issued, George Francis Train sailed for England. He was almost immediately put in prison because of his Irish sympathies and was kept there a year. He had left $600 with her, saying that Mr. Mellis would furnish the necessary funds during his absence. Mr. Mellis did his best to fulfill his obligations, but the *Revolution* began running into debt. It was very hard to get advertisements, for the circulation was small and the management was firm in its decision to advertise no quack remedies and nothing which it could not recommend. This was a courageous policy in days when even religious periodicals advertised anything and everything.

Meanwhile Elizabeth was steadily and happily at work writing editorials and articles. The *Revolution* gave her the opportunity to champion unpopular causes, causes indisputably connected with the crusade for woman's freedom, but which more cautious, less discerning minds would have ignored. She had always taken an interest in the problems of working women, had always believed that every occupation should be opened to them. She knew that financial dependence was one of the chief reasons for women's abject subservience, and so in every possible way she brought up the subject, calling attention to women's low wages, and demanding equal opportunities and equal pay for equal work. She hailed with delight every new occupation open to women.

Susan was as interested in the working woman as Elizabeth and organized a Working Woman's Association with members from the different trades—typesetters, printers, bookbinders, factory workers, milliners, seamstresses, embroidery workers, and rag pickers. Both tried to make these working women see that the ballot was the most effective means of improving working conditions and wage standards for women, but the question of woman suffrage was not a popular one and at first they took it up rather gingerly. Susan attended the National Labor Union Congress as a delegate of this Association and presented strong resolutions including a demand for woman suffrage which was turned down.

A few months later they championed a cause which brought upon them a great deal of censure—that of Hester Vaughn, a young servant girl who, accused of murdering her child, born out of wedlock, was sentenced to hang. Hester Vaughn's tragic story aroused Elizabeth's sympathy at once. In impassioned editorials in the *Revolution* she pleaded for Hester Vaughn, calling attention to the injustice of the sentence.

At a meeting of the Working Woman's Association, Anna Dickinson, the popular orator, vividly and sympathetically told the story of this unfortunate girl. Twenty-year-old Hester Vaughn had come from England to Philadelphia with her husband who shortly deserted her. She found it difficult to earn her living, worked as a servant girl in several families, and was seduced by one of her employers who, as soon as he learned she was pregnant, discharged her. She wandered about the streets sick and desperate, working when she could. She found refuge in an unheated garret and there in midwinter her child was born. For twenty-four hours she lay on the floor in a stupor, occasionally rousing herself to call for help. When found at last, she was in a critical condition and the baby was dead. She was imprisoned at once for infanticide. Ill and ignorant of her legal rights, she was tried without proper defense, and convicted. There was no proof that she had deliberately killed her child.

The Association sent the well-known author, Eleanor Kirk, and a woman physician, Dr. Clemence Lozier, to Philadelphia to investigate the case. They were convinced of Hester Vaughn's innocence and worthiness. Then the Working Woman's Association called a large meeting in Cooper Institute on her behalf, and Eleanor Kirk and Dr. Lozier made their reports. Resolutions were enthusiastically adopted demanding a new trial or unconditional pardon for Hester Vaughn, that women be tried by a jury of peers, have a voice in the making of laws, and that capital punishment be abolished. Elizabeth Cady Stanton and Elizabeth Smith Miller personally presented these resolutions to the Governor of Pennsylvania. They visited Hester in prison, had a long talk with her, and were completely won over by her gentleness and pitifulness. And after many months of continuous effort by her friends, she was pardoned and sent back to her home in England.

This case stirred Elizabeth so deeply and seemed so much a part of woman's fight for equality that she wrote a great deal in the *Revolution* about the issues it raised. She pointed out fearlessly that Hester Vaughn's seducer was as guilty as Hester. She demanded equal moral standards for men and women and jury service for women. She wrote:

> If we look over the history of jury trial, we find in all ages, and nations, the greatest stress laid on every man being judged by his equals.... If nobles cannot judge peasants, or peasants nobles, how can man judge woman? But, cannot woman trust her own father, husband, brother for wise laws and just judgments? The Hester Vaughns—the very class that most need protection—are often bound to earth by no ties like these. Their betrayers may be their judges and their jurors.

There was a great deal of criticism because the *Revolution* championed Hester Vaughn so unreservedly. The press was none too friendly, casting aspersions upon those who were attempting to interfere with the administration of justice. Conservatives felt it not only unwise but unbecoming to be involved in and besmirched by such a criminal case. Others, who sympathized with Hester Vaughn, thought it unnecessary to connect her case with the cause of woman's rights.

So many letters came in to the *Revolution,* asking whether the paper was opposed to marriage, that Elizabeth answered them in the editorial, "The Man Marriage," in which she listed her objections to the present marriage system:

> First, I object to the teachings of the Church on this question. Its interpretation of the Bible, making man the head of the woman, and its forms of marriage, by which she is given away as an article of

merchandise, and made to vow obedience as a slave to a master, are all alike degrading to my sex.... Second, the position of the State on this question is quite as objectionable as that of the Church.... There is not a man in this nation, who, knowing what the laws are, but would repudiate for himself a relation that would so wholly merge his individual existence in that of another human being.

The social customs which had grown out of these false creeds and codes, she regarded as not only degrading to women but demoralizing to the race and dangerous to the state. She continued:

Marriage today is in no way viewed as an equal partnership, intended for the equal advantage and happiness of both parties. Nearly every man feels that his wife is his property, whose first duty, under all circumstances, is to gratify his passions, without the least reference to her own health and happiness, or the welfare of their offspring; and so enfeebled is woman's judgment and moral sense from long abuse, that she believes so too, and quotes from the Bible to prove her own degradation.

Such frank, true statements on the subject of marriage did not win friends for Elizabeth or for the *Revolution*. However, at this time George Francis Train severed all connection with the paper and thus the main cause of criticism was removed. He had written from England in December 1868:

You no longer need my services. The *Revolution* is a power. Would it not be more so without Train? Had you not better omit my name in 1869? Would it not bring you more subscribers and better assist the noble cause of reform?

But the manager and editors of the *Revolution* were loyal to the man who had helped them when no one else would and continued to print his letters and news of him until May 1869, when he insisted that his name be omitted. Elizabeth announced his retirement in an editorial:

Our partnership dissolves today. Now we shall look for a harvest of new subscribers, as many have written and said to us again and again, if you will only drop Train, we will send you patrons by the hundreds. We hope that the fact that Train has dropped us will not vitiate these promises. Our generous friend starts for California on the seventh in the first train over the Pacific road. He takes with him the sincere thanks of those who know what he has done in the cause of woman, and of those who appreciate what a power the *Revolution* has already been in raising public thought to the importance of the speedy enfranchisement of women.

The *Revolution* had moved its offices to the Women's Bureau at 49 East Twenty-third Street, near Fifth Avenue, at the request of Mrs. Elizabeth B. Phelps, a wealthy woman who felt that a place should be provided which would be a rallying point for women's organizations and for women from all parts of the country. For this purpose she had bought a large house which she called the Women's Bureau. The *Revolution* occupied the first floor, although Susan warned Mrs. Phelps that its presence might have an adverse influence on the popularity of the Women's Bureau. She was right. The feeling was so strong among the more conservative women against those two agitators, Susan B. Anthony and Elizabeth Cady Stanton, and their too liberal *Revolution* that not even the open-minded Sorosis, the first woman's literary club founded in this country, would hold its meetings at the Women's Bureau. After one year Mrs. Phelps had to abandon the project which should have been of such value to the women of New York.

The year at the Women's Bureau was a very happy one for the staff of the *Revolution*. Their friends gathered there: Alice and Phoebe Cary, who were devoted to Susan; Elizabeth Tilton, who selected the poetry for the paper; and Anna Dickinson, who always burst into the office with a smile and boundless energy whenever she was in New York. It was a center for a group of forward-looking women who had confidence in Elizabeth and Susan. The *Revolution* gained in literary reputation; its contributors were among the best-known women writers of the day —Alice and Phoebe Cary, Anna Dickinson, Laura C. Bullard, Lillie Devereux Blake, Paulina Wright Davis, Eleanor Kirk, Olive Logan, Mary Clemmer, and Matilda Joslyn Gage. There were foreign correspondents who sent the latest news about women from Europe. It gained subscribers but not enough to ease the increasing financial burden. The retirement of Train and the omission of the column of Wall Street gossip, which had been so offensive to many, did not bring in a host of new supporters, for the Abolitionist suffragists were still at odds with the *Revolution* in regard to the amendments to the Federal Constitution which were to enfranchise the Negro. This difference of opinion, more fundamental and important than George Francis Train or Elizabeth's frank editorials and her espousing of troublesome causes, widened the breach between them.

XVI

A WOMAN SUFFRAGE AMENDMENT

THE Fourteenth Amendment had been ratified July 28, 1868, and settled the status of citizenship. It definitely recorded the word male three times in connection with citizenship, thereby excluding women. But even the Negro was not safely enfranchised under the Fourteenth Amendment and it soon became evident that a Fifteenth would be necessary.

Elizabeth and Susan were determined that the Fifteenth Amendment be written to include women. From the *Revolution* office they sent petitions to all parts of the country for signatures. When Gerrit Smith refused to sign their petition asking that any amendment extending suffrage make no distinction between men and women, Elizabeth was incredulous. Gerrit Smith, whom she had always regarded as the noblest, the fairest, the most liberal of men! Another idol shattered. First Wendell Phillips and Garrison and now Gerrit Smith. She wrote a long editorial in the *Revolution* criticizing her Cousin Gerrit's position. She spared no one who differed with her on this issue. But she loved her Cousin Gerrit too well to bear him any ill will. She wrote him:

> I am glad to hear that you think you were annihilated in the *Revolution* but I intended to leave enough of you to reply.... If I go to Chicago I will stop and bind up your wounds, pouring in oil and wine, for I admire you more than any living man though you do persist in putting Sambo, Hans, Patrick, and Yung Fung above your noblest countrymen.

George W. Julian of Indiana in December 1868 had introduced an amendment in the House of Representatives which would enfranchise all citizens whether native or naturalized "without any distinction or discrimination whatever founded on race, color, or sex." Senator Pomeroy of Kansas had offered an amendment making citizenship the basis of suffrage, and a little later Senator

Wilson of Massachusetts and Mr. Julian had introduced bills to enfranchise women in the District of Columbia. It looked as if at
last women might slip in with the Negro. But Senator Pomeroy's
and Mr. Julian's bills were ignored, not even debated, and a
Fifteenth Amendment, enfranchising the Negro and omitting
women, gave every promise of being passed. It read:

> The right of citizens of the United States to vote shall not be de-
> nied or abridged by the United States, or by any State, on account
> of race, color, or previous condition of servitude.

It would have been so easy to include the word sex.

Elizabeth came out strongly against this proposed amendment in
a long editorial in the *Revolution*. To Abolitionists this was heresy.
Even women were saying, "We must stand by the Negro although
our own claims are neglected." In fact only a few women stood
by Elizabeth and Susan in their insistent demand for woman
suffrage at this crucial time—Lucretia Mott, Martha C. Wright,
Olympia Brown, Josephine Griffing, Paulina Wright Davis, Matilda
Joslyn Gage, Ernestine Rose, and Clarissa Howard Nichols. Even
Lucy Stone had deserted them because they opposed the Fifteenth
Amendment. She was now advocating two amendments, one to
enfranchise the Negro and the other to enfranchise women, and was
urging that the two causes be kept separate. Again Elizabeth spoke
out plainly in the *Revolution* against any such policy, citing the
case of Kansas to show how two separate issues stir up ill feeling
against each other and inevitably are both defeated.

Feeling that this was an opportune time to hold a convention in
Washington and bring all possible pressure to bear on Congress,
they made plans with the woman suffrage association which had
recently been organized by Washington women.

On January 19, 1869, the first Woman Suffrage Convention ever
held in Washington convened with Senator Pomeroy in the chair.
He soon retired in favor of Lucretia Mott, who was elected president. Lucretia Mott was now seventy-six, and although a little less
vigorous than formerly, had lost none of her eloquence. She directed
the convention perfectly, giving it the serenity and consecration

that her presence always inspired. She was loved and reverenced by everyone.

The three pioneers, Lucretia, Elizabeth, and Susan were the attraction of the convention. Each made a telling speech. Grace Greenwood, reporting the convention for the *Philadelphia Press* said:

> Of all the speakers Mrs. Stanton seemed to me to have the most weight. Her speeches are models of composition—clear, compact, elegant, and logical. She makes her points with peculiar sharpness and certainty, and there is no denying or dodging her conclusions. . . . Indeed, it seems to me, that while Lucretia Mott may be said to be the soul of this movement, and Mrs. Stanton the mind, the "swift keen intelligence," Miss Anthony, alert, aggressive, and indefatigable, is its nervous energy—its propulsive force. Mrs. Stanton has the best arts of the politician and the training of the jurist, added to the fiery, unresting spirit of the reformer. She has a rare talent for affairs, management, and mastership. Yet she is in an eminent degree womanly, having an almost regal pride of sex. In France, in the time of the Revolution or the first Empire she would have been a Roland or a de Staël.

It was a large, enthusiastic convention. Twenty states were represented. New recruits for the cause were won, among them Clara Barton. There was a spirited debate as to whether it was the duty of women to withdraw from the field until the Negro was enfranchised. Robert Purvis, wealthy Philadelphia Negro, as true as ever to the women, demanded for his daughter all that he asked for his son and himself. But his son was not as just, nor was George Dowling, a young colored man who announced that God intended the male to dominate the female everywhere.

As the Fifteenth Amendment had passed Congress and was waiting for the President's signature before being submitted to the states, Mrs. Stanton pleaded at the convention for a Sixteenth Amendment to enfranchise women, and she and Miss Anthony persuaded Mr. Julian to introduce a Sixteenth Amendment in the next Congress. He introduced this Amendment on March 15, 1869, after the Fifteenth Amendment had been submitted to the states. This marked an epoch in the history of woman suffrage. At last a definite bill enfranchising women was before Congress. It read:

The Right of Suffrage in the United States shall be based on citizenship, and shall be regulated by Congress; and all citizens of the United States whether native or naturalized shall enjoy this right equally without any distinction or discrimination whatever founded on sex.

Mrs. Stanton wrote in the *Revolution:*

Since our famous Bill of Rights was given to the world declaring all men equal, there has been no other proposition, in its magnitude, benevolence, and far-reaching consequences, so momentous as this. The specific work now before us, is to press Woman's Enfranchisement, and petitions should be circulated in every school district from Maine to California, praying the adoption of the Sixteenth Amendment, that when the Forty-second Congress assembles, it may understand the work before it.

Not only did Elizabeth and Susan have petitions printed and sent to all parts of the country, but they made a tour of several western states to urge the passage of the Sixteenth Amendment. They were so well received everywhere that it seemed almost like a triumphal tour. Many new suffrage organizations were formed. Elizabeth sent interesting letters to the *Revolution* telling of their meetings in Chicago, Springfield, Bloomington, Galena, St. Louis, Madison, Milwaukee, and Toledo. From Chicago to St. Louis they had their first experience in the new Pullman cars and with enthusiasm she wrote:

Sunday night we left Chicago for St. Louis in the palace cars, where we slept as comfortable as in our own homes and breakfasted on the train in the morning. The dining room was exquisitely arranged and the cooking excellent. The kitchen was a gem, and the cook, in the neatness and order of his person and all his surroundings was a pink of male perfection. It really did seem like magic to eat, sleep, read the morning papers, and talk with one's friends in bedroom, dining room, and parlor, dashing over the prairies at the rate of thirty miles an hour. While men can keep house in this charming manner, the world will not be utterly desolate when women *do* vote.

They found valuable workers in the West—Virginia Minor of St. Louis, whom they had known since the Kansas campaign; Phoebe Couzins of St. Louis, known as the Anna Dickinson of the West; Myra Bradwell, who edited the *Chicago Legal News;*

and Mary Livermore, who was planning a woman suffrage paper for the West, which she would call the *Agitator*.

In spite of the support in the West, Elizabeth and Susan found that their old friends and supporters in the East remained almost solidly against them. Hardest of all to bear and understand was Lucy Stone's attitude. Both sides did their best to avert an open break. In answer to a letter from Thomas Wentworth Higginson, Elizabeth wrote:

> I received your kind note and hasten to say that I fully agree with you as to the wisdom of keeping all our misunderstandings to ourselves. No word or pen of mine shall ever wrong or detract from any woman, especially one who has done so good a work for woman as Lucy Stone. I rest assured that time will vindicate our own position. I accept all things patiently, for I see that human nature is the same inside and outside the reform world. Our Abolitionists are just as sectarian in their association as the Methodists in their church, and divisions are always the most bitter where there is the least to differ about. But in spite of all, the men and women who have been battling for freedom in this country, are as grand and noble as any that have ever walked the earth. So we will forget their faults and love them for their many virtues.

When it looked as if most of the old friends of woman suffrage were deserting women for the Negro, a new champion arose. John Stuart Mill made a speech before Parliament on the subjection of women, asking for their enfranchisement. He was an advocate who commanded attention. The reports of his speech in American papers were very meager, but Elizabeth and Susan sent to England for a verbatim report, which they reprinted as a tract. In 1869, *The Subjection of Women* was published in book form in England, and Elizabeth with deep gratitude for Mill's espousal of woman's cause wrote him:

> I wish to thank you for your noble work on *The Subjection of Women*. To my mind, no thinker has so calmly, truthfully, and logically revealed the causes and hidden depths of woman's degradation, and so clearly pointed out the secret springs of the sycophancy of the more fortunate woman to man. It is my earnest hope that progress will vouchsafe to all men the power of seeing as clearly as you do the demoralizing effect on all alike of the idea that man is to be served and woman to serve. I lay the book down with a

peace and joy I never felt before, for it is the first response from any man to show he is capable of seeing and feeling all the nice shades and degrees of woman's wrongs, and the central point of her weakness and degradation.

She invited him to attend the convention of the Equal Rights Association in New York in May 1869 and was overjoyed to find in his letter of regret these lines on the Fifteenth Amendment:

It is not to be believed that the nation which is now engaged in admitting the newly liberated Negro to the plenitude of all political franchise, will much longer retain woman in a state of helotage, which is more degrading than ever, because being no longer shared by any of the male sex, it constitutes every woman the inferior of every man.

She made use of this at once in an editorial for the *Revolution*. From the *Revolution* office hundreds of letters were sent to all parts of the country urging the friends of woman suffrage to attend the Equal Rights Association Convention. To one of her friends Elizabeth wrote:

We have written to every one of the old friends, ignoring the past and urging them to come. We do so much desire to sink all petty considerations in the one united effort to secure woman suffrage. Though many unkind acts and words have been administered to us, which we have returned with sarcasm and ridicule, there are really only kind feelings in our souls for all the noble men and women who have fought for freedom during the last thirty years.

An unusually large number of delegates attended the Convention of the Equal Rights Association in Steinway Hall, May 14, 1869. The West was well represented under the leadership of Mary Livermore. In the absence of the president, Lucretia Mott, Elizabeth presided. She had acquired a poise and a command as presiding officer which might have been the envy of many a man.

After the usual eloquent speeches and reports, Stephen Foster of Massachusetts arose and objected because officers had been nominated who, he believed, had repudiated the principles of the Society. He mentioned first in this connection the presiding officer.

In a clear calm voice, Elizabeth replied to his accusation, "I would like you to say in what respect."

"I will with pleasure," answered Mr. Foster, "for ladies and gentlemen, I admire our talented president with all my heart, and love the woman." At this, the audience laughed heartily. "But I believe," he continued, "she has publically repudiated the principles of the Society."

Again, Elizabeth repeated, "I would like Mr. Foster to state in what way."

Mr. Foster then explained that he objected to the *Revolution's* advocacy of educated suffrage. Mrs. Stanton and Miss Anthony should stand for universal suffrage. He objected to the article, "That Infamous Fifteenth Amendment." "I am not willing," he declared, "to take George Francis Train on this platform with his ridicule of the Negro and opposition to his enfranchisement."

"Is it quite generous," asked Mrs. Livermore, "to bring Mr. Train on this platform when he has retired from the *Revolution?*"

"If the *Revolution,*" retorted Mr. Foster, "which has so often endorsed George Francis Train will repudiate him because of his course in respect to the Negro's rights, I have nothing further to say. But it does not repudiate him. He goes out; it does not cast him out."

"Of course it does not!" interposed Susan.

"My friend says yes to what I have said," continued Mr. Foster. "I thought it was so. Then I have other objections to these women being officers of this Society. When we organized this Society, we appointed a committee for the purpose of having a body which would be responsible for the funds of the Society and we appointed a treasurer to take care of the funds. But if you look into that committee's report, you will find that it shirked its duty. That committee put its funds in the hands of an individual person, and let her run the machine."

"That is true," said Susan.

"And she never kept any books or account of the expenditures," charged Mr. Foster.

"That is false!" Susan vehemently retorted. "Every dollar ever received by me and every dollar expended, item by item, was presented to the trust fund committee of Boston, of which this gentleman is a member. The account was audited, and has been reported to me, by Wendell Phillips, Parker Pillsbury, Abby Kelly Foster, and Charles F. Whipple, and they voted me a check of $1000 to balance the account."

"I would be glad to believe Miss Anthony," continued Mr. Foster, "but her statement is not reliable, for Wendell Phillips and Abby Kelly Foster told me so."

Elizabeth, calm but indignant that this matter so unfair to Susan was being aired before the convention, called Mr. Foster to order. Voting on the question of order, the convention sustained her ruling.

Mr. Foster then attempted to tell why the Massachusetts Society could not co-operate with this organization and why Miss Anthony and Mrs. Stanton should retire and give place to officers whom the Society could respect. "If you choose to put officers here," he said, "who ridicule the Negro, and pronounce the Fifteenth Amendment infamous, why I must retire. I cannot work with you."

All eyes turned to Henry Blackwell, who was waiting to express his opinion. He had a reputation for fairness. "The facts of the case," he said, earnestly, "are these. During the early portion of the Society Miss Anthony was given full power over the funds of the Society to spend them as she thought best. Some of us thought her expenditures were not judicious; no one doubted the purity of her motives. The whole financial matter, however, has been settled in this way. Miss Anthony brought in a statement of her expenditures to the Society. No one doubts that all the expenditures were actually made as she reported. Her statement made due to herself from the society $1000. Now, Miss Anthony, for the sake of harmony and the good of the cause has given up her claim for this $1000. In regard to this we have to say that we are entirely satisfied with the settlement thus made. When a person for the good of a cause will make a pecuniary sacrifice of expenditures made, which expenditures many might consider perfectly wise, although some of us did not, it shows such a spirit that I think this question might well have been kept back.

"In regard to the criticism of our officers," he continued, "I will agree that many unwise things have been written in the *Revolution* by a gentleman who furnished part of the means by which that paper has been carried on. But that gentleman has withdrawn, and you, who know the real opinions of Miss Anthony and Mrs. Stanton on the question of Negro suffrage, do not believe that they meant to create antagonism between the Negro and the woman question. If they did disbelieve in Negro suffrage, it would be no reason for excluding them. We should no more exclude a person from our platform for disbelieving Negro suffrage than a person should be excluded from the antislavery platform for disbelieving woman suffrage. But I know that Miss Anthony and Mrs. Stanton believe in the right of the Negro to vote. We are united on that point. There is no question of either money or principle between us."

After this tense debate, the nominations were approved by a large majority, but the atmosphere was still charged, ready to flare up at the slightest provocation.

The attempt on the part of a group of men to get the endorsement of the convention for the Fifteenth Amendment started another battle which was opened by Frederick Douglass, when he said, "I must say that I do not see how anyone can pretend that there is the same urgency in giving the ballot to woman as to the Negro." He cited Julia Ward Howe's generosity as an example for all women, quoting from her speech at the Boston Convention, "'I am willing that the Negro shall get the ballot before me.'"

Quick as a flash Susan was on her feet. "Mr. Douglass," she declared, "talks about the wrongs of the Negro; but with all the outrages that he today suffers, he would not exchange his sex and take the place of Elizabeth Cady Stanton."

To this he retorted, "I want to know if granting you the right of suffrage will change the nature of our sexes."

"It will change the pecuniary position of woman," insisted Susan, and applause rang through the hall. "It will place her where she can earn her own bread. She will not then be driven to such employments only as man chooses for her."

Then Lucy Stone voiced her opinion. "Mrs. Stanton," she said, "will of course advocate the precedence for her sex, and Mr. Douglass will strive for the first position for his, and both are perhaps right. . . . Woman has an ocean of wrongs too deep for any plummet, and the Negro, too, has an ocean of wrongs that cannot be fathomed. . . . But I thank God for that Fifteenth Amendment, and hope that it will be adopted in every State. I will be thankful in my soul if *any*body can get out of the terrible pit. But I believe that the safety of the government would be more promoted by the admission of women as an element of restoration and harmony than the Negro. I believe that the influence of women will save the country before every other power."

Phoebe Couzins, young law student from St. Louis, protested against the "half-loaf" policy just proposed. "The advocates of the Fifteenth Amendment," she said, "tell us we ought to accept the half loaf when we cannot get the whole. I do not see that woman gets any part of the loaf, not even a crumb that falls from the rich man's table. . . . I regard it as neither just nor generous eternally to compel women to yield on all questions (no matter how humiliating) simply because they are women."

Susan then in her decisive manner voiced her opposition to the Fifteenth Amendment on the grounds that it was not equal rights and put two million more men in the position of tyrants over two million women who had until now been the equals of the men at their side.

Finally after hours of debate, a resolution endorsing the Fifteenth Amendment was adopted over the protests of this small but determined group of women. The convention had been dominated by men. Elizabeth and Susan now realized, as they had years ago in their New York State Temperance Society, that women must have their own organization. Unconquered, they made their plans.

XVII

THE PARTING OF THE WAYS

ANY of the women attending the Convention of the Equal Rights Association visited the office of the *Revolution* at the Women's Bureau, discussed the waning fortunes of woman suffrage, saw the need of a separate woman suffrage association, and demanded that some action be taken before they returned to their homes.

At a reception held at the Women's Bureau for members of the Equal Rights Association, Elizabeth and Susan saw the opportunity of crystallizing this healthy discontent into action, and when the parlor, halls, and stairway were crowded with guests, Susan announced that at the urgent request of many present a formal meeting would be held. Elizabeth was called to the chair and discussion started at once. All were agreed that woman suffrage had been sadly neglected by the Equal Rights Association and that women must take a definite stand.

The result was the formation of the National Woman Suffrage Association, with an enrollment that evening of one hundred members, including women from eighteen states. This new organization, it was planned, would work primarily for the Sixteenth Amendment enfranchising women. It was to be distinctly a woman's organization. No men were to hold office or direct its policies. For president, just one name was proposed, that of Elizabeth Cady Stanton. Susan, Ernestine Rose, Anna Dickinson, Mrs. Horace Greeley, Matilda Joslyn Gage, Virginia Minor, and Elizabeth Smith Miller, all took an active part in the new association. There were many women glad to give Elizabeth and Susan free reign in directing the affairs of the organization, for they trusted them implicitly and relied on their judgment. These two intrepid workers with the *Revolution* at their command seemed better equipped than anyone else to plan special campaigns or to act quickly when the occasion demanded.

Weekly meetings of the Association were held at the Women's Bureau, branches were formed in the states, and petitions for the Sixteenth Amendment were widely circulated. But opposition to the Fifteenth Amendment was also part of their program and at one meeting this resolution was passed:

> RESOLVED, That while we rejoice in every step toward an end, on the Continent, of an aristocracy of color, we repudiate the Fifteenth Amendment, because by its passage in Congress the Republican Party propose to substitute an aristocracy of sex, the most odious distinction in citizenship that has ever yet been proposed since governments had an existence.

Again and again Elizabeth spoke through the *Revolution* in strong editorials against the Fifteenth Amendment. She wrote:

> All wise women should oppose the Fifteenth Amendment for two reasons: 1st, Because it is invidious to their sex. Look at it from what point you will, and in every aspect it reflects the old idea of woman's inferiority, her subject condition. . . . 2nd, We should oppose the measure, because men have no right to pass it without our consent. . . . If women understood this pending proposition in all its bearings, theoretically and practically, there would be an overwhelming vote against the admission of another man to the ruling power of this nation, until they themselves were first enfranchised.

These continued attacks on the Fifteenth Amendment were unforgivable to those who were Abolitionists first and feminists afterward.

Lucy Stone, Thomas Wentworth Higginson, William Lloyd Garrison, Wendell Phillips, Stephen and Abby Kelly Foster, and other members of the New England Suffrage Association felt that Elizabeth and Susan were overstepping their authority when they presumed to speak for a National Woman Suffrage Association. The new National Woman Suffrage Association was to them a blatant ignoring of a large number of workers who had been in the movement for years. To be sure those who were out of sympathy with an immediate demand for woman suffrage had not been consulted in regard to the organization of the new Association. The New England group had made it plain that they would tolerate no opposition to the Fifteenth Amendment and would not press actively for woman suffrage until the Negro was enfranchised. They resented the autocratic control, which, it seemed to them, Susan was exercising over the woman's rights movement. They deplored the way Elizabeth flaunted her liberal ideas, and for a long time had felt that her interest in marriage and divorce was detrimental to the cause. With Susan in control, Elizabeth's ideas were bound to be in the foreground. They wanted an organization in which all the members had more opportunity to dictate policy.

The bitterness between the two factions was increased by Elizabeth's ruthless criticism in the *Revolution* of those who differed with her in regard to woman's rights. Wendell Phillips was so offended that he refused to shake hands with her when they met in Boston, declaring emphatically, "Mrs. Stanton is no friend of mine." And she, who heartily disliked hurting anyone, least of all an old friend, wrote him:

> I regret that you feel any personal bitterness about my articles in the *Revolution*. I see with a vividness and an intensity that no words could express, the consequences of the political action which you and others advocate. The influence upon our government of degrading one half of the citizens of the Republic will indeed be far-reaching. If our bravest men today can speak of freedom for women only in weak and vacillating words, what think you, will be the result when millions trained under despotism and ignorant of the philosophy of self-government, shall be our rulers.

It was impossible to weld together two such divergent viewpoints, and before long plans were under way for a second national woman suffrage association. Lucy Stone sent out letters to many old workers and new to ascertain their feelings in the matter. To Esther Pugh she wrote:

> You will see by the circular within, that we are arranging to form a Woman's Suffrage Association, national in character, to unite those who will work steadily to one end, who will not weaken our claim by opposition to the Fifteenth Amendment or by raising side issues. It is especially to unite those who cannot use the methods, and means, which Mrs. Stanton and Susan use, but who, in separate

organizations, each in harmony with itself, will be more effective than is possible at present. Will you please say what you think of the plan, and if you approve, give your name to a call for a Convention to form such an association.

When Elizabeth received a circular letter asking for her signature to the call for a convention in Cleveland, November 24 and 25, to form an American Woman Suffrage Association, she refused and replied that a national organization was already in existence.

Some weeks later, when the call was issued, the *New York World* asked:

Where are those well-known American names, Susan B. Anthony, Parker Pillsbury, and Elizabeth Cady Stanton? Not one of them appears. In fact, it is clear that there is a division in the ranks of the strong-minded, and that an effort is to be made to ostracize the *Revolution,* which has so long upheld the cause of Suffrage through evil report and good....

The *Rochester Democrat* commented:

Can it be possible that a National Woman Suffrage Convention is being called without Susan's knowledge or consent? Whether the meeting will be legitimate without her sanction is a serious question. A National Woman's Suffrage Association without speeches from Susan B. Anthony and Mrs. Stanton will be a new order of things. The idea seems absurd.

Elizabeth, in a signed editorial in the *Revolution,* deplored a division in the ranks of the suffragists at this time, feeling that instead of rending each other, they should fight the common enemy together. She wrote:

When the Boston malcontents first consulted me on this point, I said, if your hostility to the National Woman Suffrage Association is one of leadership alone, as it seems to be, and any other woman desires to be president of the Association, I shall gladly resign at any moment. As I do not hold this post by inheritance, or divine right, at the end of the year when all new officers are voted in, if I did not resign of my own free will, I could easily be supplanted by the voice of the majority....

That the difference is one simply of leadership and personalities is well known to all behind the scenes, for the American Woman Suffrage Association proposes no new or different principles from those accepted in the Association already formed. Although the circular letter asserts that there is no antagonism between the old and the new, yet the contrary is well known to every worker in the movement. The names of persons are appended to that circular letter who have been sedulously and malignantly working for two years to undermine certain officers and their journal in the minds of all those who affiliate with them....

We have a National Woman's Suffrage Association already; representing in its officers the leading workers from eighteen states at its formation; numbering thousands of members and friends; with auxiliaries in different parts of the country. In the *Revolution* we have a mouthpiece circulating from Maine to California, in the Old World and New World....

In conclusion, she said:

If there are people who can not come up to our broad, catholic ground, and demand Suffrage for All—*even negro suffrage, without distinction of sex,* why let them have another association until they are educated for the higher platform the present Association occupies. I have said this much to let our friends generally understand the situation.

Of course, the New England group felt that theirs was the higher platform, that by the formation of a new organization they were saving the woman suffrage movement and were rescuing it from the clutches of two radical women who would run it into the ground. It was simply the clash of strong personalities with divergent policies. Both were sincere in their belief that what they did was for the good of the cause.

In the meantime, the activities of the National Woman Suffrage Association continued. Efforts were redoubled to get signatures for petitions to be presented to Congress. Elizabeth had impressive plans for this presentation, suggesting that the petitions be carried to the Capitol by young girls, twenty-one years of age—one from every state—strong, well-developed girls, "with sensibly large waists." Successful conventions were held in Saratoga and Newport where men and women of wealth and social position gathered for the summer. Society had always looked down upon woman-suffrage workers, forming its opinions from the ridiculous stories of the press. These dignified conventions with speakers of refinement and ability did much to break down this false prejudice and win new friends.

Isabella Beecher Hooker, the half-sister of Henry Ward Beecher, had been very much prejudiced against Elizabeth and Susan from newspaper reports and from the remarks of mutual friends. Paulina Wright Davis, who was a firm friend and admirer of all three, determined that they should meet, feeling sure that acquaintance would bring about a change in Mrs. Hooker's feeling. She invited them to visit her for several days at her home in Providence. The result was even more successful than she had anticipated, and from then on Mrs. Hooker was one of their loyal allies. She wrote to Caroline Severance about this meeting:

> I have studied Miss Anthony day and night for nearly a week.... She is a woman of incorruptible integrity and the thought of guile has no place in her heart. In unselfishness and benevolence she has scarcely an equal, and her energy and executive ability are bounded only by her physical power, which is something immense. Sometimes she fails in judgment, according to the standard of others, but in right intentions never, nor in faithfulness to her friends. I confess that after studying her carefully for days, under the shadow of ————'s letters against her, and after attending a two-days' convention in Newport engineered by her in her own fashion, I am obliged to accept the most favorable interpretation of her which prevails generally, rather than that of Boston. Mrs. Stanton, too, is a magnificent woman, and the truest, womanliest one of us all. I have spent three days in her company, in the most intense heart-searching debate I ever undertook in my life. I have handled what seemed to me to be her errors without gloves, and the result is that I love her as well as I do Miss Anthony. I hand in my allegiance to both as leaders and representatives of the great movement.

Having been won over to Susan and Elizabeth, she must do everything in her power to bring about a reconciliation between them and the New England group. She called a Woman Suffrage Convention in Hartford, on October 29, inviting all of the old workers to take part, but the breach had become too wide. It could not be healed at this time. Elizabeth, describing the convention with her characteristic humor said:

> Mrs. Hooker wrote each a letter of instructions re dress, manners, and general display of all the Christian graces. I did my best to obey orders, and appeared in a black velvet dress with real lace, and the most inoffensive speech I could produce; all those passages that would shock the most conservative were ruled out, while pathetic and

aesthetic passages were substituted in their place. From what my friends said, I believe I succeeded in charming everyone but myself and Susan who said it was the weakest speech I ever made. I told her that was what it was intended to be.

The atmosphere of the convention was somewhat strained as there were rumors of the establishment in Boston of a new woman suffrage paper, the *Woman's Journal,* which would necessarily compete with the *Revolution* for subscribers. But sparks flew only once when William Lloyd Garrison denounced the *Revolution* and ignored the existence of the National Woman Suffrage Association.

On November 24, 1869, the much-discussed convention to form an American Woman Suffrage Association was held in Cleveland. Although none of the officers of the National Woman Suffrage Association had been invited to attend, Susan was determined to be there, for was not the suffrage organization in this country her child? Had she not with years of hard work built up the movement?

Elizabeth did not attend the meetings. She was in the West on a lecture tour for the New York Lyceum Bureau, but as she read the reports of the convention in the *Revolution* her heart swelled with pride at Susan's pluck.

Judge Bradwell of Chicago, seeing Susan in the audience, moved that she be invited to take a seat on the platform. Thomas Wentworth Higginson, who was presiding, said he thought this unnecessary, as a general invitation had been extended to all desiring thus to identify themselves with the movement. Judge Bradwell, however, insisted, and his motion was carried. As Susan walked up to the platform, applause resounded through the hall.

A long letter was read from William Lloyd Garrison in which he asked only those interested in forming a new organization to enroll as delegates. The organ of the new organization, should it have one, he said, "will not mistake rashness for courage, folly for smartness, cunning for sagacity, badinage for wit, unscrupulousness for fidelity, extravagance for devotion, effrontery for heroism, lunacy for genius, or an incongruous melange for a simple palatable dish."

To Susan this was a thrust at her beloved *Revolution*.

A little later she asked permission to speak. She hoped, she said, that the work of this association, if one should be organized, would be to go in strong array up to the Capitol at Washington and demand a Sixteenth Amendment to the Constitution. "We must remember," she said, "that by the Fifteenth Amendment millions of ignorant men, who know less than any other class of men on the face of the globe as regards the great principles of human rights, have to stand in judgment over us...."

"So help me Heaven!" she continued, "I care not what may come out of this Convention, so this great cause shall go forward to its grand consummation! And though this Convention, by its action, shall nullify the National Association of which I am a member, and though it shall tread its heel on the *Revolution,* to carry on which I have struggled as never mortal woman or mortal man struggled for any cause which he or she advocated, though you here assembled declare that the one is null and void—a bogus and a sham, and that the other is unworthy of your patronage and should be ground into the dust—still, if you will do this work in Washington so that this amendment shall be proposed, and go with me to the several legislatures and compel them to adopt it, I will thank God for this Convention as long as I have the breath of life."

A storm of applause broke forth.

The convention continued. It organized the American Woman Suffrage Association with a man as president, the popular Henry Ward Beecher, and Lucy Stone, chairman of an executive committee of twenty-four members. It stipulated that before any business could be undertaken by the Association it must be approved at a meeting of at least five members of the executive committee after fifteen days' notice to all members of the committee, and the action of these five must be ratified in writing by at least fifteen members of the committee. To Susan such methods were too slow and too involved. The American Woman Suffrage Association also decided to work for woman suffrage in the states rather than for a federal amendment. Susan and Elizabeth felt that there could never be a more opportune time for Congressional action. Two amendments to the Constitution had been ratified within two years. The Fifteenth was pending. With sufficient pressure brought to bear, a Sixteenth could be passed. But the ranks were hopelessly divided.

The National Woman Suffrage Association continued its conventions. Susan had planned one in Washington for January 1870, and Elizabeth on her lecture tour longed to be relieved of taking part. She was tired of conventions. She was tired of being told that she harmed the cause. She was ready to let anyone else who wanted to, manage the woman suffrage movement. Susan, however, must keep her hands on the organization and Elizabeth must stand by Susan. She wrote Susan:

> It does not seem to me worth while for me to take that long trip to Washington when I have all I can do all winter out here in the West. This field is ripe for harvest. I am doing more good in stirring up these Western women than in talking to those old Washington politicians....I stand ready to pay anybody you can get to go to Washington in my stead. But of course I stand by you to the end. I would not see you crushed by rivals even if to prevent it required my being cut into inch pieces....If your life depends on me, I will be your stay and staff to the end. No power in heaven, hell, or earth can separate us, for our hearts are eternally wedded together. Ever yours, and here I mean *ever*.

Elizabeth attended the Washington Convention, and before the joint committees for the District of Columbia made an eloquent plea for woman suffrage. This time she struck a new note, one which had been suggested by Francis Minor, a St. Louis lawyer, at a St. Louis Woman Suffrage Convention—that the Constitution, especially since the passage of the Fourteenth Amendment, actually enfranchised women and that in asking for the ballot women were asking merely for their rights under the Constitution. Thus the Fourteenth Amendment, which feminists had fought so fiercely because of its introduction of the word "male" into the Constitution, was now proposed as a weapon in the contest for woman suffrage.

"While the Constitution of the United States," Elizabeth declared, "leaves the qualifications of electors to the several States, it nowhere gives them the right to deprive any citizen of the elective franchise. The Constitution of the United States expressly declares that no

State shall make or enforce any law that shall abridge the privileges or immunities of citizens of the United States; hence those provisions of the several State constitutions that exclude women from the franchise are in direct violation of the Federal Constitution. Even the preamble recognizes, in the phrase, 'We, the people,' the true origin of all just government.... Are not women people? ...."

For the first time the New York papers sent women reporters to cover a woman suffrage convention. They were most complimentary in their reports of the convention and the Congressional hearing. So general had been the feeling that "woman's righters" were uncouth and vulgar, that they dressed like men and were utterly unattractive, that these well-dressed, beautiful, refined, able women made a great impression. Jessie Benton Frémont watching them file into the dining room of the Arlington Hotel, said to Susan later, "Now tell me, did you hunt the country over and pick out a score of the most beautiful women you could find to melt the hearts of our Congressmen?" And Charles Sumner, pacified by the imminent ratification of the Fifteenth Amendment, remarked, "I have been in this place, ladies, for twenty years; I have followed or led in every movement toward liberty and enfranchisement; but this meeting exceeds in interest anything I have ever witnessed." Woman suffrage was becoming respectable.

Repeated efforts were made to effect a reconciliation between the National and American Woman Suffrage Associations. Western suffragists wanted one organization. There were still a few suffragists in the East who felt that union might be possible. Once more Theodore Tilton tried to arrange matters. He called a conference for representatives of both associations. Even Lucretia Mott, who now seldom left home because of her age, came to New York to do what she could to bring the two organizations together. Elizabeth and Susan were lecturing in the West at the time. Elizabeth sent a letter to the conference:

> I will do all I can for union. If I am a stumbling block, I will gladly resign my office. Having fought the world twenty years, I do not now wish to turn and fight those who have so long stood together through evil and good report. I should be glad to have all

united, with Mr. Beecher or Lucretia Mott for our general.... I am willing to work with any and all or to get out of the way entirely, that there may be an organization which shall be respectable at home and abroad.

Susan telegraphed:

The entire West demands united national organization for the Sixteenth Amendment, this very Congressional session, and so does Susan B. Anthony.

Nothing came of the conference. The representatives of the American Association said they had made overtures at the time of their convention in Cleveland, suggesting that the National become an auxiliary of the American, and had been refused. They now took no interest in a merger with a new constitution and new officers. They were satisfied with their own organization and the new woman suffrage paper, the *Woman's Journal*, which was being issued in Boston with Mary Livermore as editor, Lucy Stone, Julia Ward Howe, Thomas Wentworth Higginson, and William Lloyd Garrison as assistant editors, and Henry Blackwell as business manager. They saw no reason for making concessions. In fact they rather resented and laughed at Theodore Tilton's efforts for union.

When Theodore Tilton's proposition for a Union Woman Suffrage Association was discussed at the anniversary meeting of the National Woman Suffrage Association in New York in May 1870, Elizabeth and Susan were on hand. Just prior to the meeting, Elizabeth had put this notice in the *Revolution*:

It is a great thing for those who have been prominent in any movement to know when their special work is done, and when the posts they hold can be more ably filled by others. Having in my own judgment reached that time, at the present anniversary of our association, I must forbid the use of my name for president or any other official position in any organization whatever.

Many of the younger suffragists, however, were opposed to any organization which did not put either Mrs. Stanton or Miss Anthony at its head. Phoebe Couzins of St. Louis declared: "They have felled the trees and cleared the forests. Shall they be set aside for these newcomers?"

But both Elizabeth and Susan were determined to step aside for the present at least, and Theodore Tilton was elected president of the new Union Woman Suffrage Association. These two veteran suffragists knew better than to put a man at the head of their organization. They had tried that sort of thing before. A woman suffrage association needed an active woman as a leader. But they were willing to do anything to still the clamor for union, to let the younger generation learn by experience what they had learned long ago.

The Union Woman Suffrage Association, however, proved to be a union in name only, for the American Woman Suffrage Association at its annual meeting refused to merge. The Union Association was then forgotten, and the National continued its activities as if nothing had happened, with Elizabeth and Susan at the head. No more attempts at union were made for twenty years. These two groups could do far better work separately. The National, with its more militant methods, its insistence on Congressional action, and its willingness to discuss any subject related to woman's emancipation, appealed to a more liberal group of women. The American, with its elaborate organization machinery, its policy of state action, and its determination to concentrate on the one subject, woman suffrage, attracted the more conservative. Both did valuable work in the long-drawn-out struggle for woman's enfranchisement.

XVIII

THE LECTURE CRUSADE

THE *Revolution* was in deep waters financially, simply because there was no real interest in a woman suffrage paper. Women had not been aroused sufficiently to support a paper of their own, and it was not yet important for advertisers to make an appeal to women as purchasers.

For the past year Susan had done her best to raise money to continue its publication. Her family had loaned her several thousand dollars. Anna Dickinson and Paulina Wright Davis made large contributions. Susan, herself, had put into it every dollar she could scrape together, barely allowing herself enough to live on. Elizabeth was not able to give financial assistance because of the demands of her large family, but contributed her editorial services.

All sorts of plans were in the air. Mrs. Hooker and Harriet Beecher Stowe would give the paper financial aid and prestige if the name were changed. Susan wrote to Elizabeth about this and she replied:

> As to changing the name of the *Revolution,* I should consider it a great mistake. . . . There could not be a better name than *Revolution.* The establishing of woman on her rightful throne is the greatest revolution the world has ever known or ever will know. To bring it about is no child's play. You and I have not forgotten the conflict of the last twenty years—the ridicule, persecution, denunciation, detraction, the unmixed bitterness of our cup for the past two years when even friends crucified us. A journal called the Rosebud might answer for those who come with kid gloves and perfumes to lay immortal wreaths on the monuments which in sweat and tears others have hewn and built; but for us and for that great blacksmith of ours [Parker Pillsbury] who forges such red-hot thunderbolts for Pharisees, hypocrites, and sinners, there is no name like the *Revolution!*

Then came the Richardson-McFarland murder case, and Elizabeth's comment on it in the *Revolution.* This decided Mrs. Hooker and Mrs. Stowe. They could not be associated with such a paper.

The shooting in the *Tribune* office by Daniel McFarland of Albert D. Richardson, a well-known journalist on the staff of the *Tribune,* caused a great stir in New York. Mr. Richardson had been befriending Mrs. McFarland since her divorce from Mr. McFarland, whose brutality and dissolute habits had made it impossible for her to live with him. This friendship roused the jealousy of Mr. McFarland and was the reason for the shooting. Mrs. McFarland married Mr. Richardson on his deathbed. The ceremony was performed by Henry Ward Beecher and O. B. Frothingham in the presence of Horace Greeley and Joshua Leavitt. The press at once raised a storm of protest expressing sympathy for the outraged husband, casting aspersions upon his divorced wife, a refined, talented woman who had suffered greatly by her marriage with him.

Elizabeth's impetuous comments in the *Revolution* estranged others besides Mrs. Hooker. She wrote in part:

> I rejoice over every slave that escapes from a discordant marriage. With the education and elevation of woman we shall have a mighty sundering of unholy ties that hold men and women together who loathe and despise each other. Such marriages are a crime against both the individual and the State, the source of discord, disease, and death, of weakness, imbecility, deformity, and depravity.... One would really suppose that a man owned his wife as the master the slave, and that this was simply an affair between Richardson and McFarland, fighting like two dogs over one bone.... This wholesale shooting of wives' paramours should be stopped.... Suppose women should decide to shoot their husbands' mistresses, what a wholesale slaughter of innocents we should have of it! I wonder how long justice would halt in our courts in their case, and how long public sentiment would sustain such action.... If I had a word to say in regard to Mr. McFarland, I should put him in some safe asylum, or prison, where he could never deceive another woman, nor take the life of another man....

Several months later Mr. McFarland after a trial of nationwide interest was acquitted on the plea of insanity and at the same time given the custody of his child, a boy of twelve years. Such an insult to a woman, Elizabeth and Susan could not allow to go unchallenged. Susan arranged a mass meeting of 2000 women at Apollo Hall with Elizabeth as the principal speaker. They made a mighty protest against the unjust decision of the court, against the scurrility of the press and the popular idea of marriage. All this was reported in the *Revolution*.

The *Woman's Journal* did not comment at all on the social aspects of this case. Its editors saw no reason for connecting it in any way with woman suffrage, especially since none of the people involved were interested in the movement. But Elizabeth and Susan could not possibly remain aloof from a controversey which was such a glaring example of woman's enslavement under law and custom.

As time went on it became more evident that Susan must lose the *Revolution*. She worried so much and worked so hard that she was utterly worn out. She had personally shouldered a $10,000 debt for the paper and yet could not give it up. Elizabeth tried to show her the folly of hanging on to it when its debts were swallowing up her spirit and energy.

But to Susan, giving up the *Revolution* was defeat, especially since the Boston group, now so hostile to her, had founded the *Woman's Journal*. However, she was finally obliged to part with it, and on May 22, 1870, for the consideration of one dollar turned it over to Clara Curtis Bullard, who had been one of their literary contributors and whose large fortune, accumulated from Dr. Winslow's Soothing Syrup, enabled her to undertake this publishing experiment. The day of the transfer, she wrote in her diary, "It was like signing my own death warrant"; and to a friend she wrote, "I feel a great calm sadness like that of a mother binding out a dear child that she could not support." The *Revolution* now became a literary and society journal and continued as such for eighteen months. After that it was taken over by the *New York Christian Enquirer*.

Elizabeth wrote Susan:

> You and Parker Pillsbury gone and our *Revolution* no more! There is a sadness, though relief in the fact....And think of our sacred columns full of the advertisements of quack remedies! The present owners have asked me and urged me a dozen times to write for them. But I do not feel moved by the spirit. Theodore Tilton told me that in writing for the paper he wished I would be careful

not to shock those good Baptists and to say nothing on divorce, but to be "spicy and brilliant on some pleasant topics." Greeley once offered me the columns of the *Tribune* in the same way. I am very busy reading, and writing my speeches, and I have no time to prepare articles nor any desire to submit my ideas to the pruning knife of youngsters. Now do for my sake let them manage matters in their own way, and remember that you did not sell my pen in your transfer of the *Revolution*. I am not to be bought to write at anybody's dictation. You know when I drop anything, I drop it absolutely. You cannot imagine what a deep gulf lies between me and the past.

Susan, aside from her sentiment and love for their paper, felt that they needed an organ to expound their views. Elizabeth was convinced that she could get her articles published in ordinary channels and that a propagandist journal was no longer necessary. She knew they could spread their message of equal rights and equal opportunity for women by lecturing even better than by the *Revolution*. She had proved this for herself for the past few months. Lyceum lecturers were now in demand everywhere. Informing the public on all sorts of subjects, they almost took the place of books and newspapers, and injected as well a dramatic personal element which impressed people more than the printed word.

Just before the Cleveland Convention, she had been engaged by the New York Lyceum Bureau to make a lecture tour of the West. The fee was most alluring and would help toward the college education of her younger children. Because Henry's law practice and editorial writing did not provide sufficient income for the education which they both wanted their children to have, she felt she should not refuse such an opportunity to earn. She was now in her prime as a public speaker and her name was known throughout the country. It was hard to leave her children for such long periods as the lecture tours required, but they were in good hands, for Amelia Willard, her faithful housekeeper, was still in charge. It was hard to leave the new house which she had built in Tenafly, in the hills of New Jersey. It had been such a joy to come to Tenafly from the crowded city, to breathe the pure air of New Jersey, and to look out from her windows upon the trees, hills, and brilliant sunsets. She dreaded the long uncomfortable train rides, the weary hours in railroad stations, waiting to make connections, the poor coffee, the ill-kept hotels. But there would be compensations —the stimulation of holding the attention of every kind of audience, making new friends, and everywhere leaving a kernel of woman's rights. It was good to be undertaking new work in the face of the dissension in the suffrage ranks. She had learned a good lesson in her youth—to spend no time mulling over disagreeable happenings. She did not sigh over the past. She looked into the future with new hope.

For twelve years, from 1869 to 1881, eight months every year, from October to June, Elizabeth Cady Stanton lectured for the Lyceum Bureau.

At the end of the first seven months she wrote Gerrit Smith, "I have made $2,000 above all expenses since the middle of November, besides stirring up the women generally to rebellion." She earned from $3,000 to $4,000 a year and this made it possible for Theodore to continue at Cornell, for Robert to look forward to a course there, and for Margaret to enroll at Vassar, the new woman's college.

The question of educating her daughters was a serious one. She often discussed it with Elizabeth Smith Miller, and wrote her:

> I am disgusted with the whole system of education, and am pondering the same problem as yourself concerning the mental development of our girls. . . . I have looked all around, and the best schools I know of for girls are Vassar College and Swarthmore. Suppose we send our daughters to the latter? It is a quiet Quaker institution, in a healthy, warm situation, thorough in its teachings, where boys also go. You know I am a firm believer in the benefits of co-education of the sexes, which is peculiar to our country, and which we should never abandon.

But Margaret and Harriot went to Vassar.

Between lecture engagements, whenever she was near Poughkeepsie, she visited them. The authorities at Vassar were too conservative to ask her to address the students, but she managed to plant her seed of woman's rights within the well-guarded walls. Harriot and Margaret, very proud of her, always invited a large group of girls to meet her. Comfortable in an easy chair, beaming upon the girls sitting on the floor about her, she told them stories out of her own experience, illustrating the discriminations against women. She left with them the thought that they had a responsibility to bring about a change in law and custom.

Her life as a Lyceum lecturer was strenuous. She filled as many engagements as the Bureau could crowd into her schedule, traveling night and day at all hours in all kinds of weather, sleeping in poor hotels, and eating unsavory food. Almost every night, she spoke for one or two hours, then hurried to her hotel, put on her traveling clothes, and took the midnight train.

She was very fastidious about her platform appearance. Her dress was of black silk with the inevitable lacey white collar and cuffs. Her white hair, beautifully arranged, always impressed everyone who saw her. There was something so radiant and motherly about her that she won the hearts of her audience the moment she appeared. Her delivery was excellent; her voice clear, powerful, and persuasive. There was never any difficulty in hearing every word she said, and yet one never thought of her voice as loud and jarring. She was earnest and logical, not facetious, as were many lecturers. She had a keen sense of humor which brought roars of laughter and applause from her listeners.

Her most popular lecture was "Our Girls," and it was her favorite one, for in it she could expound all her views on a full and free life for girls. She told how young girls start life with enthusiasm, with eagerness to learn, with plans for a career—only to find they are a subject race. If a daughter has a talent for drawing and wants to cultivate it, her father will probably tell her to be satisfied with charity work. "All women," she admonished, "are not made for sisters of mercy, and it is not best for any to watch the shadows and sorrows of life forever." She pleaded for a free and independent life for every girl, for clothes that would give her freedom of action, for an education which would enable her to support herself, for an equal opportunity in business and the professions. "Marriage as a profession," she said, "nine cases out of ten proves a sad failure, because the wife is pecuniarily dependent."

"Woman, as she is today," she continued, "is man's handiwork. When men see a woman with brains and two hands in practical life, capable of standing alone, earning her own bread and thinking her own thoughts, conscious of the true dignity and glory of womanhood, they call her unsexed."

She entered her protest against the prevalent attitude toward marriage—that it was a condition of subjection for woman, not spiritual and mental companionship. She made it plain that she was unalterably opposed to the word "obey" in the marriage ceremony and to the custom of giving the bride away. "The world will talk to you of the duties of wives and mothers and housekeepers," she said, "but all these incidental relations should ever be subordinate to the greater fact of womanhood. You may never be wives, mothers, or housekeepers, but you will be women. Therefore labor for the grandeur and more universal fact of your existence."

Here was a lecture, not full of platitudes, but brimming over with challenging ideas and practical advice. No wonder women flocked to hear her. She did not antagonize the men. The men of the West whose wives and daughters had shared with them the dangers and hardships of pioneer life were free from many of the prejudices and conventions of an older civilization.

"Our Boys" was another lecture much in demand, full of good common sense and understanding of youth. A mother of five well-brought-up boys could speak with authority. Yet "Our Boys" was not as spontaneous as "Our Girls" and she worked hard over it before it really satisfied her. She wrote her daughter Margaret from Iowa:

> At West Salem I had three whole days and I boned down to expanding and improving my lecture on "Our Boys." I wrote two hundred pages and made the whole much better. I begin to think that in time I shall succeed in throwing as bright a halo round "Our Boys" as is the case already with "Our Girls."

She worked out many other lectures, for there must be variety and the right lecture for each occasion. She often wrote them on scraps of paper as she was traveling, in railroad stations, or whenever the ideas occurred to her. A popular subject was "Thurlow

Weed, William H. Seward, and Horace Greeley," especially interesting because these men were her personal friends. Others were
"The True Republic," "Prison Life," "Coeducation," "Home Life,"
"The Subjection of Women," "Marriage and Divorce," "Marriage
and Maternity." On Sunday, if she could not have a free day, she
delivered an address on the famous women of the Bible or on the
Bible and woman's rights. Occasionally she was asked to occupy
the pulpit, and she always accepted. "I have never let an occasion
slip to storm a pulpit," she wrote a friend, "though the storm generally breaks after I have taken a back seat." Very often she
distressed the clergy. She told Susan:

> I had a magnificent audience at Ulrichville, where I so vexed the
> Presbyterian minister by telling what the General Assemblies and
> Synods of that church had done against women that he vowed he
> would get up a protest. But the people were delighted with what
> I said, and after I finished, flocked up to tell me so.

After the famous McFarland-Richardson trial, she frequently
delivered her lecture on "Marriage and Divorce." She wrote Susan:

> When I spoke in Brooklyn on this subject, I had a splendid audi-
> ence. . . . Women respond to this divorce speech as they never did to
> suffrage. In a word, I have had grand meetings. Oh, how the women
> flock to me with their sorrows. Such experiences as I listen to, planta-
> tion never equalled.

She found women so ignorant about the care of babies that she
planned "Marriage and Maternity" especially for them and delivered
this lecture afternoons to women only. But her missionary work
for babies was not confined to lectures; it went on continually,
especially on trains. Through her efforts, they received their first
drink of water and were freed from woolen hoods, veils, tight
strings under their chins, and endless swaddling bands. Whenever
she saw a tired mother trying to quiet a crying baby, she went to
her at once and offered to hold the baby. The first thing was a
drink of water for the parched throat; then she loosened the tight
bands, and sometimes on hot days even gave the baby a bath. Soon
the baby was crowing and smiling, the mother was sleeping, and
she was happy.

She also gave her attention to the stifling air on the crowded trains. Passengers were content only when every window and ventilator was shut tight. Religiously she made the rounds, opened every ventilator, and in the winter, surreptitiously closed the dampers in the stoves in the sleeping cars at night.

Mrs. Clara B. Colby often told the story of seeing Elizabeth Cady Stanton for the first time on a train in the West. She was impressed at once with her dignity, self-possession, and independence, especially as during a long wait, she walked up and down the car for exercise. In those days air and exercise were the prerogative of men travelers only. Women remained modestly seated so that they would not attract attention. Elizabeth's natural, sensible independence taught Mrs. Colby a lesson in self-respect which she never forgot. Later when Elizabeth lectured in Beatrice, Nebraska, Mrs. Colby met her and was at once interested in the cause of woman's rights. As the years went by they became firm friends, Mrs. Colby founding the *Woman's Tribune* and taking an active part in the National Woman Suffrage Association.

Elizabeth was in Lincoln, Nebraska, during the Constitutional Convention of 1875 when the proposition to strike the word "male" from the constitution was being considered. She addressed the Convention and answered the questions which the members asked her. All of the men but one were serious and respectful and he tried to be witty at her expense. He was small, unprepossessing, and very pompous. She noticed that the other members were annoyed at his behavior and she resolved to humble him if an opportunity arose. Finally he brought his chair directly in front of her and mockingly asked: "Don't you think that the best thing a woman can do is to perform well her part in the role of wife and mother? My wife has presented me with eight beautiful children; is not this a better lifework than that of exercising the right of suffrage?"

Surveying him from head to foot, she answered promptly, "I have met few men worth repeating eight times." At this the members of the committee roared with laughter, and for days to come they and the newspapers made his life miserable.

Lincoln, Nebraska, at this time was celebrating the opening of a railroad. Crowds gathered from miles about to pay tribute to the work of the early settlers. No mention was made of the courage of the pioneer women or the hardships they endured. "This state," declared one speaker, "was settled by three brothers, John, James, and Joseph, and from them have sprung the great concourse of people that greet us here today." Stirred as she always was by indifference to and neglect of the work of women, Elizabeth turned to the Governor and quietly asked him if all these people had sprung Minerva-like from the brains of John, James, and Joseph. He urged her to put that question to the speaker and she did. The crowd cheered, the women beamed with satisfaction, and the remaining speakers gave due credit to Anne, Jane, and Mary.

Her part in the celebration was a toast to the women of Nebraska, expressing her appreciation of the part they had played in the settlement of the West.

She said:

Here's to the mothers, who came hither by long tedious journeys, closely packed with restless children in emigrant wagons, cooking the meals by day and nursing the babies by night, while the men slept. Leaving comfortable homes in the East, they endured all the hardships of pioneer life, suffered with the men, the attacks of the Dakota Indians and the constant apprehension of savage raids, of prairie fires, and the devastating locusts. Man's trials, his fears, and losses, all fell on woman with double force; yet history is silent concerning the part women performed in the frontier life of the early settlers. Men make no mention of their heroism and divine patience; they take no thought of the mental or physical agonies women endure in the perils of maternity, oftimes without nurse or physician in the supreme hour of their need, going, as every mother does, to the very gates of death in giving life to an immortal being!

Many other popular lecturers, men and women, were traveling about the country at this time for the Lyceum Bureau—Anna Dickinson, Olive Logan, Kate Field, Mary Livermore, Julia Ward Howe, Susan B. Anthony, Bronson Alcott, Wendell Phillips, Frederick Douglass, Theodore Tilton, George William Curtis, and Henry Ward Beecher. Susan had not thought of herself as a Lyceum lecturer but, obliged to substitute for Elizabeth one month when she was ill, found that she too was in demand, and continued the work as the best means of paying up the debt of the *Revolution*. Occasionally they met on their travels, sometimes unexpectedly, as when in Columbus in the railroad station she found Elizabeth sitting on a bench fast asleep, "her gray curls sticking out." Whenever possible several of the lecturers would meet in some city at a comfortable hotel to spend Sunday, and there, glorying in clean, comfortable beds and good food, would tell of their adventures.

One winter when Elizabeth had many lecture engagements in Iowa, the railroads were blocked for weeks with heavy snow. She was determined to get through but when she asked for a sleigh, two good horses and a skillful driver, she was told that she could not stand a six-hours' drive in the piercing wind. Remembering the snowy winters in Johnstown with the thermometer twenty degrees below zero, she had no fear of winds and drifts, and insisted on making the trip. Bundled in a fur coat, a fur hood, and a large buffalo robe, with a thick veil over her head and a hot oak plank at her feet, she started off in a sleigh with an experienced driver. Just as the clock struck eight, she drove up to the hall where her lecture was to be delivered. The audience had gathered. None the worse for her adventure, but supperless and in her traveling clothes, she stepped on the platform.

She continued her travels by sleigh, driving forty and fifty miles a day and filling all her engagements. Returning to Chicago, she found at the Sherman House, Charles Bradlaugh and General Kilpatrick, who were advertised to precede her all through Iowa. They were waiting for the roads to be opened and had lost three weeks' engagements. She commented:

> As the General was lecturing on his experiences in Sherman's march to the sea, I chafed him on not being able in an emergency to march across the State of Iowa. They were much astonished and somewhat ashamed, when I told them of the long, solitary drives over the prairies from day to day. It was the testimony of all the Bureaus that the women could endure more fatigue and were more conscientious than men in filling their appointments.

She lectured anywhere and everywhere. In the larger cities of the East and West, in little frontier villages from Michigan to Texas, in opera houses, in halls, churches, and schoolhouses, to men,

women, and children, who had driven from twenty to forty miles
to hear her, to students in the new coeducational colleges and universities of the West, to prisoners in state penitentiaries. She had a
message for them all, and through her own ability and through
her consistent high estimate of women, she planted a new thought
in the minds of many.

One cold night the crowded ferry on which she was crossing the
Mississippi was caught in the ice for hours. To still the excitement
and impatience of the passengers, a committee asked her to entertain them with a speech on woman suffrage. Always ready to instruct anyone on that subject she began at once. Soon they were
eager listeners, asking questions and laughing at her humorous
jibes.

From Chicago she wrote Susan:

> I had a magnificent audience at the Grand Opera House, with
> people on the stairs, sidewalks, and even out into the street who
> could not get into the building. I was in the depths all night and the
> day before lest the speech should not be up to the occasion. But
> when I was fairly launched, and every eye on me, I could feel the
> pluck slowly rising, and I went through the ordeal with credit to
> myself and to you; for I believe you are always quite as anxious
> about me as I am myself.

One of the compensations on these arduous lecture tours was
meeting so many interesting and worth-while people. She soon had
good friends in all parts of the country. She felt like a mother
to them all. They came to her with their troubles and asked her
for advice. She visited in pretentious homes and humble cottages.
She saw how comfortable and happy people could be in frontier
towns away from all the luxuries and so-called niceties of life.
In many of the homes in which she visited there were no servants.
She knew how much work this meant for her hostess especially
when she served an elaborate dinner in her honor. On these
occasions she was always asked to say grace. At first she refused.
Then when she realized that even through a blessing she could
spread her message, she made up one of her own. She told the
story this way:

I often saw weary little women coming to the table after most exhausting labors, and large, bumptious husbands spreading out their hands and thanking the Lord for the meals that the dear women had prepared, as if the whole came down like manna from Heaven. So I preached a sermon in the blessing I gave. You will notice that it has three heresies in it: "Heavenly Father and Mother, make us thankful for all the blessings of this life, and make us ever mindful of the patient hands that oft in weariness spread our tables and prepare our daily food. For humanity's sake, Amen."

This blessing always caused a little flurry of astonishment. She noticed it as she glanced from face to face about the table. The hostess beamed and held her head higher. It brought to every obscure homemaker added self-respect and paid her the homage she so much deserved. Women everywhere asked her for copies. Several had it framed and hung in their dining rooms. She inscribed it in many an autograph album.

Autograph albums were then at the height of their popularity, and after each lecture many were presented for sentiments and signatures. To most lecturers this was a deadly bore, but Elizabeth took great satisfaction in inscribing on the gayly decorated and gilded pages sentiments which would preach her gospel of woman's equality with man. All through the country over her signature written in a bold hand, she scattered lines like these, "Man and woman a simultaneous creation"; "The masculine and feminine elements are equal in the Godhead"; "We have proved it possible to have a state without a king, a church without a pope, a currency without a gold basis, and a family without a divinely ordained head"; "I am a citizen of the United States and demand the right to vote."

Sundays were often desperately lonely days, far from home, in small western towns. She treasured every letter that came from Henry and from her boys and girls in college and at work. She spent these days writing them and reading. From a small town in Ohio she wrote Harriot:

I sit today in a forlorn old hotel, poor bed and worse fare, and yet I am comfortable, for I have spent the day outside of my surroundings. These trips have taught me one thing in regard to myself and that is that I can be happy under most conditions. I see so many people fretting and discontented under the most promising circumstances that I have come to the conclusion that heaven and hell depend more on our organization than on our environment.

To Margaret at Vassar, she wrote from Austin, Minnesota:

Imagine me today sitting in a small comfortable room in the railroad hotel about a half mile from this little Minnesota town, where I do not know one soul. But as everybody is polite and attentive, I suppose they all know me. I spoke last evening at Waterloo, and in order to reach here, my next place, I was obliged to leave at midnight. So after my lecture, I had an oyster supper, packed up my finery, and, all ready to start, took a short nap on the sofa. I was called at two. But as the horses were sick and I was the only guest going from the hotel westward, I was toted, I and my baggage, in a little cart drawn by a mule through a fearful snow storm, the wind cutting like particles of glass. Having arrived safely at the depot, my escort, a good natured, over-grown boy, deposited me and mine beside a red-hot stove. Learning then and there that the train was two hours behind, I rolled my cloak up for a pillow, lay down on the bench and went to sleep, listening to a discussion in an adjoining room on the merits of my lecture. One man vowed in a broad Irish brogue that he would leave the country if the women voted. Gracious, I thought to myself as I dozed into slumber, what would become of our experiment if one "white male" should desert the flag! In due time I was awakened by some gentle Patrick—perhaps my very critic—tickets bought, valise checked and I transferred to a sleeping-car, where, in a twinkling, I at once "flopped" asleep again, without even taking my bonnet off. At eight, I was roused by an African for this place, where, it being Sunday, the train lies over. So I ordered a fire, washed my face, ate breakfast, undressed regularly, went to bed and slept soundly until one, when I arose, took a sponge bath, had dinner, read all the papers I could procure and now sit down to answer your letter, which was the only one I received at Waterloo. I read it alone at midnight, and, though I am always advising you to write short letters, I did wish this time you had written more at length. You ask if it is not lonely traveling as I do. It is indeed, and I should have enjoyed above all things having Hattie with me. But you see, dearest, that would double my expenses, and as I am so desirous of making money for the household, I must practice economy in some direction. And above all considerations of loneliness and fatigue, I feel that I am doing an immense amount of good in rousing women to thought and inspiring them with new hope and self-respect, that I am making the path smoother for you and Hattie and all the other dear girls. You would laugh to see how everywhere the girls flock round me for a kiss, a curl, an autograph. They all like so much my lecture, "The Coming Girl." I am so glad, dearest, to know that you are happy. Now, improve every hour and every opportunity, and fit yourself for a good teacher or professor, so that you can have money of your own and not be obliged to depend on any man for every breath you draw. The helpless dependence of women generally makes them the narrow, discontented beings so many are.

One bright spot in these western trips was a visit with her son, Gerrit, who because of his health had settled on a farm in Iowa, inherited from Grandfather Cady. Life in the open had done him a world of good and he was very happy on Starlight Plantation, as he called his farm. Not far away lived her sister, Madge, and her husband, Duncan McMartin, who also had been obliged to come West for his health after the Civil War. The McMartins owned a beautiful farm of 2,000 acres, run in the most scientific manner. She found much of interest in their life on the Iowa prairies. She wrote Margaret from Starlight Plantation:

> I wish you could have seen Gat [Gerrit] and me coming over the prairies. Imagine a lumber wagon laden with a chest of drawers, a spring bed, a box of groceries, a package of meat, two bags of flour, a bag of sundries, a box of freight, my trunk and handbag, bundles for a half dozen neighbors, a hundred trees from the nursery and a lot of small fruits—all this looming up behind us. We moved along as if in a funeral procession, for the load was heavy, the roads bad and head winds blowing a hurricane. My hair and veil stood out to the four points of the compass. Everybody is in bed now, though it is only eight P.M. But they will be up at four tomorrow morning and breakfast at five. Of course I shall not join this matutinal feast, but will appear on the scene much later, as I did this morning, when I had for my meal a broiled chicken, some flour "gems" as light as a feather, stewed peaches, excellent coffee, cream as yellow as gold and butter as sweet as clover.

During these years while Elizabeth and Susan were busy lecturing, their love and appreciation for each other never lessened, although they were able to spend very little time together. As they traveled through the country, their popularity grew. Susan, the uncompromising crusader, unmarried, angular, plainly dressed, neat but thoughtless of her appearance, had more prejudice to overcome than Elizabeth. The fact that Elizabeth was the mother of seven children won over the public at once, as did her good nature, her smiling face, her faultless appearance, and her real gift for oratory. She was soon one of the most popular Lyceum lecturers and the most loved woman in the United States.

"As I go dragging around in these despicable hotels," she wrote Susan, "I think of you and often wish we had at least the little comfort of enduring it together."

Before long her wish was granted, and in the summer of 1871, they set out together for California. Susan very naturally assumed her role as manager. In spite of the fact that experience had proved that she had something to say which people wanted to hear, she still considered herself the secondary attraction, and Mrs. Stanton the drawing card.

The long days on the train gave these two old friends, now fifty-six and fifty-one, ample opportunity for heart-to-heart talks. They recalled with satisfaction the bitterly criticized campaigns of their younger days. They planned for the future. They discussed women thoroughly and unsparingly. They discussed education, marriage, home life, financial independence, and that glorious future when men and women as equals would walk hand in hand down the road of life. Susan wrote of their trip:

> We have a drawing-room all to ourselves, and here we are just as cozy and happy as lovers. We look at the prairie schooners slowly moving along with ox-teams, or notice the one lone cabin-light on the endless plains, and Mrs. Stanton will say: "In all that there is real bliss, if only the two are perfect equals, two loving people, neither assuming to control the other." Yes, after all, life is about one and the same thing, whether in the prairie schooner and sod cabin, or the Fifth Avenue palace. Love for and faith in each other alone can make either a heaven, and without these any home is a hell.

From Des Moines, Iowa, Elizabeth wrote to her cousin, Elizabeth Smith Miller:

> Since I left you, I have filled twenty engagements, speaking twice in nearly every place, once on suffrage and once to women alone. This idea of mine of addressing women by themselves should produce a rich fruitage in the future. What radical thoughts I then and there put into their heads, and as they feel untrammeled, these thoughts are permanently lodged there! That is all I ask.

When they reached Wyoming, the first territory to enfranchise its women (1869), they felt they were truly in the land of the free. With real joy and gratitude they lectured in Cheyenne. At Laramie one hundred women escorted them to the station, and Elizabeth delivered an address from the platform.

They spent a week in Salt Lake City just at the time of the Godbe secession, when a group of liberal Mormons renounced the doctrine of polygamy. They were invited to address a large group of women in the Tabernacle. No one before had had the opportunity to speak to Mormon women alone and they made the most of it. Their meeting lasted from two until seven. Elizabeth covered the ground thoroughly. She gave these puzzled, questioning women a brief history of the marriage institution in all times and countries, of the matriarchate, of the patriarchate, of polyandry, polygamy, monogamy, and prostitution. These sad-faced, careworn pioneer women called out her sympathy at once. They personified woman's utter dependence on and subjection to man. Here was an opportunity for real missionary work, and as Susan so well expressed it, "No Phariseeism, no shudders of Puritanic horror, no standing afar off; but a simple, loving, fraternal clasp of hands with these struggling women, and an earnest work with them—not to ameliorate but to abolish the whole system of woman's subjection to man in both polygamy and monogamy."

While they were in Salt Lake City, Governor Leland Stanford of California sent them a pass to California and through the state. They proceeded at once to San Francisco, where they were enthusiastically welcomed and royally entertained. Elizabeth made her first speech there to an audience of 1200. The press was very complimentary. But they soon stirred up a tempest. The whole state at this time was very much concerned over the murder of A. P. Crittenden by Laura Fair. Hearing of this and always eager to learn the woman's side of the case, they went to the jail to talk with Laura Fair. At once the press was up in arms. An immense crowd gathered at Susan's first lecture, determined that there should be no defense of Laura Fair. She spoke on "The Power of the Ballot," emphasizing the fact that woman could not depend on man to protect her but must learn to protect herself. She showed clearly, citing example after example, that man's so-called protection of woman was a farce. "If all men," she declared, "had protected all women as they would have their own wives and daughters protected, you would have no Laura Fair in your jail tonight." The hissing that greeted this statement reminded Susan of antislavery days. She stood her ground calmly until it ceased and then courageously repeated her remark. Again the hisses burst forth, but a few cheers were intermingled. When the tumult died down, she made her challenging statement for the third time, and the audience, admiring her courage, burst into applause.

The next morning, however, she was denounced by the press and accused of condoning the murder and the life Mrs. Fair had led. So bitter and continuous was the abuse that she had to give up all thought of further lectures in and about San Francisco at that time. In California Susan bore the brunt of the criticism, but eastern papers denounced Elizabeth, who as usual expressed herself freely and fearlessly to reporters. They sought refuge in the Yosemite for some days and then continued their lectures in a few of the smaller California towns. The last of August, Elizabeth left for home, stopping in Johnstown to spend a few days with her mother, who was very feeble and who passed away a week later.

Susan continued her lectures in Oregon and Washington, for there was still a big debt to be paid off on the *Revolution*. She was lonely without Elizabeth, but she was now being appreciated for herself alone. Wherever they went together, Elizabeth was lionized while she basked in her glory; and even the best of friends sometimes secretly resent such an overshadowing. Susan wrote home:

> I miss Mrs. Stanton, still I cannot but enjoy the feeling that people call on *me,* and the fact that I have an opportunity to sharpen my wits a little by answering questions and doing the chatting, instead of merely sitting a lay figure and listening to the brilliant scintillations as they emanate from her never exhausted magazine. There is no alternative—whoever goes into a parlor or before an audience with that woman does it at the cost of a fearful overshadowing, a price which I have paid for the last ten years, and that cheerfully, because I felt our cause was most profited by her being seen and heard, and my best work was making the way clear for her.

XIX

VICTORIA WOODHULL AND THE BEECHER-TILTON CASE

ELIEVING that with more tactful methods she could accomplish
for woman suffrage what Elizabeth and Susan had failed to
do, Isabella Beecher Hooker had volunteered to relieve them of the
responsibility of the Washington Convention in January 1871. With
all the confidence of the Beechers, she was certain that woman
suffrage could be quickly won, if a few women of the right type
guided the destiny of the suffrage organizations. She wrote
Elizabeth:

> I fully expect to accomplish far more by a convention devoted to
> the purely political aspect of the woman question, than by a woman's
> rights convention, however well managed; and this because the time
> has come for practical work....

Amazed and a little annoyed at Isabella's attitude, Elizabeth
commented to Martha Wright:

> You can imagine what success Mrs. Hooker will have with those
> wily politicians. She thinks they will come serenely from their seats
> to the lobby when she tries all the means known to an honest
> woman! I fear the means known to the other sort would meet a
> readier response....Mrs. Hooker will find it no easy matter to hook
> them on to her platform, but she will be wiser after trying. She is
> mistaken in considering the cause so nearly won....

Elizabeth was ready to let Isabella try her wings. She had no
intention of breaking into her lecture tour to attend the meetings
and offered to send $100 as a substitute for her presence. This was
wholly satisfactory to Isabella, if not to Susan, who for her part
had no intention of letting the woman suffrage movement get out
of her hands. Impatient with Elizabeth's indifference, Susan wrote
her a scathing letter:

> To my mind, there never was such a suicidal letting go as has
> been yours these last two years. But I am now teetotally discouraged

and shall make no more attempts to hold you up to what I know is not only best for our cause, but equally so for yourself, from the moral standpoint if not the financial. . . . How you can excuse yourself is more than I can understand.

But even this did not bring Elizabeth to Washington. Instead she commented to Martha Wright:

For your instruction in the ways of the world, I send you Susan's letter. You see I am between two fires all the time. Some are determined to throw me overboard, and she is equally determined that I shall stand at the masthead, no matter how pitiless the storm.

The convention was a great success and a sensation as well, as Elizabeth learned from the press and from Susan, who soon afterward spent a day with her in Chicago. By a strange twist of circumstances, Isabella Beecher Hooker's convention, which was to have been a model of propriety and good judgment, was dominated by the personality of the notorious, bewitching lady broker of Wall Street, Victoria Claflin Woodhull. In comparison, George Francis Train and the *Revolution* had been mild and harmless associates.

For the past year Victoria Woodhull had entertained the New York press with her escapades. She appeared apparently from nowhere, opened an office on Wall Street with her sister, Tennessee Claflin, made a fortune, and lived in luxury and in an aura of mystery and glamour. A sordid childhood, spent traveling about like a gypsy, telling fortunes, tipping tables, communicating with spirits, and living by her wits; an early marriage to Canning Woodhull, disregarded when she met Colonel James Blood, president of the Society of Spiritualists, with whom the spirits advised an alliance—these were the events preceding Victoria Woodhull's spirit-directed appearance in New York. The office on Wall Street would never have materialized had it not been for sister Tennessee's skill as a magnetic healer, practiced on Cornelius Vanderbilt, who started them out on their venture in finance. Wall Street, however, was only a means to an end for Victoria, whose real interests were spiritualism, free love, and self-glorification. She must keep her views and Colonel Blood's before the public, and so, on May 14,

1870, *Woodhull & Claflin's Weekly* was issued, announcing itself as "primarily devoted to the vital interests of the people," treating all matters freely and without reservation, supporting Victoria Woodhull for President, and advocating suffrage without distinction of sex.

For the first few months the paper was mild enough, urging women to be independent, reprimanding Elizabeth Cady Stanton for giving a lecture to "Ladies Only," adding in explanation, "It is a pity for women to set the example of discourtesy." Nor was the discussion of spiritualism or new social theories anything unusual at the time, for it was an era of great interest in spiritualism, in Utopian communities, in mysticism, and in impractical social theories designed to build a better world. But as time went on, *Woodhull & Claflin's Weekly* grew bolder in its language as it attacked the social evil and began muckraking.

Victoria Woodhull had announced herself as a candidate for the Presidency of the United States in April 1870 in the *New York Herald*:

> While others of my sex devoted themselves to a crusade against the laws that shackle the women of the country, I asserted my individual independence ... while others argued the equality of women with man, I proved it by successfully engaging in business. ... I therefore claim the right to speak for the unenfranchised women of the country, and believing as I do that the prejudices which still exist in the popular mind against women will soon disappear, I now announce myself as a candidate for the Presidency. ...

Nobody paid much attention, and the suffragists did not hail her as their prophet. But Victoria had a way with her. She was beautiful, she was daring, and she was disarming. She readily found men to champion her. This time General Benjamin Butler came to the rescue and planned a coup for her. She appeared in Washington with a memorial, praying Congress to enact such laws as were necessary to enable women to exercise the right to vote already vested in them by the Fourteenth Amendment. She was granted the privilege of addressing the Judiciary Committee of the House of Representatives on the day in January 1871 when Isabella Beecher Hooker's genteel, discreet woman suffrage convention was to convene.

Susan thought they should attend the hearing to find out what Mrs. Woodhull's plans were; Mrs. Hooker did not think it wise to have anything to do with her; but Senator Pomeroy, before whom they were discussing the matter, warned them that men never stopped to consider each others' antecedents and associates before working together politically. Mrs. Hooker was won over, and the next morning, she, Susan, and Paulina Wright Davis appeared at Victoria Woodhull's hearing. They had expected to find a bold, aggressive woman decked out in bright colors and furbelows. Instead they saw a beautiful young woman, plainly and tastefully dressed, with every appearance of refinement. She read her able address in a clear musical voice. She captivated them all and there was nothing to do but to invite her to repeat the address at the National Woman Suffrage Convention, where again she and her sister, Tennessee, in their dark dresses and blue neckties, with their short curly brown hair and jaunty Alpine hats, won the hearts of the suffragists.

Victoria Woodhull's arguments on woman's rights under the Fourteenth Amendment fitted in very well with the ideas of the National Woman Suffrage Association. Virginia Minor and her husband, Francis Minor of St. Louis, had raised the point and were planning to test it in the courts. Elizabeth Cady Stanton had emphasized it in her last speech before a Congressional committee. Now Victoria Woodhull's memorial focused the attention of the public upon it.

However, the Judiciary Committee reported adversely on the Woodhull memorial, maintaining that Congress did not have the power to act. Benjamin Butler and William Loughridge of Iowa handed in a minority report, a strong argument for woman's right to vote under the Constitution.

Susan was again in the West lecturing when she read the Minority Report, and she wrote Victoria Woodhull praising Benjamin Butler and expressing her delight at this latest effort to gain suffrage for women under the Fourteenth Amendment.

The connection of a notorious character such as Victoria Woodhull with woman suffrage was just what an unfriendly press was looking for. Free love, spiritualism, and woman suffrage were now bandied about together. It was far worse than the New England group ever dreamed possible, and they were grateful to be safe and proper in their own American Woman Suffrage Association.

Although Elizabeth was not in Washington to witness Victoria Woodhull's admission to the suffrage ranks, she welcomed her to the fold on the enthusiastic recommendations of Susan, Isabella Beecher Hooker, and Paulina Wright Davis. She was always eager to welcome a new and able recruit to the cause—always ready to champion a woman who was criticized for unconventionality, glad for an opportunity to insist that she be judged by the same standards as a man. She met Victoria Woodhull for the first time in May 1871 prior to the New York meeting of the National Woman Suffrage Association, when the suffragists were being mercilessly criticized by men, sympathetic to the cause, for linking such an adventuress up with woman suffrage.

This was all that Elizabeth needed to rouse her. She came to Victoria Woodhull's defense at once. To one of these men she wrote:

> In regard to the gossip about Mrs. Woodhull I have one answer to give all my gentlemen friends. When the men who make laws for us in Washington can stand forth and declare themselves pure and unspotted from all the sins mentioned in the Decalogue, then we will demand that every woman who makes a constitutional argument on our platform shall be. If our good men will only trouble themselves as much about the virtue of their own sex as they do about ours, if they will make one moral code for both men and women, we shall have a nobler type of manhood and womanhood in the next generation than the world has yet seen.

Victoria Woodhull was on hand for the woman suffrage meetings at Apollo Hall, New York, in May 1871. Some of the suffragists objected to her presence and refused to sit on the platform with her, but Elizabeth, trying her best to make the newcomer acceptable and respectable, seated her between Lucretia Mott and herself.

Victoria's speech electrified her audience. Enemies were won over. She was beautiful. Her personality compelled. She spoke to them like a prophetess aflame with her message. "If the very next Congress refuses women all the legitimate results of citizenship," she warned, "we shall proceed to call another convention expressly to frame a new constitution and to erect a new government. . . . We are plotting revolution; we will overthrow this bogus republic and plant a government of righteousness in its stead." In her enthusiasm she saw herself as President of this new republic. But Elizabeth and her colleagues, who loved to talk of social revolutions, were oblivious of the ambition that was driving Victoria. Instead they were visioning the women of the nation aroused to demand their rights, triumphant at last.

The *New York Tribune,* now as vindictive as it had been friendly in the past, assumed that the suffragists had adopted all of Victoria Woodhull's "free love" doctrines and worked itself up into a white heat. Headlines called it "The Woodhull Convention." Victoria was getting all the publicity. Woman suffrage had temporarily been eclipsed.

Had Elizabeth seen more of Victoria Woodhull, she would undoubtedly have fathomed her ambitious, self-seeking nature, but their acquaintance was purely formal. With other liberals she had made her one visit to the Woodhull home at 15 East 38th Street, and there in the glitter of gilt sensed that everything was not as it should be. She could not take very seriously Victoria's dabblings in psychic realms or her communion with her guiding spirit, Demosthenes; still, these did not trouble her. But Victoria's family squabbles, which were continually being aired in court at most unfortunate times, were constant reminders of the poor stock from which she sprang. Although Elizabeth tried to reason that a pure prophetess might arise out of the mire, her own good common sense, when she used it, put her on her guard, and eager as she was to defend Victoria and her views, she could not whole-heartedly believe in her. Victoria, however, had a way of winning over her friends when they began to doubt. She could be so charming, so refined, and so naïve that they were sure she was a genius who could be developed by association with superior people. After all, to Elizabeth, she was primarily a misunderstood woman who needed to be championed by women of courage. And in addition it was stimulating to discuss marriage, divorce, and the relation of the sexes with a woman who dared to be frank and liberal and had the courage to put her beliefs into practice. There was a great deal to talk over now, for reports of immorality in high places were leaking out.

For a year Elizabeth had known of a scandal which concerned Henry Ward Beecher and Elizabeth Tilton, the wife of her good friend, Theodore Tilton. Theodore had told the story to her and to Laura Curtis Bullard. He had told it to Victoria Woodhull, with whom he was infatuated. Elizabeth Tilton had confided it to her mother, who spread it broadcast, and to Susan B. Anthony. It was rumored in newspaper offices, but left alone out of deference to the beloved preacher. As Henry Ward Beecher grew in popularity and power and the attacks on Victoria Woodhull became more and more bitter, the social aspects of the case were often discussed by the suffragists. Here was a woman, Victoria Woodhull, openly advocating what Henry Ward Beecher, it seemed, lived in secret. She was persecuted. He went free.

Henry Ward Beecher was using his power to protect himself, and the first step was to crush and discredit Theodore Tilton. Tilton was dismissed from the editorship of the *Independent*. He was encouraged to write a biography of Victoria Woodhull for the *Golden Age,* a new magazine which Beecher temporarily financed— this to flatter Victoria and keep her quiet; but the biography brought the two together and this was incriminating. His lecture engagements fell off. Plymouth Church wanted to expel him.

In her motherly way Elizabeth longed to comfort and help Theodore and Elizabeth Tilton, to guide these confused young children over the impasse which was threatening their married life. She understood so well what they were going through, for she herself, many years ago, before her marriage, had been so tempted to defy the conventions and run away with Edward Bayard. She knew what a struggle it took to combat human weakness and desire, and this knowledge had made her kind and tolerant and eager to help other puzzled men and women. She urged the Tiltons to build a little house in New Jersey in the country as she had done. She wrote Theodore:

I know Elizabeth and the children would enjoy a new peace and happiness in a little country home of their own, where they could sit under shady trees and hear the birds sing, far from care and company and all the restraints of city life. Rest and quiet, time for thought and study would be good, dear Theodore, for you too. Let the dead past go, waste no energies in regret, but garner up the wisdom that comes from experience, for future worth. You do not know how much interest and sympathy I feel for you and your little wife and how happy I should be to do anything to strengthen and shelter you from this kind of persecution.

Catherine Beecher and Harriet Beecher Stowe, infuriated by Victoria Woodhull's views, assailed her in the press whenever possible, little realizing that they were driving her to reveal a secret which might ruin their famous brother's life. Victoria was seething under these attacks. She was being financially ruined and was obliged to move from her pretentious home to a boardinghouse. But she was biding her time. She published her warning in the *New York Times:*

I do not intend to be made the scapegoat of sacrifice to be offered up as a victim to society by those who cover the foulness of their lives and the feculence of their thoughts with a hypocritical mantle of fair profession, diverting public attention from their own iniquity in pointing the finger at me.... My judges preach against "free love" openly, and practice it secretly.... For example, I know of one man, a public teacher of eminence, who lives in concubinage with the wife of another public teacher of almost equal eminence. All three concur in denouncing offenses against morality.... I shall make it my business to analyze some of these lives, and will take my chances in the matter of libel suits.

The situation was tense for Henry Ward Beecher, the Tiltons, and their friends.

Theodore Tilton sent Elizabeth his biographical sketch of Victoria Woodhull, published as a *Golden Age* tract. This sentimental eulogy, recounting Victoria's struggles and sufferings, moved her deeply, and when she was deeply moved, she usually had to express herself in an article or a letter to some newspaper or magazine. This time the result was an article in the *Golden Age,* December 1871, which gave Victoria a thorough whitewashing. She wrote:

Some people carp at the "National" organization because it endorses Mrs. Woodhull. When our representatives at Washington granted to Victoria C. Woodhull a hearing before the Judiciary Committees of both Houses—an honor conferred on no other woman in the nation before—they recognized Mrs. Woodhull as the leader of the woman suffrage movement in this country. And those of us who were convinced by her unanswerable arguments that her positions were sound, had no choice but to follow.

Mrs. Woodhull's speeches and writings on all the great questions of national life are beyond anything yet produced by man or woman on our platform. What if foul-mouthed scandal, with its many tongues, seeks to defile her? Shall we ignore a champion like this? Admit for the sake of argument that all men say of her is true— though it is false—that she has been or is a courtesan in sentiment and practice. When a woman of this class shall suddenly devote herself to the study of the grave problems of life, brought there by profound thought and experience, and with new faith and hope struggles to redeem the errors of the past by a grand life in the future, shall we not welcome her to the better place she desires to hold?...Victoria C. Woodhull stands before us today a grand, brave woman, radical alike in political, religious, and social principles. Her face and form indicate the complete triumph in her nature of the spiritual over the sensuous. The processes of her education are little to us; the grand result is everything.

The fears of women of one another, lest they should be compromised by those they imagine less reputable than themselves is as amusing as pitiful....Now I think we had better agree to fight this battle just as our fathers and husbands have their two revolutions— enroll all that are loyal to the principle. How much of an army should we have had for the rebellion, if every man who came to enroll himself had been asked, "Do you smoke, chew, drink, steal, lie, swear? Are you low-bred, illiterate, or licentious? If so, you cannot fight for freedom." Was it not just this element we swept into the army? And were they not the better for suffering and dying for a noble cause? Churches and reform associations are just the places to draw in the sinners, and inspire them with a new and moral purpose.... Jesus, the good and perfect one, ate and talked with publicans and sinners, and was ever kind and merciful to the erring and unfortunate Magdalens of his times. Let us, one and all, follow his example.

Victoria C. Woodhull was one of the prominent figures at the convention of the National Woman Suffrage Association in Washington in January 1872. In her blue broadcloth suit with its double-breasted chinchilla cloth coat, she was very proper and very alluring. She was now president of the National Association of Spiritualists, and as she addressed the suffragists, she mentioned this fact. She talked a great deal about the "better government which shall descend from heaven." She proposed a constitution of the United States of the World.

Susan, who had just returned from a long western lecture tour, took the opportunity offered by the convention, to say a word in commendation of Victoria, voicing sentiments similar to those expressed by Elizabeth in the *Golden Age*. "I have been asked by many," she began in her blunt way, "Why did you drag Victoria C. Woodhull to the front? Now bless your souls, she was not dragged to the front. She came to Washington with a powerful argument. She presented her memorial to Congress and it was a power. I should have been glad to call it the Dickinson memorial, or the Beecher memorial, or even the Anthony memorial, since it was a mighty effort of which any woman might be proud.... I was asked by an editor of a New York paper if I knew of Mrs. Woodhull's antecedents. I said I didn't, and that I did not care any more for them than I do about those of the members of Congress. Her antecedents will compare favorably with any member of Congress." But Susan was careful to add that the National Woman Suffrage Association did not endorse all of Victoria's ideas—temperance, labor reform, or spiritualism. Its one object was woman suffrage.

At this time Susan requested the privilege of addressing the Senate and the House on woman's right to vote under the Fourteenth Amendment. To her group of suffragists and to many able lawyers, such an interpretation of the Amendment looked extremely promising, but to the Senate and the House the issue was not sufficiently important to warrant the breaking of precedent to the extent of allowing women to address them. Instead they merely granted the suffragists a hearing before the Senate Judiciary Committee at which Elizabeth spoke with her usual force and intelligence. The Committee, true to form, reported adversely on the question.

Soon after the Washington Convention both Susan and Elizabeth continued their lecture tours in different parts of the country; and Victoria Woodhull lectured at the New York Academy of Music on "The Impending Revolution," to an audience that fairly stampeded to hear her. Then Victoria's family troubles were again aired in court. The press was virulent. But this did not keep her from making plans for the anniversary meeting of the National Woman Suffrage Association in New York in May. She talked so much and so well about the need of a new political party that she worked up Isabella Beecher Hooker and Matilda Joslyn Gage almost to her own pitch of enthusiasm. Elizabeth, who for some time had been thoroughly disgusted with the present political parties and their treatment of women's demands, was an easy convert. Susan, in Leavenworth, Kansas, far away from the magnetic personality of Victoria Woodhull, could view the matter dispassionately. She wrote Elizabeth and Mrs. Hooker:

> We have no element out of which to make a political party, because there is not a man who would vote a woman suffrage ticket if thereby he endangered his Republican, Democratic, Workingmen's or Temperance party, and all our time and words in that direction are simply thrown away. My name must not be used to call any such meeting.... I tell you I feel utterly disheartened—not that our cause is going to die or be defeated, but as to my place and work. Mrs. Woodhull has the advantage of us because she has the newspaper, and she persistently means to run our craft into her port and none other. If she were influenced by *women spirits,* either in the body or out of it, in the direction she steers, I might consent to be a mere sail hoister for her; but as it is, she is wholly owned and dominated by men spirits and I spurn the control of the whole lot of them, just precisely the same when reflected through her woman's tongue and pen as if they spoke directly for themselves.

Elizabeth had had sufficient political experience to know that the formation of a new political party could not be effected by amateurs with a small following, no matter how worthy their platform or ideals. She had seen the slow and feeble rise of the Liberty party out of the ranks of fiery Abolitionists. She knew how long it took for the Republican party to evolve and unite the discontented elements of other parties. But she was not being practical. She was being carried away by her enthusiasm for a revolution which would give woman her political and civil rights, and this enthusiasm was fanned by Victoria Woodhull.

The more Victoria was vilified by the press and criticized by Elizabeth's friends, the less Elizabeth analyzed the character of this astonishing woman and the more eager she was to defend her. She wrote Lucretia Mott at this time:

> I have thought much, since leaving you, of our dear Woodhull, all the gossip about her, and have come to the conclusion that it is great impertinence in any of us to pry into her affairs.... We have had women enough sacrificed to this sentimental, hypocritical prating about purity. This is one of man's most effective engines for our division and subjugation. He creates the public sentiment, builds the gallows, and then makes us hangman for our sex. Women have crucified the Mary Wollstonecrafts, the Fanny Wrights, the George Sands, the Fanny Kembles, the Lucretia Motts of all ages, and now men mock us with the fact, and say we are ever cruel to each other. Let us end this ignoble record and henceforth stand by womanhood. If Victoria Woodhull must be crucified, let men drive the spikes and plait the crown of thorns.

In this frame of mind she signed the call to the May anniversary meeting of the National Woman Suffrage Association and allowed Susan's name to be appended. The call read in part:

> The undersigned citizens of the United States, responding to the invitation of the National Woman Suffrage Association, propose to hold a Convention at Steinway Hall, in the city of New York, the 9th and 10th of May.
> We believe the time has come for the formation of a new political party whose principles shall meet the issues of the hour, and represent equal rights for all. As the women of the country are to take part for the first time in political action, we propose that the initiative steps in the Convention shall be taken by them....
> This Convention will declare the platform of the People's Party, and consider the nomination of candidates for President and Vice-President of the United States, who shall be the best possible exponents of political and industrial reform....

Susan, in a little town in the West, read this call in *Woodhull & Claflin's Weekly*. Indignant that her name, without her consent, was signed to something of which she so thoroughly disapproved, she telegraphed immediately to have it removed, and wrote sharp letters remonstrating with Elizabeth and those arranging the convention. Now that she was fully awake to Victoria Woodhull's machinations, she was determined to put a stop to them.

As soon as possible she returned to New York and took over the final arrangements of the convention. She went to Tenafly to thrash the matter out with Elizabeth. When Susan was so in earnest, Elizabeth usually listened, even though she was not wholly convinced.

It had been the custom at all suffrage conventions, as previously at all antislavery meetings, to glorify the theory of free speech. Hence anybody and everybody was allowed to speak. Victoria had gathered about her a motley array of spiritualists, radicals, and dissatisfied members of society, ready to do her bidding. With these allies, she planned to assume control of the suffrage organization. But she had not reckoned with the astute and determined Susan. As Susan had rented Steinway Hall specifically for a suffrage meeting, she did not intend to let it be used for a People's Convention and she made this plain. Victoria and her supporters, therefore, were obliged to engage Apollo Hall for their meetings. Both Elizabeth and Isabella Beecher Hooker felt that Susan had been very unreasonable, and Elizabeth refused to act as president any longer. Susan was elected to take her place, grateful to have complete control of affairs.

Elizabeth, however, presided at the first meeting of the convention and made the opening speech. Susan had not been able to stamp out her enthusiasm for a new political party. Talk of new political alignments filled the air, not only among Victoria Woodhull's supporters. Liberal Republicans, appalled at the corruption under the Grant administration, had called a convention in Cincinnati. The trouble with Elizabeth was—she was too near the wrong band wagon. She began her speech:

> We are not here today to rehearse old arguments for woman suffrage, which we have advocated for the last twenty-five years, but to inaugurate a new political party. It is not probable that during this Convention we shall nominate candidates. But we propose to take the initiatory steps for a convention of new forces, such as we have never had before. The politicians who are afraid that our support will not be given them say that our cause is so holy and should be kept so high in the clouds that we could never see our flags. But now we propose to descend to the political business of life. Today we are combined with the Liberal Reformers, with Prohibitionists, and the Internationalists—with all classes of men who will help to roll back the constitutional doors that we may enter and enjoy the rights that belong to every free citizen of the United States. We claim under the Fourteenth and Fifteenth Amendments that we are citizens of the United States today, and we have as good a right to

go to the polls, register our names, and if our votes are refused, we will contest it in the Supreme Court of the United States....

Somehow or other Susan managed to hold the meeting in check and keep it for the most part on the subject of woman suffrage. But Victoria Woodhull was as determined as Susan. She was not going to be separated from the National Woman Suffrage Association without a struggle, nor lose the support of the suffragists for her new party. At the close of the first evening session when Susan was presiding, Victoria suddenly appeared on the platform and moved that the convention adjourn to meet the next morning with her colleagues in Apollo Hall. One of her allies in the audience seconded the motion, but Susan refused to put it. After an appeal was made from the decision of the chair, Victoria, herself, put the motion and it was carried by a large majority. Undaunted, Susan pronounced the proceeding out of order as the greatest number of those voting were not members of the Association. In a clear, ringing voice she announced that the convention would adjourn to meet in the same place the next morning. Then, as Victoria kept on talking, she ordered the janitor to turn out the lights, and the crowd dispersed. She had conquered Victoria.

News that came from the People's Convention the next day proved that she had been right in her estimate of Victoria's ambitions and plans and that she had saved the National Woman Suffrage Association from being the laughingstock of the entire country. The People's party chose for a permanent name the Equal Rights party. Amid cheers, stamping, and the waving of handkerchiefs and hats, Victoria C. Woodhull was nominated for President of the United States, and Frederick Douglass, without his consent, for Vice-President. The ovation which Victoria received from her ardent supporters was all she could have wished, but there it ended. No one else took her seriously.

The *Woman's Journal,* commenting on the turbulent convention of the National Woman Suffrage Association, said:

We hope they have got rid of the "Free Love" incubus which has done incalculable harm to the cause of Woman Suffrage. Women, like men, are known by the company they keep. The withdrawal of

ELIZABETH CADY STANTON AND HER SON HENRY IN 1854

Victoria Wocodhull Presenting Her Memorial Before the Judiciary
Committee of the House of Representatives in 1871
(From *Frank Leslie's Illustrated Newspaper*)

Mrs. Woodhull and her so-called "radical reformers" will result we hope in bringing to the front of the New York Society, women whose intellect and character command public respect.

This incensed Victoria. Her fortunes were waning. She had not been able to climb to fame on the reputation of the suffragists. She resented this and blamed her troubles on them. Since they criticized her, she would publish unpleasant things about them in *Woodhull & Claflin's Weekly*. With the proof of an article, "Tit for Tat," she tried to frighten and extort money from Mrs. Phelps, Lillie Devereux Blake, and Laura Curtis Bullard, but she did not succeed. This caused a rift in her friendship with Theodore Tilton. He was indignant at her designs on his friends. Theodore, however, was now too deep in politics to be of use to Victoria. He was not supporting her candidacy. With other liberal Republicans he was looking forward to the nomination of Horace Greeley.

In June, *Woodhull & Claflin's Weekly* was obliged to suspend publication temporarily, and Victoria and her family were put out of their boardinghouse. Wherever they sought lodgings, they were turned away. Victoria, when she attended the meeting of the National Spiritualists' Association at Boston in September, felt driven to the wall, but she had one more card to play. According to the press, her speech "poured out like a stream of flame." She told her story of the Beecher-Tilton scandal. She shocked and thrilled her audience with her accusations and her theories. They re-elected her president of their Association. The Boston papers did not print one word of the alleged Beecher-Tilton scandal, and it continued to smolder. But Victoria Woodhull had not yet done her worst.

On November 2, 1872, *Woodhull & Claflin's Weekly* resumed publication with her sensational story of the Beecher-Tilton scandal. It was in such demand that by evening it sold on the streets at forty dollars a copy.

Elizabeth was featured in that startling issue of the *Weekly* as one of Victoria's informants who had her facts directly from Theodore Tilton. But Victoria had so colored the story with her own vivid, sensual language that Elizabeth warmly denied that version. The press distorted her denial so that Susan, reading the reports, accused her of deserting Victoria. Emphatically she replied:

> I had supposed you knew enough of papers to trust a friend of twenty years' knowledge before them.... I simply said I never used the language Mrs. Woodhull put in my mouth, that whatever I said was clothed in refined language at least, however disgusting the subject. I have said many times since the denouement that if my testimony of what I did know would save Victoria from prison I should feel compelled to give it. You do not monopolize, dear Susan, all the honor there is among womankind. I shall not run before I am sent, but when the time comes, I shall prove myself as true as you. No, no, I do not propose to shelter a man when a woman's liberty is at stake.

Anthony Comstock, defender of virtue, could not allow this story of the Beecher-Tilton scandal to endanger the morals of a nation. The passage of a federal law earlier in the year, declaring the transmission of obscene matter through the mails a misdemeanor, gave him his weapon. Through his efforts Victoria Woodhull was arrested. Then followed a series of court cases and arrests which kept her busy for many months. When she was free again, she told her story through *Woodhull & Claflin's Weekly,* through the press, and through her lecture, "The Naked Truth," which she delivered to enormous audiences throughout the country. There was a glamour about Victoria which could not be resisted.

But she was no longer invited to attend the conventions of the National Woman Suffrage Association. This group of suffragists had not repudiated her because of her revelation of the Beecher-Tilton affair. Many of them still believed her a sincere, much-persecuted reformer, but they now realized the wisdom of keeping her machinations out of their conventions. Nor did she try to force her way in. She had learned that she could not dominate that organization, but she recognized that it was not well to sever all connections, and so she published reports of the woman suffrage conventions in her paper.

The public, now well-aroused over the Beecher-Tilton scandal, was divided in three camps. The minority wanted to get at the truth of the matter; a group of wealthy men dependent upon Beecher's good name for the safety of their investments in the church property, in his religious magazine and his published writings, were determined to see him vindicated; and the great majority, closing their eyes to the possibilities of his guilt, insisted that his purity and sanctity must be upheld at any cost to keep the social institutions—the church, marriage, the home, morality—from tottering.

It was a tragic story. Theodore Tilton, a handsome, magnetic young man, a brilliant writer and speaker, had been Henry Ward Beecher's best friend and protégé. Both he and his young wife, brought up in Plymouth Church, looked upon Beecher as their spiritual advisor. Their home was a refuge to him after the unhappiness and austerity of his own. Here he met intellectuals and liberals and enjoyed stimulating conversation. He found peace in the company of Elizabeth Tilton, who knew so well how to make her home radiate hospitality. Often he wrote his sermons at Theodore's desk while she sat near by darning the children's stockings. He frolicked with the children and brought them toys. He brought her flowers, pictures, and books. He was grateful for the home life shared with him.

One winter while Theodore was away, he came almost daily to read to Elizabeth Tilton the draft of his novel, *Norwood,* which he had contracted to write for Bonner's *Ledger* for the amazing sum of $20,000. To her this was an undreamed-of honor; to him it was inspiration. She looked upon him as a God who could do no wrong. She satisfied his hunger for love and companionship, and almost without realizing it, they drifted into more intimate relations. At least so Elizabeth Tilton later confessed to Theodore. Then, because these two emotionally distraught young people could not keep their unhappy secret to themselves, it became public property, and people and circumstances would not let them live it down. To complicate matters the reputation of a great preacher was at stake.

A popular idol, such as Henry Ward Beecher, could not easily be shattered. The man who had drawn thousands to his church every Sunday, who had held his congregation in the hollow of his hand, swaying the emotions of the strong as well as the weak until they regarded him almost as a second Christ, could not lose his power in a moment by the circulation of a scandal. His personal magnetism was a mighty defense. Desperately frightened inwardly, he fought to retain his power. He would crush anyone to save himself. He had ruthless, astute lawyers at his command. They did the necessary work. Theodore Tilton, Elizabeth Tilton, and the suffragists were defamed to whitewash Henry Ward Beecher, and he continued to preach the gospel of Christ to admiring congregations.

The suffragists were the stumbling block to proving his innocence. Susan B. Anthony, Elizabeth Cady Stanton, and his half-sister, Isabella Beecher Hooker, had first-hand knowledge of the affair, and while they would not hound him as did Victoria Woodhull, yet he knew they discussed the matter in their group. He knew they believed him guilty of immoral relations with Elizabeth Tilton. They were women of integrity and prominence. Their word bore weight. He could not manipulate them nor buy them off. They would stand by the woman in the case at all costs. Their knowledge was like the sword of Damocles hanging over him. There was but one thing to do—damage their reputations in the eyes of the public—call them free lovers. His henchmen took care of this. Isabella, who did her best to comfort him and to persuade him to confess, was branded as an irresponsible person verging on insanity.

The press was avid for news. It printed anything and everything. The Beecher-Tilton scandal covered pages of the metropolitan papers. People eagerly expressed their opinions in letters and interviews—all but Susan B. Anthony, who would in no way violate the confidences which Elizabeth Tilton had revealed to her in a moment of desperation. Elizabeth Cady Stanton both commented and wrote freely on the subject. Negotiations, intrigues, accusations, and denials continued month after month. Henry Ward Beecher at first appeared to maintain a dignified silence, but finally he declared his innocence; and Susan, reading the press report, wrote Isabella Beecher Hooker, "Wouldn't you think if God ever did strike anyone dead for telling a lie, he would have struck then?" Even this letter, without Susan's consent, later appeared in the *New York Graphic*—one of the many personal letters on the subject flaunted by the press.

A reporter of the *Brooklyn Argus* called on Elizabeth Cady Stanton at Tenafly to get her story. By this time she was so incensed by the slanderous attacks on the suffragists and so disgusted by Beecher's treatment of Elizabeth Tilton, that she was ready to tell all she knew and to express her views freely. She told among other things what Elizabeth Tilton had confided to Susan and Susan in turn had related to her.

Hearing of this, Susan berated her soundly, and she replied in explanation:

> Offended Susan, come right down and pull my ears. I shall not attempt a defense. Of course I admit that I have made an awful blunder in not keeping silent so far as you were concerned on this terrible Beecher-Tilton scandal. The whole odium of this scandalum magnatum has in some quarters been rolled on our suffrage movement, as unjustly as cunningly; hence I feel obliged just now to make extra efforts to keep our ship off the rocks. There was never anything so base and cowardly as that statement of some of Beecher's supporters, building a footstool for him to stand upon out of the life, character, aspirations, and ambition of a large circle of reputable women. This terrible onslaught on the suffrage movement has made me feel like writing for every paper daily. From the silence on all sides, I saw it was for me to fight alone. I have in fact written several articles, incog., in the *Graphic*. . . . When Beecher falls, as he must, he will pull all he can down with him. But we must not let the cause of woman go down in the smash. It is innocent.

By the summer of 1874, matters had become so complicated that Henry Ward Beecher appointed a committee of six members of his church to investigate the charges made against him. Their report pronounced him innocent. "We find nothing whatever in the evidence," it read, "that should impair the perfect confidence of Plymouth Church or the world in the Christian character and integrity of Henry Ward Beecher."

Such hypocrisy was more than Elizabeth could endure. She was familiar with the fabrications foisted on the investigating committee. She saw the reputations of Theodore and Elizabeth Tilton being utterly ruined.

To a friend in the West who had asked for her views, she sent a pertinent interpretation of the Plymouth Church investigation. It was published in the *Transcript* of Earlville, Illinois, and reprinted in the *Chicago Tribune,* thus reaching thousands of readers who respected her opinions. It was one of the ablest statements issued— a fearless analysis of a social problem:

I have a double interest in this sad page of domestic history; first, because it involves great principles of social ethics; second, because those who have accidentally been forced to illustrate our ignorance of these principles are among my personal friends. To those who take a surface view of "the scandal," it is probably "prurient," "disgusting," "nauseating," as our refined Metropolitan press affects to consider it, although the first news sought for by the reading public, by gentlemen and ladies alike, has, I presume, during the last two months, been "the Plymouth Church investigation." This, to my mind, is an evidence, not of a depraved popular taste, but of a vital interest in the social problems that puzzle and perplex the best of us.

The true relations of men and women, the foundations of the family and home, are of more momentous importance than any question of State or Church, can possibly be.... The true social code, whatever it is, must be the same for both sexes. If the testimony given in this case be all true, and it be proven that such men as Henry Ward Beecher and Theodore Tilton find the marriage laws of the State of New York, too stringent, both being in discordant marriage relations, might it not be well to review the laws, as well as their violations? To compel unhappy husbands and wives, by law and public sentiment, to live together, and to teach them that it is their religious duty to accept their conditions, whatever they are, produces, ever and anon, just such social earthquakes as the one through which we are now passing....

What a holocaust of womanhood we have had in this investigation! What a football the Committee, the lawyers, Mrs. Beecher, and her husband have made of Elizabeth R. Tilton! What statements and counter-statements they have wrung from her unwilling lips; then like a withered flower, "the Great Preacher" casts her aside and tells the world "she thrust her affection upon him unsought"—the crowning perfidy in that bill of impeachment that blackens everyone who dared to hear or tell the most astounding scandal of the 19th century! In common with the rest of the world, members of the National Woman's Suffrage Association heard and repeated the scandal as other men and women did; and forsooth Mr. Beecher dubs them "human hyenas" and "free lovers," though his own sister, Isabella Beecher Hooker, was one of the number, and who, by letters and conversations that through him and his brother were published to the world, is presented as "insane," "deluded," "weak-minded." Those who know Mrs. Tilton—her natural delicacy and refinement—will readily believe her true story, that through months of persuasion and argument, her love was sought—and sealed....

You ask if it is possible for Mr. Beecher to maintain his position in the face of the facts. His position will be maintained *for* him, as he is the soul and center of three powerful religious rings, as he tells you himself in his statement: (1) Plymouth Church; (2) the *Christian Union;* (3) *The Life of Christ.* The church property is not taxed, its bonds in the hands of wealthy men of that organization are valuable, and the bondholders, alive to their financial interests, stand around Mr. Beecher, a faithful, protecting band, not loving truth and justice less, but their own pockets more. They are shrewd enough to know that in Mr. Beecher's downfall their bonds must be of little value. Next the *Christian Union*—a dull paper that represents no new thought in morals, religion, or politics....If then his good name is shadowed, another circle of suffering stockholders would be brought to grief. As to *The Life of Christ,* in the words of one of the fold, that would indeed be blown "higher than a kite" were the author proved an unworthy shepherd. I have heard that he was paid $20,000 for that work before he put pen to paper....

If the secret history of this tragedy is ever brought to light, we shall have such revelations of diplomacy and hypocrisy in high places as to open the eyes of the people to the impossibility of securing justice for anyone when money can be used against him.

When a refined gentleman and scholar like Theodore Tilton can be hurled in a day from one of the proudest positions in the country—the able editor of a great journal—and become the target for the jibes and jeers of the nation, without one authenticated accusation of vice or crime against him, his downfall is the result of no lack of moral rectitude in himself. They who try to see Theodore Tilton vindicated do but maintain the claims of common justice for those who have not the money to buy it....

The expression of such views, while a great relief to Elizabeth, did not enhance her reputation among the conservative suffragists. By using this opportunity to advocate a revision of divorce laws—still a forbidden subject—she drew fire. Jane Grey Swisshelm, voicing the opinions of a large group, wrote to the *Chicago Tribune:*

Of course, Mrs. Stanton has a right to her opinions; but I question her prerogative to load the Woman-Suffrage movement with their dead weight, and if she would magnanimously relieve that cause from the odium of her adherence, she would thereby do more for humanity than anything her long, earnest but often-mistaken advocacy of human rights has hitherto accomplished. Any right-minded person who can believe that the enfranchisement of woman would bring such philosophy as Mrs. Stanton teaches in her Earlville letter into popular favor, must pray and labor to prevent that catastrophe.

The American Woman Suffrage Association was grateful that Elizabeth Cady Stanton could not speak for them. The *Woman's Journal* gave very little space to comments on the Beecher-Tilton controversy. Its sympathies were with Henry Ward Beecher, who had been the first president of the American Woman Suffrage Association. Toward Theodore Tilton it was venomous. It did, however, stanchly uphold Elizabeth Tilton. Both Lucy Stone and Julia Ward Howe stood by the woman who they felt had been unspeakably wronged.

Eventually the Beecher-Tilton controversy reached the law courts. The case of Tilton vs. Beecher was called for trial on January 11, 1875, in the Brooklyn City Court and continued for 112 days. The testimony was front-page news in all the papers. Pamphlets of letters relating to the case were printed and sold at the news stands. Cartoonists were busy caricaturing the principal actors in the stupendous melodrama that gripped the nation. Victoria Woodhull could not have stirred up a more devastating tempest. Her *Weekly* prospered printing news of the trial. She was summoned as a witness, appeared very decorously, and gave the testimony called for in a most proper, unsensational manner.

When Theodore Tilton in his testimony repudiated her, saying that he had done favors for her to silence her and to protect his wife and Beecher, and that his relationship with her was foolish, Elizabeth Cady Stanton was so disgusted with him that she reprimanded him in the *Newark Call*. She was not going to have Victoria Woodhull, Elizabeth Tilton, or any woman blackened to save the reputation of any man. She wrote:

> Theodore Tilton need not have shirked an acknowledgment of his association with Mrs. Woodhull. Victoria Woodhull's acquaintance would be refining to any man. . . . Victoria Woodhull has done a work for woman that none of us could have done. She has faced and dared men to call her names that make women shudder, while she chucked principle, like medicine down their throats. . . . Theodore Tilton was ashamed to acknowledge Victoria Woodhull; but in the annals of emancipation the name of which he was ashamed will have its own high place as a deliverer. . . . I have worked thirty years for woman suffrage, and now I feel that suffrage is but the vestibule of woman's emancipation.

The case dragged on week after week, piling up testimony. Counsel warred. Reputations were blackened. There were tensely dramatic moments. Henry Ward Beecher assumed a jocular manner throughout, as if it were all an amusing play. On the witness stand he gave a facetious turn to his statements whenever he could, sniffing now and then a bunch of wild violets which he held in his hand. Witness after witness was called, but never Susan B. Anthony, who was credited with first-hand knowledge of the affair. So well-established was Susan's reputation for integrity and honesty that obviously neither side wished to run the risk of her testimony.

Nor did Mrs. Stanton appear as a witness although she too was involved in the drama. Theodore Tilton had written her:

> My friend, Judge Morris, who passed his legal examination before your father and who is a great admirer of your father's most brilliant daughter, wants you to come to court and say that Elizabeth and I had a happy home for years, as you knew it to be. This testimony will be ladylike to give on your part and will be a great benefit to me, while it cannot but reflect credit at the same time on Elizabeth. I have no power to summon you, as you live out of the State. But remember how much I would do for *you* if you were in the supreme trial of your life....

She, however, did not accede to Theodore Tilton's request, probably because she could not testify as he wished. She knew him well, knew that, likable as he was, he was vain and self-centered, not a man who would make home life happy. Her sympathy was not with her good friend Theodore Tilton, although she felt his reputation and fortune had suffered unduly through Beecher's machinations, but with Elizabeth Tilton, who had been crushed and cast aside by two dominating men.

That Elizabeth Tilton, whose good name had been ruined by her husband and Henry Ward Beecher, could not take the witness stand in her own defense, Mrs. Stanton felt was an insult to her sex. The law held her incompetent as a witness for or against her husband, and yet he could charge her with gross crimes. In one of her lectures at this time, Mrs. Stanton declared:

> Nothing more touching and dramatic has transpired in that Brooklyn court than the woman's appeal to be heard in her own defense.

Ruled out of court as a witness by a technicality of law, Elizabeth Tilton determined to be heard through a letter to the Judge, and rising like an apparition in their midst, she addressed the Judge and requested that a letter be read aloud. "I ask," said she, "for a few words in my own defense. I feel very deeply the injustice of my position before the law and before the court now sitting. My soul cries out before you!" Oh from how many women the same hopeless helpless wail is echoed round the world and no one heeds their cry. The men in power mock their griefs like the Judge who cruelly returned the letter and pointed the victim to the law, a law that his coadjutors quote with respect, sustain and perpetuate, a law that is a disgrace to the statute books, to the lawyer who pleads and to the Judge whose ruling is based on the narrowest interpretation of the letter and spirit.

Again and again in her lectures in all parts of the country, Elizabeth Cady Stanton called attention away from Henry Ward Beecher and Theodore Tilton to Elizabeth Tilton and woman's helplessness under existing statutes. Her part in the Beecher-Tilton case was on the lecture platform and in the newspapers, where she lifted pertinent points out of the welter of personalities and applied them to the life of the people.

The jury was unable to agree regarding Henry Ward Beecher's innocence or guilt. The public drew its own conclusions. The majority preferred to think him innocent and Beecher propaganda smoothed the way. Theodore Tilton, financially ruined, could not carry the case further. He left the country and spent the rest of his life in Paris. Elizabeth Tilton lived hers in sorrow and obscurity.

Victoria Woodhull, who first dragged their personal relationships into the limelight, soon began following the path of respectability, married a wealthy Englishman, and as Mrs. John Biddulph Martin, spent the remainder of her life in England. Little if anything had been accomplished by all this heart-breaking exposure of private lives. Through it all the cause of woman suffrage passed unharmed.

XX

MILITANCY

MILITANCY was abroad in the land in the early seventies with women attempting to vote and refusing to pay taxes, adopting the slogan "no taxation without representation." Dr. Harriot K. Hunt of Massachusetts had for years refused to pay taxes on these grounds, and now other women were following her example: Lucy Stone, Abby Kelly Foster, whose house in Worcester was sold for taxes, and Julia and Abby Smith of Glastonbury, Connecticut, who entered into a contest with the tax collectors which attracted attention and provoked comment throughout the country. Women in Rochester, New York, formed a Women Tax-Payers Association.

Elizabeth also refused to pay taxes but she adopted different tactics. On the legal ground that she was a feme covert, she claimed that her husband was responsible for them. Many criticized her for this, but the *Boston Post* commented approvingly:

> In combating the tyrant man, Mrs. Stanton shrewdly turns upon him the weapons of his own forging. It may seem out of character for her, while claiming her equal responsibilities as a citizen with Mr. Stanton, to shift on his shoulders burdens which she herself has incurred; but a moment's reflection will show that this is the most effective argument she could use to oppose the unequal distribution of accountability according to existing statutes.

But the militant action which roused nationwide interest was the voting of Susan B. Anthony in the national election of 1872. Elizabeth had prophesied at the woman suffrage convention in May that women would no longer stand quietly by but would claim their rights under the Fourteenth and Fifteenth Amendments and vote. She was right. In different parts of the country, determined, courageous women went to the polls and presented their ballots. In some instances the ballots were refused, in others the proceeding was regarded as a huge joke, but in Rochester, where fourteen women voted, marshaled by Susan, the matter was taken so seriously that it developed into a legal contest between the United States and Susan B. Anthony.

Susan wrote Elizabeth about it:

> Well I have been and gone and done it!! Positively *voted* the Republican ticket—straight—this A.M. at 7 o'clock—*and swore my vote in at that*—was registered on Friday and fifteen other women followed suit in this ward.... Twenty or thirty other women tried to register, but all save two were refused.... Hon. Henry R. Selden will be our counsel. He has read up the law and all our arguments and is satisfied that we are right.... So we are in for a fine agitation in Rochester on the question. I hope the morning's telegrams will tell of many women all over the country trying to vote....
>
> How I wish you were here to write up the funny things said and done.... When the Democrats said my vote should not go in the box, one Republican said to the other, "What do you say, Marsh? I say put it in." "So do I," said Jones. And "we'll fight it out on this line if it takes all winter."... Not a jeer, not a word, not a look disrespectful has met a single woman. If only now *all the Woman Suffrage Women* would work to *this* end, of *enforcing the existing constitution,* supremacy of *national law* over state law, what strides we might make this very winter.

Later she heard the whole story in detail from Susan: How two weeks after election Susan was arrested and summoned for a hearing; how she refused to furnish bail of $500, applying for a writ of habeas corpus, how the judge denied the writ and raised her bail to $1000; how her counsel took the matter out of her hands and went her bond, because he could not bear to see her go to jail; how this action prevented her case from going to the Supreme Court.

Before the case came to trial Susan lectured throughout the country on the subject, "Is It a Crime for a Citizen of the United States to Vote," and newspapers far and wide discussed the case pro and con. Matilda Joslyn Gage came to her assistance with her lecture, "The United States on Trial, not Susan B. Anthony." Elizabeth, out on the Lyceum circuit, could help only by brief references to the case in her lectures, by an occasional letter to a newspaper, and by discussing it with people whom she met on her travels. She did not make the trip to Canandaigua to attend the trial on June 17, 1873, as she had just come home from a long, hard lecture tour. Not being on the spot, she was not aroused to such indignation as were Susan and Mrs. Gage by the way Judge Hunt took the case out of the hands of the jury and charged them to find a verdict of guilty. In fact she had reached the point where she almost despaired of expecting justice for women.

She preached militancy everywhere she could. She was ready to turn society upside down to obtain rights for women. At the anniversary meeting of the National Woman Suffrage Association in New York in May 1873, she preached this doctrine:

> Let women assist themselves as they have never assisted themselves before. Let them take care of their own interests. They have too long let their benevolent instincts work toward the church and men; let them now attend to themselves. Let the churches alone; don't carpet churches, don't have fairs to deck them with painted windows, don't give your ministers donation parties. Put all your energies into earnest work for your own emancipation. Make a social revolution. Carry the war if need be, into your own families; let the baby go without bibs, the husband's shirt without buttons, the home without care, until the men give in. When they find their comfort depends on allowing us the ballot, they will wheel into line and give it to us. Women have too long petitioned and begged of men; let them now make siege and carry the war into their own homes. It is coming to that, sirs, and it is going to be a dear piece of business for you. We are going to vote, peaceably if we can, but with war if we must.

Readers of the *Woman's Journal* were troubled by this belligerent attitude and wrote letters in protest which were published in that paper. In reply, she sent a letter to the *Woman's Journal* by which she meant to sweep away all objections:

> Is there an instance in all history of an oppressed class being secured in all their rights without assuming a "belligerent attitude"? Earnestness, determination, true dignity ofttimes require a "belligerent attitude." Just imagine some writer in the old *Boston Gazette,* saying in the height of the Revolution of '76, "I am sorry James Otis, John Adams, Patrick Henry and George Washington are so belligerent. How disgraceful to the memory of the Puritans, for New England men to rush on board a vessel and pitch a whole cargo of tea into the harbor; what spiteful child's play was that! How much better to have petitioned King George and his Parliament in a dignified manner for a 'respectful consideration' of their grievances."

When William Lloyd Garrison was fired with the wrongs of

2,000,000 men, he used bold words to denounce the tyrants and declare his action. He called the United States Constitution "a covenant with death, and an agreement with hell." His *Liberator* was a firebrand among tyrants. With the Bible in one hand and the Republican theory in the other, he defied the whole nation, the State, the Church, and the social institutions of the South.... He told black men to take the law into their own hands, to strike for freedom at all hazards, and rush to the Canadas, at the risk of their lives. Gerrit Smith told them to steal anything they needed in their flight—horses, boats, bread, fire arms—they had a right to anything that would help them to the land of freedom.

Wendell Phillips, in a speech in Boston on the Anthony Burns case, fired with the cruelty and wickedness of sending that man back to slavery, exclaimed "God damn the Commonwealth of Massachusetts," and Lydia Maria Child is said to have clapped with such vehemence as to break her wedding ring.

And what, I ask, are the battles of the fathers, or the Abolitionists, compared with the one we are fighting today? It was a grand thing for a handful of men to lay the foundations of a Republican government in this Western world. It was a grand thing to strike the last blow at an aristocracy of race on Southern plantations. But it is a greater work to roll off the public mind the mountains of ignorance and superstition that, for Ages, have made the mother of the race the bond slave of her own sons, held by the triple cord of a political, religious and social serfdom—that have made her a pliant, patient victim by the utter perversion of the highest and holiest sentiments of her nature.

When we can get all our women up to the white heat of a "belligerent attitude," we may have some hope of our speedy enfranchisement....

Another militant movement was also sweeping the country. Bands of earnest women, roused by the drink evil, gathered in front of saloons, singing hymns and kneeling in the dust, prayed fervently for the abolition of these breeders of iniquity. Often they walked boldly through the saloon doors, sang their hymns and prayed, until the jeers of the patrons ceased and one by one they slipped away. Sometimes they were able to work the saloon keeper up to such a pitch that he would empty his liquor in the street and pray with them to be saved. This crusade, started in a small Ohio town, eventually developed into that powerful organization, the Women's Christian Temperance Union.

Both Elizabeth and Susan believed heartily in temperance, both believed in militancy, but both realized that women could not be a power for reform until they had the ballot. Therefore, first enfranchisement, then afterward temperance and other reforms.

To a friend in the West, Elizabeth wrote:

> These praying bands are not exactly to my taste. Lifting humanity up to a higher plane, is to be done by the slow process of education, which can be accomplished not by praying, but *working....* This temperance revival, I am glad to see for some reasons, though I do not approve the mode of warfare.

Susan, addressing a group of women crusaders in Rochester, gave them this good advice:

> Now my good women, the best thing this organization will do for you will be to show you how utterly powerless you are to put down the liquor traffic. You can never talk down or sing down or pray down an institution which is voted into existence. You will never be able to lessen this evil until you have votes.

The conservative women of the country also felt the need of gathering together in the year 1873 and called a Congress of Women in New York "to meet a pressing demand for interchange of thought and harmony of action among women interested in the advancement of their sex." Elizabeth at their request signed the call. Susan did not.

It was a learned, impressive gathering, discussing all such safe subjects as the household, enlightened motherhood, woman's dress, education, literature, art, science, women in the professions and industry, in reform, in the church. Mary E. Livermore presided. Julia Ward Howe and Maria Mitchell were among the prominent speakers. Elizabeth addressed the congress on one of her favorite subjects, "Coeducation." This was done with propriety, but as she also took part in the discussion of other subjects, she managed to inject a little too much liberalism into this conservative convention.

At one session she asked what would be thought of an artist who filled his studio with distorted forms, and declared, "That is what American mothers are doing, filling the world with cripples and monsters. Men have taught that it is woman's greatest glory to bear children, but as John Stuart Mill said, 'It is greater to give the world one lion than ten jackasses.'" She insisted that women teach the rising generation of girls that quality is important and there is no glory in numbers.

Then she made the heretical statement that it is not the duty of all men and women to be parents and that because this had been regarded as their duty, infanticide was common and would continue to be until there was a changed attitude in regard to child-bearing. "If a woman is diseased," she continued, "if she has a husband who is intemperate and licentious, the fewer children she has the better."

This recommendation of birth control was bad enough, but the mention of infanticide was far worse. Julia Ward Howe, distressed that such subjects had been introduced, announced that she would be mortified if any sanction of infanticide went forth from that meeting.

Instantly Elizabeth replied: "I hope I have not been understood by the majority as speaking in favor of infanticide. I mentioned it only as a fact. There is as much of it as ever, and it will continue until woman is the sovereign of her own person."

This was embarrassing. Such subjects were not publicly discussed among "ladies."

Nevertheless, Elizabeth Cady Stanton, undaunted, here and elsewhere, continued her role of advance guard, injecting new and startling ideas, which, although they roused antagonism, eventually were accepted as a matter of course.

When the hundredth anniversary of the founding of the Republic was celebrated in 1876 by a large centennial exposition in Philadelphia, conservative as well as radical suffragists felt that the only suitable commemoration of the founding of the Republic was conferring equal rights on its unfranchised citizens—women.

Although women had contributed generously to the Exposition fund, no special building was at first assigned to them to record their achievements and progress. As an afterthought, a special fund was raised to erect a woman's pavilion, but its exhibit was unsatisfactory as it showed only a small portion of woman's accomplishment in business, invention, and manufacture, and in no way noticed woman's long struggle for civil and political rights. The suffragists of Massachusetts sent for exhibit the taxation protests of Harriot K. Hunt, Lucy Stone, Abby Kelly Foster, Sarah E. Wall, and Julia and Abby Smith, but the authorities declared that anything that savored of protest was not suited to the time and place. Although they finally relented and placed the tax protests, they hung them so high that they could not be read.

The National Woman Suffrage Association, alert to every opportunity to spread its message, established headquarters at 1431 Chestnut Street, Philadelphia. Here suffragists gathered, made plans, and distributed literature. After the close of her lecture tour in June, Elizabeth joined Susan and Matilda Joslyn Gage there. Lucretia Mott came in frequently from her country home, bringing eggs, cold chicken, and tea for their lunch. With these irreconcilables conferring together, something important was bound to happen. They decided that a Woman's Declaration of Rights should be presented after the reading of the Declaration of Independence at the public celebration of the Fourth of July in Independence Hall. Elizabeth, Mrs. Gage, and Susan set to work at once to prepare a Declaration of Rights, and it was a masterful document with Mrs. Stanton's ringing phrases and the pertinent points thought out by all three. They applied to the authorities for a place on the program, for seats for at least one representative woman from each state, and for permission to read their Declaration of Rights immediately after the reading of the Declaration of Independence. They were sent six tickets and told that the program had already been arranged and could not be changed.

After this rebuff Elizabeth and Lucretia Mott determined to have nothing to do with the public Fourth of July celebration and to attend only their own mass convention which had been called for the same day at the First Unitarian Church. Not so Susan. She, carrying the Woman's Declaration of Rights and supported by Matilda Joslyn Gage, Sara Andrews Spencer, Lillie Devereaux Blake, and Phoebe Couzins, entered Independence Hall on that historic Fourth of July, and there, in an audience composed almost entirely of men, listened respectfully to the reading of the Declaration of

Independence by Richard Henry Lee of Virginia. As soon as he had finished, these five determined women marched to the platform, and Susan, with a few appropriate remarks, presented the Woman's Declaration to the presiding officer, Senator Ferry. It all happened so quickly and unexpectedly that Senator Ferry could do nothing but receive the document, and thus it became part of the day's proceedings. Susan and her allies then left the hall quietly, scattering printed copies of the Declaration throughout the curious audience.

A platform had been erected for the musicians in front of Independence Hall. The five militants mounted it, and to an eager, applauding crowd, Susan in a clear voice read the Woman's Declaration, while Mrs. Gage held an umbrella over her to shield her from the blazing sun.

Then hurrying over to the church, where delegates to their own convention had already gathered, they gave them a full and spirited report of the proceedings. It was an enthusiastic, harmonious convention that made a lasting impression upon the many visitors from afar. Lucretia Mott, now eighty-four, presided, calm, dignified, and saintly in her soft gray Quaker dress. Elizabeth Cady Stanton, with much feeling, read once more the Woman's Declaration of Rights. Twenty-eight years had passed since she, with the eagerness and optimism of youth, had read the first Declaration of Rights to the small group assembled at the Seneca Falls Convention. During the intervening years she and Lucretia Mott had fought and pleaded well for the emancipation of women. Martha C. Wright, who had so loyally stood by them, was gone. New workers had joined them, and the most valiant and consecrated was Susan B. Anthony, whose zeal had been fired by Elizabeth.

When later in July a meeting was held in Philadelphia to commemorate that first Woman's Rights Convention, Elizabeth, unable to attend, sent a letter giving her conclusions regarding woman's progress. She wrote:

> Looking over these twenty-eight years, I feel that what we have achieved, as yet, bears no proportion to what we have suffered in the daily humiliation of spirit from the cruel distinctions based

on sex. Though our state laws have been essentially changed, and positions in the schools, professions, and world of work secured to woman, unthought of thirty years ago, yet the undercurrent of popular thought, as seen in our social habits, theological dogmas, and political theories, still reflects the same customs, creeds, and codes that degrade women in the effete civilizations of the old world. Educated in the best schools to logical reasoning, trained to liberal thought in politics, religion and social ethics under republican institutions, American women cannot brook the discriminations in regard to sex that were patiently accepted by the ignorant in barbarous ages as divine law.... As I sum up the indignities toward women, as illustrated by recent judicial decisions—denied the right to vote, denied the right to practice in the Supreme Court, denied jury trial—I feel the degradation of sex more bitterly than I did on that July 19, 1848....

Women, aided by some of the ablest lawyers in the country, had made every effort to claim their right to vote under the Fourteenth and Fifteenth Amendments. The adverse decision in the case of Susan B. Anthony vs. the United States had been their first serious setback. Another important case, brought by Virginia Minor and her husband, Francis Minor, because Mrs. Minor had not been allowed to register for the Presidential election in 1872, was passed on adversely by the United States Supreme Court in 1875. This showed suffragists the futility of further efforts along this line. To Elizabeth, Susan, and their colleagues there was but one thing to do—to work for an amendment to the Constitution which would prohibit the states from disfranchising women on the grounds of sex.

Elizabeth, as president of the National Woman Suffrage Association, sent out a plea to women of the United States to roll up a mammoth petition for a Sixteenth Amendment. During the winter of 1877 petitions were presented to Congress signed by 10,000 women, and the important event of the National Woman Suffrage Association Convention in January 1878 was the introduction of the Sixteenth Amendment by Senator Sargent of California.

Elizabeth, who had been lecturing in the West, came to Washington for the convention in answer to the insistent demands of Mrs. Hooker and Mrs. Spencer, who were in charge. Susan was kept in the West by her lecture engagements. This was one of the few conventions she did not attend.

Elizabeth was the guest of the Sargents while she was in Washington. She and Susan had met them in California in 1871 and since then they had been very helpful friends. Elizabeth conferred with Senator Sargent regarding the Amendment and probably drafted it. It was simply worded, patterned after the Fifteenth Amendment, which enfranchised the Negro, and read: "The right of citizens of the United States to vote shall not be denied or abridged by the United States or by any State on account of sex."

Senator Sargent introduced the Amendment on January 10, 1878, and Elizabeth spoke for it forcefully in the convention and before the Senate Committee.

She wrote Susan:

> I suppose you are waiting to hear about the convention. It went off well; there were crowded houses as usual and $200 in the treasury after all bills were paid. I prepared the resolutions a week before and had them in print, so that there was no worry at the last moment over them. I devoted my whole vacation to the speech to be made before the committee [Senate Committee on Privileges and Elections]. All said, "Very good." The day before, Senator Sargent had presented in the Senate a resolution proposing the following amendment: Article 16, sec. 1 "The right of citizens of the United States to vote shall not be denied or abridged by the United States or by any State on account of sex." . . . I reached home Saturday night and found a telegram asking for my speech as the committee intends to print it. So I sat up last night until four o'clock in order to copy it and sent off this morning 150 pages of manuscript.

An adverse report on the Amendment was presented by Senator Wadleigh of New Hampshire, but the minority report—the most favorable consideration even given the question by the Senate— brought the suffragists a slight ray of hope. "The people of the United States," it declared, "are committed to the doctrine of universal suffrage by their constitution, their history, and their opinions, and by it they must stand or fall."

Suffragists did not rally whole-heartedly in support of the Amendment. The American Woman Suffrage Association, guided by the Boston group and the *Woman's Journal,* was committed to state action. Only the National Woman Suffrage Association insisted on the direct method of an amendment to the Constitution. At their

conventions held yearly in Washington, more and more pressure
for the Amendment was brought to bear on Congressmen and Senators. Elizabeth Cady Stanton, Susan B. Anthony, and their coworkers were listened to respectfully when they delivered their well-
thought-out speeches at hearings. But when the subject of woman
suffrage was debated for a few moments in Congress, only a few
regarded it as a matter for serious consideration. The majority had
a hilarious time over it, making use of the opportunity to display
their wit and sarcasm.

Year after year until 1919, when it was passed by Congress, the
Amendment was reintroduced in this same form. In later years
it was called the Susan B. Anthony Amendment by the younger
suffragists who, inspired by Miss Anthony's example, were eager to
pay her tribute. It is often assumed that it was written by Miss
Anthony, but available data does not bear this out. Even her official biographer, Ida Husted Harper, does not claim this for her.

Undoubtedly Mrs. Stanton drafted the Amendment as she wrote
everything for the National Woman Suffrage Association—appeals,
resolutions, and most of the important official papers. She was
looked upon as the scribe as well as the legal mind of the movement. Had Miss Anthony drafted it, Mrs. Stanton would not have
quoted it for her in the letter she wrote her after the convention
and would have referred to it as *your* Amendment.

For the actual wording of the Amendment, however, credit must
be given to Charles Sumner, who drew up the Fifteenth Amendment. Mrs. Stanton made use of his clear language and substituted
"on account of sex" for "on account of race, color, or previous condition of servitude."

Mrs. Stanton and Miss Anthony had of course discussed and
planned this move together previously and the Amendment was the
result of their joint efforts. In all fairness it should have been called
the Stanton-Anthony Amendment to honor also the invaluable work
of Elizabeth Cady Stanton, who not only was a sponsor of the
Amendment and one of its most ardent advocates, but also was the
first woman in this country publicly to demand woman suffrage.

XXI

"THE HISTORY OF WOMAN SUFFRAGE"

THE opinion is current in some quarters that Elizabeth Cady Stanton was the leisurely member of the woman suffrage group and during her later years had to be continually goaded into action by Susan B. Anthony. Her very busy life during the eighteen-seventies belies this. While she never had the fervor for organization that Susan had, she supported her admirably with speeches, resolutions, and appeals. Her strenuous lecture tours through the country, while not always direct work for woman suffrage, were the means of preparing the thought of the nation for the emancipation of women. Some idea of the active life she led is given in a letter written to her son Theodore:

> Last week in Washington I sat up two nights until three o'clock in the morning to write a speech and the resolutions for the convention....I presided at all the sessions during two days. The Washington papers were very complimentary to me as a presiding officer, and Susan says I never did so well. I came home by the night train and now have until Monday—this is Saturday—in which to get ready for a five months' trip in the West.

The lecture tours lost some of their novelty as the years went on, and the discomforts and continuous travel were very wearing. Susan felt the strain of her long lecture tours even more than Elizabeth. She was so worn and tired that Elizabeth was concerned about her. "Do be careful, dear Susan," she wrote her. "You cannot stand what you once did. I should feel desolate indeed with you gone." Susan finally paid up the $10,000 debt on the *Revolution* and was gradually building up a small fund for work ahead. Elizabeth had sent Margaret to Vassar and Theodore and Robert to Cornell with her lecture fees.

It was a great satisfaction to Elizabeth to know that her children were being well educated. It was her ambition to give them the best possible start in life; and she gave them understanding companionship as well as education. Their father too was a good companion. One of the most dependable and able editorial writers of the *New York Sun,* he always had interesting news to tell of world affairs, politics, and people in the public eye. Devoted to his own work, he was willing that his wife should be equally devoted to hers, and so as always, they followed their own interests, leaving each other free. Their home life was happy, never dull.

Their younger children were now starting out on their careers. Margaret had graduated from Vassar, married Frank E. Lawrence, and moved to Omaha, Nebraska. Theodore received his master's degree at Cornell, went abroad to study, became foreign correspondent for the *New York Tribune,* and married a charming young Frenchwoman, Marguerite Berry. Harriot, after graduating from Vassar, studied public speaking in Boston and occasionally accompanied her mother on a lecture tour. When Harriot was with her, Elizabeth was supremely happy. Harriot was following in her footsteps with her zeal for woman's emancipation and reform. She was a natural orator and often, with great success, tried out her powers on her mother's audiences. Later she went to Europe as tutor to a group of girls and to continue her own studies.

To Harriot and Theodore, who more than any of her children sympathized with her work and ideals, Elizabeth wrote on her sixty-fifth birthday, November 12, 1880:

> This is my birthday. I am sixty-five years old, nearing the seventies. Looking back through life, I feel that our troubles are fully compensated by our joys. I have had an existence of hard work, but I think it has been a success. I began a diary today, which I shall hope to keep up with more or less regularity—I fear the latter!—so that, when I have passed away, you children will have a better knowledge of some of the things I have thought and done during the final years of my life.

She wrote in her diary that day:

> Today I am sixty-five years old, am perfectly well, am a moderate eater, sleep well, and am generally happy. My philosophy is to live one day at a time; neither to waste my forces in apprehension of evils to come, nor regrets for blunders of the past. Once in a while, in thinking of what I might have done for my children, I feel sud-

denly depressed. But as I did not see, when I myself was young, all that I now see with age and experience, I dismiss the thoughts from my mind with the reflection that I then knew no better than to have seven children in quick succession. I have no sympathy with the old idea that children owe such immense gratitude to their parents that they can never fulfill their obligations to them. I think the obligation is all on the other side. Parents can never do too much for their children to repay them for the injustice of having brought them into the world, unless they have insured them high moral and intellectual gifts, fine physical health, and enough money and education to render life something more than one ceaseless struggle for necessaries.

Between lecture tours Elizabeth and Susan now spent as much time as possible working on a history of the woman's movement. For a long time Elizabeth had wanted to undertake this work. She had made several attempts, but something had always interfered. Finally in 1876, she, Susan, and Matilda Joslyn Gage decided that the writing of this history must be put off no longer. They drew up an agreement. Elizabeth and Mrs. Gage were to write, collect, select, and arrange the material for the history. Susan was to secure its publication and attend to all details in that connection. The names of the three would appear on the title page and they would share equally any profits which might be realized.

But Susan did more than arrange for publication. She had collected a mass of material, letters, reports, and documents. Several trunks and boxes filled to the brim arrived at the Stanton home in Tenafly. The three got together there, sorted the material, and began work. They wrote letters to leading suffragists in all parts of the country asking for biographical sketches and accounts of the work in their localities. Elizabeth sent a request for such information to Lucy Stone, acting as if no differences had ever occurred between them.

Lucy Stone replied:

I have never kept a diary or any record of my work, and so am unable to furnish you the required dates. I made my first speech in the pulpit of my brother in Gardner, Massachusetts in 1847. I commenced my regular public work for antislavery and woman's rights in 1848. I have continued it, to the best of my ability ever since, except when the care of my child and the war prevented.

Then on the opposite page she added:

...you say "I" must be referred to in the history you are writing. If you will publish the letter which is on the opposite page, it will be a sufficient reference. I cannot furnish a biographical sketch and hope you will not try to make one. Yours with ceaseless regret that any "wing" of suffragists should attempt to write the history of the other.

On the whole Elizabeth, Susan, and Mrs. Gage received splendid co-operation from the suffragists. From all parts of the country came glowing reports of work done, of women who had single-handed in the face of bitter criticism aroused other women to action. The difficulty lay in going over the mass of hand-written manuscript in many cases almost illegible, in evaluating it, in checking historical facts, and presenting a readable account of what to them was the greatest bloodless revolution in history.

They had planned to publish their history in pamphlet form, but it soon became evident that it would spread out into several large volumes. When Elizabeth and Susan gave up their lecture engagements in the fall of 1880, they settled down at Tenafly and set themselves at their task regularly every day—often till midnight, Susan selecting and checking the material, Elizabeth doing all the writing. It was hard and monotonous for them but they knew that unless they kept at it, the record would not be saved for posterity.

It was like old times for them to be together—only now there were no children for Susan to look after so that Elizabeth could keep at her writing. The intervening years had wrought many changes. Susan no longer looked to Elizabeth for guidance. She was sure of herself now. She had become the driving force. But she still needed Elizabeth's true friendship, the solace of her companionship, and the leavening of her philosophical mind.

They worked in a large room with a big bay window. The sunshine poured in all day. A fire blazed on the hearth. They sat opposite each other at a large office desk, piled high with documents, books, and old newspapers—Susan, thin and wiry, nervously alert, working like an engine, Elizabeth calm, comfortable, but intensely in earnest, her fluffy white hair like an aura about her head.

As they looked over their material, they recalled their early struggles, laughed at the biting, sarcastic press notices, rejoiced at the progress that had been made, and still fumed over man's indifference to their demands.

Although they worked together with unusual harmony, they often came upon points and events over which they disagreed heartily. Both were strong minded. Susan was punctilious over dates and cold facts. To Elizabeth philosophizing, drawing conclusions, and pointing out causes was important. Each stuck to her point. Eyes flashed and caustic remarks were interchanged. Then down went the pens; Susan dashed out of one door, Elizabeth sailed out of the other. Both started walking over the grounds in opposite directions. By and by they returned arm in arm, pausing now and then to enjoy the view of the valley and the distant hills, and then set to work again as if nothing had happened.

When the work was too wearing, they stopped to take a bracing walk or a drive in Elizabeth's phaeton behind the good horse Jule, named after the Honorable George W. Julian, friend of the suffragists. Sometimes they sought relaxation in the kitchen, Susan making her prize dessert, apple tapioca pudding, or Elizabeth baking the squash pies for which she was famous. Evenings in easy chairs in front of the fire, they planned the next day's work, read aloud amusing press notices of themselves, or if they felt they needed a change, Susan read aloud from some interesting novel.

On Election day, November 2, 1880, they were deep in documents and reports. But when the Republican "wagon," decked with flags and evergreens, called at the Stanton home to take the men of the family to the polls, Elizabeth announced to the driver that, since her legal representatives were all absent, she would go with him to vote. Susan accompanied her. When they arrived at the polling place, she explained to the astonished inspectors that she was three times the legal voting age, had been a resident of Tenafly for twelve years, paid poll and real estate taxes, was a property holder, could read and write, and had every qualification for a voter. The inspectors, nonplussed, held a consultation on the matter. This imposing woman was trying to talk them into letting her do something that had never been done before. The polls were no place for a woman. Annoyed at the delay caused by her presence, State Senator Cooper exclaimed, "Put an end to this and go on with your voting. It has been delayed long enough for a small matter."

Her eyes flashing, Elizabeth replied with dignity, "Gentlemen, this is the most momentous question the citizens of your town have ever been called upon to decide."

By this time a curious crowd had gathered. She tried to deposit her ballot. The inspector refused to let her get near the ballot box. She remonstrated further. Susan quoted from the Constitution but with no avail. Then tossing her marked ballot toward the box, where it lighted for a moment and then fell to the floor, Elizabeth, with Susan close behind, left the polling booth, much to the relief of the bewildered inspectors.

"The whole town is agape with my act," she wrote Harriot and Theodore. "A friend says he never saw Tenafly in such excitement. The men have taken sides about equally. This is a good example of what I have often said of late that acts, not words, are what is needed to push this woman suffrage question to the fore."

Later in the month word came that Lucretia Mott had passed on. The day of her funeral, Elizabeth wrote in her diary, "Though I could not be at Lucretia Mott's funeral today to say my word, yet I have thought of her, read about her, and written of her all alone here by myself. This Sunday was with me a sacred memorial day to her, and as I consider her repose, self-control, and beautiful spirit, and recall how all through our conventions and discussions not one word to sting or exasperate anyone ever passed her lips, I have vowed again, as I have so many times, that I shall in the future try to imitate her noble example. If I go through the coming six months with this *History* work with equanimity, I shall have hopes of myself."

The first volume of *The History of Woman Suffrage,* covering the years from 1848 to 1861, was published in May 1881 by Fowler and Wells. It had been hard to find a publisher as it was not looked upon as a profitable financial enterprise. In fact the financial side of publishing the *History* was a problem, and Susan as usual assumed the responsibility. She was rewarded by a gift of a thousand dollars from Mrs. Elizabeth Thompson of New York.

The volume was dedicated to the memory of nineteen feminists, including Mary Wollstonecraft, Frances Wright, and Margaret Fuller, "whose earnest lives and fearless words in demanding political rights for women" had been an inspiration to the editors. The frontispiece was an engraving of Frances Wright, the woman whose life and ideas had been and still were held up by conservatives as a warning of the detrimental effects of freedom on women. It was a ponderous volume, packed with facts, speeches, and reports—a valuable source book. Vivid pictures of the struggles of pioneer feminists were scattered through the 878 pages. Elizabeth did her best as a writer to vivify the mass of material. Matilda Joslyn Gage contributed three chapters.

To see the first volume finished and in print after months of hard work was the greatest satisfaction. Elizabeth said:

> I welcomed it with the same feeling of love and tenderness as I did my firstborn. I took the same pleasure in hearing it praised, and felt the same mortification in hearing it criticized. The most hearty welcome it received was from Reverend William Henry Channing. He wrote to us that it was as interesting and fascinating as a novel. He gave it a most flattering notice in one of the London papers.

On July 3, 1881, she wrote in her diary:

> Today both the *Tribune* and the *Sun* have splendid notices of nearly two columns in length of the first volume of our History. We could ask for nothing better. Both compliment the Introduction, the former giving from it several entire paragraphs.

In spite of their pride in the *History,* they both realized that it was merely the bare record of a great social revolution—a source book, not literature. "We have furnished the bricks and mortar," they said, "for some future architect to rear a beautiful edifice."

Of course there were criticisms. They received many letters telling them that it was too soon to write a history of woman suffrage. To this Elizabeth replied emphatically but with that humor so characteristic of her:

> Well, we old workers might perhaps have "reminisced" after death, but I doubt if the writing mediums could do as well as we

have done with our pens. You say the history of woman suffrage cannot be written until it is accomplished. Why not describe its initiative steps? The United States has not completed its grand experiment of equality, universal suffrage, etc., and yet Bancroft has been writing our history for forty years. If no one writes up his own times, where are the materials for the history of the future?

Almost immediately after Volume I was finished, they set to work on Volume II although there was no money in sight to finance it. Then early in 1882 Susan received word that under the will of Eliza Jackson Eddy, the daughter of one of their first benefactors, Francis Jackson, she would inherit a large sum of money to be used at her discretion for woman suffrage. When this was paid a few years later, she bought out the interests of Mrs. Gage and Elizabeth in the *History,* and instead of trying to sell it, distributed copies to libraries and colleges throughout the world, to Congressmen, writers, and speakers.

The work on the second volume, demanding as it was, for the most part was a pleasure to Elizabeth, for not only was Susan with her a great deal of the time, but she could once more enjoy her home to the full, revel in its comfort, and look out at the trees that she loved and at the distant hills which were always an inspiration.

But it grew more and more difficult for Susan to stay at this task. She was a restless person, happiest when she was going from place to place conferring with people regarding her beloved cause. There were constant calls for her help and advice, and frequently she deserted Tenafly, leaving Elizabeth and Mrs. Gage deep in the *History.* They continued to do all of the writing.

Harriot arrived from Europe in the spring of 1882 and immediately made plans to return and take her mother with her. But Volume II must be finished before she could think of such a thing, and Harriot set to work reading proof and helping as much as she could. There was a question whether this volume should contain a chapter on the organization of the American Woman Suffrage Association. Elizabeth did not want to write it, feeling that her report would not meet with approval. Harriot insisted that such a chapter must be written and undertook it herself.

The result was Chapter XXVI, 106 pages, giving a concise story of the establishment and progress of the American Woman Suffrage Association and reporting speeches of its prominent members. No mention was made of the controversy which had flared up between suffrage leaders and which had ended in a division in the ranks. Elizabeth and Susan regretted the division, had no desire of airing the quarrel, and wished above everything else to have the movement for woman suffrage appear in all its greatness before the public.

Most of the proof was read by Elizabeth and Harriot in New York, at Mrs. Bayard's home at 8 West Fortieth Street, in a little room which was given over to the work. Susan dropped in for about an hour a day to help. When this work was finished, Elizabeth sailed with Harriot for France.

When she returned from Europe after an absence of a year and a half and was settled in Johnstown for the summer of 1884, Susan arrived with the inevitable documents and manuscripts and together they began work on Volume III. Susan stayed late into the fall, but they could not finish it. Then again in the summer of 1885 Susan came to Tenafly, determined to see it completed.

It grew more and more difficult for Elizabeth to keep herself at this monotonous task. She was brimming over with ideas which she wanted to put into stimulating magazine articles. It was just as trying for Susan, who longed for more active work. This sorting of reports, speeches, and clippings was drudgery. But both were determined that there be no deviation from the goal that they had set for themselves.

When Elizabeth was preparing the Preface for Volume III, she insisted on including a sentence with which Susan could not agree:

> We who have studied our republican institutions and understand the limits of the executive, judicial, and legislative branches of the government, are aware that the legislature, directly representing the people, is the primary source of power, above all courts and constitutions.

Susan argued that the Constitution came first. Neither could convince the other. Susan left Tenafly to prepare for the Washington

Convention. She consulted lawyers regarding the point over which she and Elizabeth differed. She wanted to convince her that the sentence must be changed or omitted. They continued their arguments by mail. Elizabeth wrote:

You have not made me take your position. I repudiate it from the bottom of my soul. It is conservative, autocratic to the last degree. I accept no authority of either Bibles or constitutions which tolerate the slavery of women. My rights were born with me and are the same over the whole globe.... Of the three branches of government, the legislative, representing the people, is the primal source of power. I perceive that one of the lawyers you have consulted admits one of my points—that the legislature is above the courts; and yet the courts can declare null and void the acts of the legislature. But if the legislature can be above the courts and yet at times be in conflict with them, why on the same principle can it not be above the Constitution and yet in conflict with it? How do you amend the Constitution? The legislature, directly representing the people, decides that the Constitution needs amending, frames the amendment and submits it to the people, the majority saying yea or nay. Now where is the primary source of power? In the majority of the people. All this seems so plain to me that I wonder you halt so long over it. Think of you accepting the man-made Constitution, the man-interpretation thereof, the man-amendment submitted by a convention of aristocrats, and the old secession reverence for a constitution. Why Garrison, who kicked and cuffed the old document for forty years, would turn in his grave to see printed in our *History of Woman Suffrage* your present ideas as to the authority and majesty of any of those constitutions, State or National. Ah, beware, Susan, lest as you become "respectable" you become conservative.

This time Elizabeth won. The sentence remained in the Preface. By the end of the year, 1885, the last page of Volume III was written. They had brought *The History of Woman Suffrage* up to date, and now they were free to do the work they longed to do.

Volume III was the last of the six large volumes of *The History of Woman Suffrage* to bear the name of Elizabeth Cady Stanton on the title page. Volume IV was compiled by Susan and Ida Husted Harper with Elizabeth occasionally giving valuable advice and information. The other two volumes, V and VI were published by Mrs. Harper, after Susan and Elizabeth had passed on, and fulfilled their wish that a complete record of woman's work for woman suffrage be left for the generations to come.

XXII

FRANCE AND ENGLAND

LEAVING years of hard work behind her, Elizabeth in 1882 looked forward to a real vacation in France with Harriot. The news that she was a grandmother and that Theodore and Marguerite had named their first child for her, Elizabeth Cady Stanton II, made her doubly eager to be there.

She now stepped into the medievalism of southern France. It was beautiful, mellow, and restful. She fell under its spell as one falls under the spell of a medieval romance, but her active mind would recurrently contrast this old civilization with the newness and vitality of America:

> I sometimes wonder whether the inhabitants of our American towns, whose growth and development have been free and untrammeled as that of a favorite child, appreciate the blessings that have been theirs. How true the lines of Goethe: "America, thou art much happier than our old continent; thou hast no old castles in ruins, no fortresses; no useless remembrances, no vain enemies will interrupt the inward workings of thy life!"

As Harriot wished to study for a University degree in mathematics, they settled in Toulouse, at the Convent de la Sagesse, not far from the country estate of Madame Berry where Theodore, Marguerite, and the baby were spending the summer. Elizabeth wrote in her diary:

> Quite a number of "lady boarders" are received at this convent ... in order to help pay the cost of the education of the children who are taught here. Several large buildings enclose a spacious garden filled with trees, shrubs, fruits, and flowers. The large beds of Easter lilies look just as the sisters do in their white caps and aprons when they sit round in a circle, some two or three dozen of them together, at the twilight hour to perform some homely household task.... We have large pleasant rooms in the second story of the main building of the convent with two spacious French windows in each. We could not be more delightfully situated. At eight o'clock every morning a little bonne with an immaculately white cap brings me a cup of coffee, a

252

piece of bread and some hot milk—no butter or cream—which I sip
and eat sitting up in a small high-curtained French bed. I then read a
bit, write a postal or two, bathe, dress, and take a walk in the garden.
Returned to my room, I read, write, and at half past eleven our
mignon bonne again appears and spreads a small round table where is
served a soup, some mysterious dish of meat, a vegetable, bread, fruit,
and wine. I never know what I am eating, as the little dishes are new
to me. I only know that I would give five francs for a good meal of
Amelia's cooking. I bemoan the absence of butter, which seems to be
an unknown quantity in this part of France, and I long for muffins,
and oatmeal, and cream.... In the afternoon we go on some explor-
ing expedition, visit some savant, or remain in the convent to receive
some interesting caller. Dinner is at six and consists also of soup—soup
is *the* dish in France—meat, vegetable, bread—another staple—fruit,
and wine, which I care little for, though it is very pure in this region,
one of the vineyards of France. If I grow thin on this diet, I shall
feel fully compensated for my many culinary deprivations. After
dinner, we walk in the garden, where the birds sing and the foun-
tains play, or we sit in our room, I mending stockings while Hattie
reads Emerson aloud.

The tranquillity of the convent life was very restful after the
many years in which she had planned work for every moment of
the day. She made friends at once with the sisters, who in turn tried
to convert her, pressing upon her many books about the church,
not realizing they were dealing with an arch heretic. But Professor
Joly of Toulouse University, who had become a frequent caller,
counteracted these efforts at conversion by loaning her a fine old
edition of Voltaire. Often Elizabeth, Harriot, and Professor Joly,
reinforced by Theodore, Marguerite, and Henry Blatch, a young
Englishman who was paying marked attentions to Harriot, sat
in the garden of this stronghold of the church, and discussed in
the most unorthodox manner all the political, social, and religious
reforms which should be enacted in the United States and France.
To Elizabeth, who gloried in being daringly liberal in the face of
orthodoxy, these conversations were doubly stimulating because of
their setting.

She frequently slipped from the garden into the chapel without
her hat and sat in one of the rear pews during the service. She
wanted to show the nuns that no punishment from heaven would
come down upon her for entering the chapel with an uncovered

head. She was defying what she considered the Church's benighted and degrading rule for women. And because she was a foreigner and so much older, the nuns never remonstrated with her.

She thought a great deal about religion, analyzing it as she had done ever since she had been freed from dogma by Lucretia Mott and William Lloyd Garrison. She commented in her diary:

> What a wonderful organization the Catholic Church is! In these convents and sisterhoods, it realizes in a measure the principle of cooperation. My dream of the future is cooperation. But is there any other foundation outside of religion on which it can be based? Can a belief grounded on science, common sense, and love of humanity sway the human soul as fears of the torments of hell and promises of the joys of heaven have done?

She appreciated the beauty of the ancient cathedrals, described them as "grand, wonderful, and mysterious" and added:

> I always leave them with a feeling of indignation because of the generations of human beings who have struggled in poverty to build these altars to an unknown God.

But her sense of humor always came to the rescue when she grew intense on the subject. She continued:

> In a chapel of one of these churches before the altar to one of the saints, lies a large open book in which you are invited to write your name, pay a franc, and then make a wish, which you are assured will be granted. I put down my name and the coin, and then asked that American women be enfranchised.

She presented Professor Joly with *The History of Woman Suffrage* and he wrote an enthusiastic review of it for the liberal newspaper of Toulouse. Of course she reported this to Susan, adding:

> He really shows great enthusiasm for our movement and for me as one of its representatives. When I bade him good-by the other day in the presence of the children, he asked if he might kiss me, which is quite French.... And so he kissed me! Pray do not let this fact reach the ears of Boston, for I suppose even an old man of seventy and a woman of sixty-seven, should not look at each other with feelings of regard. Let this indiscretion be known to you alone.

She spent a month with Theodore, Marguerite, and her beloved granddaughter at Jacournassy and found, much to her delight, that

Theodore was collecting material for a book to be called *The Woman Question in Europe*. Although she had come to France to rest from literary labors, she helped him edit and polish the manuscripts, which he received from all parts of Europe and which told of women's efforts for equal rights in the different countries.

When Harriot finished her studies at Toulouse, she made plans for her marriage to Henry Blatch. Late in the fall she and her mother left for England, and on November 12, 1882, in London in the Portland Street Chapel, she was married to Henry Blatch by William Henry Channing. To have him officiate made Elizabeth feel less among strangers, for he had been such a good friend to her and Susan during the early days of the woman's rights movement. She wasted no time mourning over the fact that the ocean from now on would separate her and her beloved daughter. Instead she renewed the acquaintances of her earlier visit in 1840, made new friends among the English suffragists, to whom she was well known by name and reputation, and enjoyed London to the full. She soon felt she had a second home at Basingstoke where Harriot and Henry were living on the Blatch estate.

Just at this time a great demonstration was held in Glasgow to celebrate the granting of municipal suffrage to women, and she attended with Mrs. McLaren, a sister of John Bright. Here for the first time she addressed an audience in the Old World. She wrote Harriot that she had been complimented on making the best speech of the evening, but although it was smooth and delivered without notes, it was by no means up to what she had often done. Here she met Lydia Becker, one of the leading English suffragists, with whom she had often corresponded regarding the cause, and wrote of her to Harriot, "Lydia Becker, whom you ask about, is the prototype of our precious Susan and is to the movement in this country just what Susan is in America."

Recalling her first visit to London in 1840 and the attitude toward women at the World's Antislavery Convention, she was filled with joy by the activity and progress among English women and felt that before long she might see the fulfillment of her hope that the women of the world would unite to demand their rights.

The English suffragists accepted her at once, invited her to their homes, and asked her to speak at their meetings. Harriot spoke too at occasional parlor meetings and charmed everyone with her beauty and eloquence. Priscilla Bright McLaren, Mrs. Jacob Bright, Lydia Becker, Helen Bright Clark, Mrs. Peter Taylor, Jane Cobden, Frances Power Cobbe, and Helen Taylor, stepdaughter of John Stuart Mill, were now their good friends.

She often contrasted their meetings and methods with those in her own country:

> Our system of conventions of two or three days duration, with long speeches discussing pointed and radical resolutions, is quite unknown in England. Their meetings consist of one session of a few hours, into which they crowd all the speakers they can summon. They have a few tame printed resolutions, on which there can be no possible difference of opinion, with the names of those who are to speak appended. Each of these is read and a few short speeches are made, that may or may not have the slightest reference to the resolutions, which are then passed. The last is usually one of thanks to some Lord or member of the House of Commons, who may have condescended to preside at the meeting or do something for the measure in Parliament. The Queen is referred to tenderly in most of the speeches, although she has never done anything to merit the approbation of the advocates of suffrage for women.

In England as in America, Elizabeth often startled her audiences by coming straight to the point instead of winning them gently with tactful trite phrases. One evening Helen Bright Clark invited a large number of friends to meet her and to hear her tell of the woman suffrage situation in America. A clergyman in the group asked if the Bible were not opposed to woman suffrage. This gave her the opportunity to speak freely on a subject she was never afraid to tackle. She even stated that there were limits to the Bible's authority. Mrs. Clark was very much troubled by her remarks, feeling she had irretrievably shocked the good people.

The next morning, however, a Methodist minister, who had been present, invited her to occupy his pulpit and repeat her remarks. She accepted with pleasure, convinced once more that it paid to speak out boldly and truthfully. She commented in her diary:

The minister led the services and I preached the sermon, taking as my text, Genesis 1, 27 and 28. It was plain that the congregation was pleased, especially the women, who were evidently glad to learn that man and woman were a simultaneous creation, that Eve was not an unfortunate afterthought, and that the curse was not a direct fiat from heaven, but the result of violated law, to be got rid of by observing the rules of life.

Her first visit to the House of Commons was eventful because she heard Gladstone and Parnell speak, but what impressed her most was the unsatisfactory high gallery from which she was obliged to view the scene. She wrote:

The place assigned ladies in the House of Commons is really a disgrace to a country ruled by a Queen. This dark perch is the highest gallery, immediately over the speaker's desk and government seats, behind a fine wire netting, so that it is quite impossible to see or hear anything. The sixteen persons who can crowd into the front row, by standing with their noses partly through the open network, can have the satisfaction of seeing the cranial arch of their rulers and hearing an occasional paean to liberty, or an Irish growl at the lack of it. I was told that this network was to prevent the members on the floor from being disturbed by the beauty of the women. On hearing this I remarked that I was devoutly thankful that our American men were not so easily disturbed, and that the beauty of our women was not of so dangerous a type. I could but contrast with these dingy buildings our spacious galleries in that magnificent Capitol at Washington, as well as in our grand State Capitols, where hundreds of women can sit at their ease and see and hear their rulers.

She visited the birthplace of Dean Stanley, and when the curate's two daughters took her through the church where he had preached for so many years, she made them think about customs and traditions of the Church which they had never before questioned.

When one of the daughters, pointing to the cover on the altar, remarked with pride, "Sister and I worked that," she asked designingly, "Did you place it on the altar?"

"Oh no," she replied, "no woman is allowed to enter this enclosure."

"Why?" asked Elizabeth, well knowing the answer.

"It is too sacred."

"But," Elizabeth remonstrated, "men go there; and it is said that women are purer, more delicate, refined, and naturally religious than they are."

"Yes, but women are not allowed," repeated the curate's daughter.

"Shall I explain the reason to you?" continued Elizabeth. "It is because the Church believes that woman brought sin into the world, that she was the cause of man's fall from holiness, that she was cursed of God, and has ever since been in collusion with the devil. Hence, the Church has considered her unfit to sing in the choir or enter the Holy of Holies."

And the curate's daughter, looking very thoughtful said, "I never supposed these old customs had such significance."

"Yes," concluded Elizabeth, driving her point home, "every old custom, every fashion, every point of etiquette is based on some principle, and women ignorantly submit to many degrading customs, because they do not understand their origin."

She visited her American friends, Mr. and Mrs. Moncure Conway, and preached in Mr. Conway's radical South Place Chapel. She wrote:

> I retired last night very nervous over my sermon . . . and this sensation of lack of confidence steadily increased until I reached the platform, when I again felt cool and happy, and never more enjoyed giving a speech than this one. My subject was "Has the Christian Religion Done Aught to Elevate Woman?" This idea has long been revolving in my mind. I had to give an answer in the negative, although I know there is much special pleading on the other side. My friends were all pleased with my discourse, and I had many warm compliments. Mrs. Conway said, "I think it is the finest thing I ever heard a woman do."

Elizabeth had been writing enthusiastic letters to Susan about her new experiences in France and England and about her interesting contacts with suffrage workers. She had repeatedly urged Susan to join her and to rest for a time from her strenuous campaigns. Finally Susan consented and sailed for England in February 1883, accompanied by Rachel Foster, a young girl of wealth who had recently joined the ranks of the suffragists.

Susan, described their meeting in London, in a letter to her sister:

ELIZABETH CADY STANTON WITH HARRIOT STANTON BLATCH AND NORA
1888

SUSAN B. ANTHONY AND ELIZABETH CADY STANTON ABOUT 1892

Mrs. Stanton was at the station, her face beaming and her white curls as lovely as ever.... Lydia Becker came to dinner by Mrs. Stanton's invitation, so she was the first of England's suffrage women for us to meet.

They were entertained by English suffragists, spoke at their meetings and discussed the subject so dear to their hearts, the best ways and means of furthering the cause. Elizabeth had been trying to interest English suffragists in an international conference of women, and now Susan added her efforts. Both had had such a gathering in mind for many years. At first they found English-women only lukewarm toward the project. They were much more conservative than Americans, and did not wish to be hurried by outsiders. They differed among themselves as to the best way of winning the ballot. A group, headed by Lydia Becker, asked for the vote for widows and spinsters, believing this would be more readily granted since it would not bring up the question of man's headship in the family. Mrs. Jacob Bright and Mrs. Peter Taylor, often called the mother of the woman suffrage movement in England, were not satisfied with such a demand, for they felt that married women were the greatest sufferers under the law. Elizabeth and Susan of course agreed with Mrs. Bright and Mrs. Taylor, and Elizabeth often urged them to ask for more and not be content until they had elevated the position of woman in every way.

While Susan traveled over Europe, Elizabeth spent most of her time in Basingstoke with Harriot. The quiet English country life was conducive to reading and writing. She was busy now with a sketch of Susan for *Our Famous Women,* a book to be published by A. D. Worthington of Hartford, Connecticut. A sketch of her own life was being written by Laura Curtis Bullard.

She stayed at Basingstoke until after Harriot's baby was born. The arrival of this granddaughter was an outstanding event in her life. Dearly as she loved all of her children, Harriot was especially precious. She more than any of the others seemed destined to carry on the torch which her mother had lighted. Now as she looked at little Nora, she saw in her another torchbearer. When Nora was one week old, she wrote in her diary:

As I sit beside Hattie with the baby in my arms, and realize that three generations of us are together, I appreciate more than ever what each generation can do for the next one, by making the most of itself and thus slowly building the Jacob's ladder by which the race shall at last reach the divine heights of perfection.

It was very hard to leave them. She confessed to her diary:

When Harriot and I parted we stood mute, without a tear, gazing into each other's eyes. My legs trembled so that I could scarcely walk to the carriage. My blessed baby was sleeping, one little arm over her head.

But Susan was sailing home with her and that took the edge off her loneliness. Besides during those last days in England at the farewell receptions, luncheons, and visits with suffragists, her plan and Susan's for an international association of women was accepted by a few Englishwomen with enthusiasm, and a committee was formed to correspond with women in other countries regarding the project.

So they left for America in November 1883, their hopes high, their goal to unite the women of the world in a demand for equal rights.

It was three years before Elizabeth again visited her children and grandchildren in Europe. During this time she devoted herself to writing for newspapers and magazines on controversial subjects relating to women. She found a ready market for her articles.

For the first time since the Civil War, she and Susan differed regarding their course of action. Elizabeth had come to the conclusion that building up the woman suffrage organization was no longer her task, although she was ready to make speeches when necessary. She believed that she could now do more for women through her writing. She had tired of conventions, hearings, and campaigns, and felt she had done her share of that work. She was convinced that women were getting into a rut with their conventions and suffrage organizations and needed rousing, that they needed freeing from the psychological fetters to which they unconsciously clung, although they asked for suffrage. Only a mentally liberated, militant womanhood could break down the indifference of legislators. She herself had been at it for thirty-seven years. Continuing the same methods, women would undoubtedly have to wait many years more for the political rights which should have been theirs when the Republic was founded.

To her mind there was only one thing which kept women from making a whole-hearted militant demand for complete freedom, and that was the subtle influence the Church had exercised over women's minds, filling them with a sense of inferiority and making them feel that sacrifice and submission were their lot and that their lives could be virtuous only if kept within a certain sphere. She was amazed again and again how women apparently liberal were held back by mental quirks which could always be traced back to religious domination. She knew that few women would have the courage to attack the Church's stand regarding women, while many were now willing and eager to work for the ballot. From now on her work would be to free women mentally fom these subtle bonds.

While Susan agreed with her theoretically, she knew that her work was to build up a powerful organization to keep the idea of woman suffrage continually before the people. She was convinced that victory would come only as women in their organizations clung steadfastly to the one idea, woman suffrage, and allowed nothing to cloud the issue. She was discovering young workers eager to help her and she turned more and more to them as the years went by.

These two old workers, now taking different roads to reach their goal, found fortunately that the roads often crossed and they could walk on together over some stretches, giving each other courage and inspiration as they had in the past. They continued to supplement each other. The woman's movement needed Susan B. Anthony's ability to build up a strong organization and to lobby among Congressmen and state legislators. It needed equally as much Elizabeth Cady Stanton's campaign to liberate woman's thought.

The subject of divorce was still on Elizabeth's mind and in an article in the *North American Review,* in September 1884, she championed more liberal divorce laws. Her article was written to refute a recommendation of Noah Davis, judge of the Supreme Court of New York, that an amendment to the Constitution be passed to make divorce laws homogeneous throughout the United States. She insisted that there be no further divorce legislation until women were enfranchised and could help frame the law which would affect them so vitally. In answer to Judge Davis's charge that with more liberal divorce laws there would be a great upheaval in social life, she said:

> A change in the civil code will not change all natural affections.... We have changed the foundations of the Church, too, without destroying religious sentiment in the human soul.... Though the cardinal points of our faith have been changed again and again, yet we have a Church still. So we shall have the family, that great conservator of natural strength and morals, after the present restrictive divorce laws are all swept from the statute books.... The same law of equality that has revolutionized the State and the Church is now reorganizing the home. The same process of evolution that has given us a State without a king, a Church without a Pope, will give us a family without a "divinely ordained head" in which the interests of father, mother, and child will be equally represented.

Then followed an article in the *Boston Index,* "The Christian Church and Women," and newspaper appeals to women to clean up the streets of their cities. She was always ready with practical suggestions for women which would put their executive ability to work outside of the home and improve general conditions. Clara Bewick Colby, then editing the *Woman's Tribune* in Beatrice, Nebraska, urged her to contribute as many articles as she could; and as she heartily approved of this paper and its liberal policy, she became a steady contributor, adding greatly to its prestige.

In another article for the *North American Review,* "Has Christianity Benefited Women?" she expressed views which had been evolving over many years and which she had touched on in her sermon in London in Moncure Conway's South Place Chapel. She took the ground that woman is not indebted to any form of religion for the liberty she enjoys, but that her religious feelings have been perverted for her complete subjection. She had been reading Lecky, Maine's *Ancient Law,* and Newman Lord and was well versed in the historical studies on the subject. She was not letting

her feminism nor her impatience with the Church run away with
her. Her ideas aroused a great deal of criticism, and she observed
in her diary:

> I have no fault to find with Jesus or his teachings. My complaint
> is of the so-called Christian Church, the *canon law* and the action
> and discipline of all the sects. In my article I do not leave the care-
> ful reader in the slightest doubt as to what I mean. The sectarian
> press and the pulpit dishonestly evade what I do say, and reply to
> what I do not say.

On her seventieth birthday, November 12, 1885, she was honored
by a nationwide celebration. To American women she was the
mother of woman suffrage. They loved her and revered her. They
forgave her again and again for startling and shocking them with
her advanced ideas. In gratitude for her years of work for women,
suffrage associations all over the country held meetings. Elizabeth
Boynton Harbert of Chicago, one of the capable younger workers,
devoted the November number of her magazine *The New Era*
entirely to her. Articles were contributed by people from all parts of
the world who knew her well. In prose and in verse she was lauded
as a mother, an orator, a reformer, presiding officer, patriot, statesman, friend, and writer. Elizabeth recorded her impressions:

> The day was ushered in with telegrams, letters, and express pack-
> ages, which continued to arrive during the week. From England,
> France, and Germany came cablegrams, presents, and letters of con
> gratulation, and from all quarters came books, pictures, silver, bronzes,
> California blankets, and baskets of fruit and flowers. The eulogies in
> prose and verse were so hearty and numerous that the ridicule and
> criticism of forty years were buried so deep that I shall remember
> them no more.

On the evening of November 12, suffragists gathered at the home
of Dr. Clemence Lozier, a prominent woman physician of New
York City, to pay homage to Elizabeth Cady Stanton. Dr. Lozier
told her that she owed her a lifelong debt of gratitude for a letter
on divorce which she had written years ago for a New York paper
and which had given her courage to dissolve a desperately unhappy
marriage. Other women were there who were equally grateful to
her for the spirit of freedom and self-respect which she had roused

in them. The younger women were fired by her example of service to women.

Comfortably seated, her black silk dress billowing about her, a white silk shawl over her shoulders, her white hair arranged most becomingly, her blue eyes sparkling, she talked to them that evening on the "Pleasures of Age," taking as her theme one of her favorite poems, Longfellow's "Morituri Salutamus":

> Ah! Nothing is too late
> Till the tired heart shall cease to palpitate.
> Cato learned Greek at eighty; Sophocles
> Wrote his grand Oedipus, and Simonides
> Bore off the prize of verse from his compeers
> When each had numbered more than four score years,
>
> .   .   .   .
>
> For age is opportunity no less
> Than youth itself, though in another dress,
> And as the evening twilight fades away
> The sky is filled with stars, invisible by day.

"Fifty, not fifteen," she told them, "is the heyday of woman's life. Then the forces hitherto finding an outlet in flirtations, courtship, conjugal and maternal love, are garnered in the brain to find expression in intellectual achievements, in spiritual friendships and beautiful thoughts, in music, poetry, and art. . . ."

"The young," she said, "have no memories with which to gild their lives, none of the pleasures of retrospection. Neither has youth a monopoly of the illusions of hope, for that is eternal; to the end we have something still to hope. And here age has the advantage of basing its hopes on something rational and attainable. . . . From experience we understand the situation, we have a knowledge of human nature, we learn how to control ourselves, to treat children with tenderness, servants with consideration, and our equals with proper respect. Years bring wisdom and charity; pity rather than criticism; sympathy, rather than condemnation."

But Elizabeth was not the only member of the Stanton family honored by a public birthday celebration that year. Henry Stanton, whose book, *Random Recollections,* had just been published, was given a dinner by the New York City Press Club in honor of his

eightieth birthday. She was proud of Henry and he of her. Their
lives had been useful and happy. They could look into the past
with satisfaction.

They had but one more year together. Late in October 1886, she
went to England for a visit with Harriot. In January 1887 a cable-
gram arrived announcing Henry's death. Her diary reveals her
deep sorrow:

> Death! We all think we are prepared to hear of the passing
> away of the aged. But when the news comes, the heart and pulses
> all seem to stand still. We cannot realize that those we have known
> in life are suddenly withdrawn, to be seen no more on earth. . . .
> When the boundless ocean rolls between you and the lost one, and
> the startling news comes to you without preparation, it is a ter-
> rible shock to every nerve and feeling, to body and mind alike.
> Then well up regrets for every unkind, ungracious word spoken, for
> every act of coldness and neglect. Ah! if we could only remember in
> life to be gentle and forbearing with each other, and to strive to serve
> nobly instead of exacting service, our memories of the past would be
> more pleasant and profitable. I have lived with my husband for forty-
> six years, and now he leads the way to another sphere. What the
> next life is, whether this one is all, or we pursue an individual
> existence in a higher form of development, are the questions not yet
> answered. My daughter and I have sat together and talked all day
> long of the mysteries of life and death, speculating on what lies
> beyond.

On this page of the diary she pasted part of a newspaper wrapper
which Henry had addressed to her and underneath it wrote in a
tremulous hand, "This is probably the last time Henry wrote my
name in sending to me the Sunday Sun."

She stayed on in Basingstoke, bravely adjusting herself to life
without Henry. Their affection for each other had been deep and
true. Now all the tender memories came crowding in—of their
courtship, of their early struggles together to bring up their large
family of children—of his thoughtfulness, his cheery, fun-loving
nature. But she had learned to live in the present—to put out of
her mind the sadness and distress of the past, and so she turned
her attention at once to the writing of a book which she had
planned before she left Tenafly, a woman's commentary on the
Bible.

She discontinued all work in the spring of 1887 to spend six months in Paris with Theodore in his apartment overlooking the Seine. She was enchanted with Paris, with its gaiety, its life and color. She was at home every Wednesday afternoon to her American friends and Theodore's and to the reformers who were eager to meet her. She wrote in her diary:

> To one of our receptions Bjornsterne Bjornson brought with him one of his daughters, who told me afterward in her girlish northern simplicity: "Papa said to me as we approached your door: 'Look well at this woman for she is one of the most famous of America.'" This is the kind of compliment that touches the heart and makes amends for so many rebuffs.

She played chess again with Theodore Tilton, who was living in Paris. She had long interesting talks with Frederick Douglass and his wife, a cultured white woman. Anna Klumpke, protégé and heir of Rosa Bonheur, was so attracted by her beautiful white hair that she begged her to pose for a portrait. She wrote Robert:

> I am quite pleased with the result. I sit in a large ruby-colored velvet chair, dressed in black satin and black lace around the throat and hands. Nothing white in the picture but my head and hands. My right hand rests in my lap, my left on the arm of the chair holding my gold spectacles. A little table on my left contains one volume of the Woman Suffrage History and two pamphlets.

Back again in Basingstoke in October she settled down to a more quiet life of study and writing, but she saw much of the English feminists and other English intellectuals and reformers who sought her out at the Blatch home.

She stayed on in England until Susan ordered her back to her own country for the long-hoped-for international gathering of women, to be held in the spring of 1888.

XXIII

SUFFRAGISTS UNITE

As far back as 1840, after the World's Antislavery Convention, Elizabeth began dreaming of the time when the women of the world would hold a convention and unite to improve their status. While in France and England in 1882 she urged this idea on many of the women she met, and when Susan joined her in England a year later, English feminists were ready to consider it seriously. At her instigation and Susan's, the National Woman Suffrage Association at its annual meeting, January 1887, voted to call an international conference to celebrate the fourth decade of the woman suffrage movement, and Susan, Rachel Foster, and May Wright Sewall began preparations at once. The correspondence entailed was tremendous. Invitations were sent to all organizations of women in the trades, professions, and reforms as well as those working for woman suffrage. Raising $10,000 to finance the conference was an undertaking in itself. Elizabeth in England escaped this arduous humdrum work, but she had a delicate task there. Dissensions among English suffragists made it look for a time as if England would send no delegates, but she, determined that this should not happen, negotiated until satisfactory representatives were appointed. She was now receiving almost daily letters urging her to come home for the International Convention. Susan demanded her return in no uncertain terms. She wrote Susan:

We have jogged along pretty well for forty years or more. Perhaps amid the wreck of thrones and the undoing of so many friendships, sects, parties, and families, you and I deserve some credit for sticking together through all adverse winds, with so few ripples on the surface. When I get back to America I intend to cling to you closer than ever. I am thoroughly rested now and full of fight and fire, ready to travel and speak from Maine to Florida. Tell our suffrage daughters to brace up and get ready for a long pull, a strong pull, and a pull all together when I come back.

But as the time approached for her to leave England, she dreaded going home to face the emptiness left by Henry's passing. She dreaded the winter voyage across the Atlantic. It was far less grueling to observe the world from her watch tower in England than to get into the turmoil again. She wrote Susan that she had about decided not to come.

When Susan received this letter, she was so angry that she dared not reply at once. She had planned to link the international meetings with the celebration of the fortieth anniversary of the Seneca Falls Convention. There could be no celebration of the Convention of 1848 without the woman who called it! She depended on Elizabeth to make the speech of the meeting and to bring honor to the National Woman Suffrage Association. She must rouse her from this apathy. "I wrote the most terrific letter to Mrs. Stanton," she recorded in her diary. "It will start every white hair on her head." The next night she added, "I made my own heart ache all night, awake or asleep, by my terrible arraignment, whether it touches her feelings or not."

But her letter did its work. Elizabeth cabled, "I am coming," and Susan confided to her diary: "My mind is so relieved. I feel as if I were treading on air."

Elizabeth arrived in Washington a few days before the convention, her speech unwritten. But Susan now had her where she could watch her and ordered her to stay in her apartment until it was completed. Delighted to be under Susan's orders again, she set to work immediately and produced one of her excellent speeches.

On Sunday, March 25, 1888, the delegates assembled in Albaugh's Opera House, where religious services were conducted entirely by women. It was here that Anna Howard Shaw showed her remarkable ability as an orator, and Susan first sensed her value to the woman's cause.

The next morning, the conference opened formally. It was the largest gathering of women ever assembled. Fifty-three national organizations sent delegates. England, France, Norway, Denmark, Finland, India, as well as the United States, were represented. A wide variety of subjects were discussed, including Education,

Philanthropy, Temperance, Industry, Professions, Organizations, Social Purity, Legal, Political, and Religious Conditions. Capacity crowds attended the sixteen sessions.

Susan made the opening speech. In her black dress and red silk shawl, her gray-brown hair parted and smoothed back, her face lit up with pride for her beloved cause, she stood before this enthusiastic gathering of women while applause thundered through the auditorium. Briefly she compared the past with the present and then introduced Mrs. Elizabeth Cady Stanton, "the woman who not only joined with Lucretia Mott in calling the first convention, but who, for the greater part of twenty years, has been president of the National Woman Suffrage Association." The audience rose in tribute to Elizabeth, clapping their hands and waving their handkerchiefs. She spoke to them, as she had always spoken, with dignity, with force, and with power to inspire. "We, who, like the children of Israel, have been wandering in the wilderness of prejudice and ridicule for forty years," she said in part, "feel a peculiar tenderness for the young women on whose shoulders we are about to leave our burdens. Although we have opened a pathway to the promised land and cleared up much of the underbrush of false sentiment, logic, and rhetoric intertwisted with law and custom, which blocked all avenues in starting, yet there are still many obstacles to be encountered before the rough journey is ended. The younger women are starting with great advantages over us. They have the results of our experience; they have superior opportunities for education; they will find a more enlightened public sentiment for discussion; they will have more courage to take the rights which belong to them. Hence we may look to them for speedy conquests. When we think of the vantage-ground woman holds today, in spite of all the artificial obstacles placed in her way, we are filled with wonder as to what the future mothers of the race will be when free to have complete development."

Thirty-six women and eight men who had been identified with the woman suffrage movement for forty years attended the conference. They held a pioneer meeting. A portrait of Lucretia Mott, decorated with smilax and lilies of the valley, looked down benignly upon the vast eager audience. The meeting was opened with silent prayer in her memory, and Susan, after alluding to her portrait, said: "I hope all will feel that her spirit is with us this morning. If spirits are anywhere, and I believe they are everywhere, I know we have that loved and venerated pioneer with us today." It had been Elizabeth's dream that Lucretia Mott preside at the first international gathering of women, but they had delayed too long. Lucretia had passed on eight years before, in 1880.

The conference continued with great success. Permanent national and international councils were formed, and the following resolution was adopted:

> It is the unanimous voice of this International Council that all institutions of learning and of professional instruction, including schools of theology, law, and medicine, should, in the interests of humanity, be as freely opened to women as to men, and that opportunities for industrial training should be as generally and as liberally provided for one sex as for the other. The representatives of organized womanhood in this Council will steadily demand that in all avocations in which both men and women engage, equal wages shall be paid for equal work; and they declare that an enlightened society should demand, as the only adequate expression of the high civilization which it is its office to establish and maintain, an identical standard of personal purity and morality for men and women.

What a change forty years had wrought! In 1848 a small group of courageous women voiced their demands. The press stirred up a tremendous storm of ridicule and protest. Forty years later women of the world gathered in the capital of the nation. Press reports were dignified and generous in their praise. Delegates were received by the President and his wife and by distinguished Senators. Congressional hearings were granted. Elizabeth had realized one more ambition. At last international recognition for the equal rights movement had been won and at last an international organization, the International Council of Women, had been formed which she hoped would be a power in the advancement of women.

Elizabeth had now been president of the National Woman Suffrage Association since 1869, twenty years, while Susan held the office of vice-president-at-large. These two leaders looked upon woman suffrage not as an abstract theory to be handled with gloves or spoken of only at proper times, but as a practical measure to be fought for in a practical way.

For example, when Mormon women, who had been granted suffrage in the territory of Utah in 1870, were being threatened with disfranchisement, ostensibly to stamp out polygamy, and came to Washington to protest, they appealed to the National Woman Suffrage Association and were invited to speak at the convention of 1879. Much criticism followed this action on the part of the Suffrage Association, as polygamy among the Mormons was of great concern to the nation at this time, and these women contaminated by polygamy were shunned by the virtuous. Indignant, Elizabeth wrote Susan:

> If the Congress of the United States can allow George A. Cannon to sit for Utah in that body without it being supposed to endorse polygamy, we could permit Mormon women the same privilege in our Association without our being accused of embracing their principles. If Congress can stand Cannon with four wives, we might stand the women with only the fourth part of a husband! And furthermore, when Congress proposes to disfranchise the women of a Territory, where should they go to plead their case but to the National Woman Suffrage Association?

Susan agreed. And in that spirit the work of the National Woman Suffrage Association went on.

Even with such a liberal attitude dominating the organization, there were differences of opinion regarding policies. The "prayer meeting group," which, under the leadership of Isabella Beecher Hooker, tried to introduce prayers and hymn singing in the conventions annoyed many of the members. Others were disturbed by the increasing temperance element represented. The growing strength of the religious element in the organization convinced Elizabeth more and more of the need of liberating women's thought on the subject of religion, and she consistently injected into the conventions her ideas on women and the Church. Even Susan often grew impatient with her zeal in this direction.

At the convention in Washington in 1885, Elizabeth had presented the following resolution:

WHEREAS, The dogmas incorporated in religious creeds derived from Judaism, teaching that woman was an after-thought in creation, her sex a misfortune, marriage a condition of subordination, and maternity a curse, are contrary to the law of God (as revealed in nature) and to the precepts of Christ, and,

WHEREAS, These dogmas are an insidious poison, sapping the vitality of our civilization, blighting woman, and through her paralyzing humanity; therefore be it

RESOLVED, That we call on the Christian ministry, as leaders of thought, to teach and enforce the fundamental idea of creation, that man was made in the image of God, male and female, and given equal rights over the earth, but none over each other. And, furthermore, we ask their recognition of the scriptural declaration that, in the Christian religion, there is neither male nor female, bond nor free, but all are one in Christ Jesus.

Speaking for the resolution, she said: "Woman has been licensed to preach in the Methodist Church; the Unitarian and Universalist and some branches of the Baptist denomination have ordained women, but the majority do not recognize them officially, although for the first three centuries after the proclamation of Christianity, women had a place in the Church. They were deaconesses and elders, and were ordained and administered the sacrament. Yet through the Catholic hierarchy those privileges were taken away in Christendom and they have never been restored. Now we intend to demand equal rights in the Church."

A heated debate continued into the second day of the convention. Jewish women resented the reference to Judaism. Susan was opposed to the resolution. "I was on the old Garrisonian platform," she declared, "and found long ago that this matter of settling any question of human rights by peoples' interpretation of the Bible is never satisfactory. I hope we shall not go back to that war. No two can ever interpret alike, and discussion upon it is time wasted. We all know what we want, and that is the recognition of woman's perfect equality—in the Home, the Church, and the State. We all know that such recognition has never been granted her in the centuries of the past. But for us to begin a discussion here as to who established these dogmas would be anything but profitable. Let those who wish go back into the history of the past, but I beg it shall not be done on our platform."

The discussion continued pro and con, and Elizabeth again defended the resolution. "You may go over the world," she argued, "and you will find that every form of religion which has breathed upon this earth has degraded woman. There is not one which has not made her subject to man. . . . What power is it that makes the Hindoo woman burn herself on the funeral pyre of her husband? Her religion. What holds the Turkish woman in the harem? Her religion. By what power do the Mormons perpetuate their system of polygamy? By their religion. Man of himself could not do this, but when he declares, 'Thus saith the Lord,' of course he can do it. So long as ministers stand up and tell us that as Christ is the head of the church, so is man the head of the woman, how are we to break the chains which have held women down through the ages. . . . Observe today the work women are doing for the churches. *The Church rests on the shoulders of women.* Have we ever yet heard a man preach a sermon from Genesis 1: 27-28, which declares the full equality of the feminine and masculine element in the Godhead? They invariably shy at the first chapter. They always get up in their pulpits and read the second chapter.

"Now I ask you if our religion teaches the dignity of woman? It teaches us that abominable idea of the sixth century—Augustine's idea—that motherhood is a curse; that woman is the author of sin, and is most corrupt. Can we ever cultivate any proper sense of self-respect as long as women take such sentiments from the mouths of the priesthood. . . . In republican America, and in the light of the nineteenth century, we must demand that our religion shall teach a higher idea in regard to woman. . . . We want to help roll off from the soul of woman the terrible superstitions that have so long repressed and crushed her."

In spite of this eloquent appeal, clear and straight to the point, the resolution was laid on the table. Women were not yet ready to face the issue, for the majority were convinced that the ballot could more readily be won without antagonizing the Church.

The press, always looking for a spicy news item from a woman suffrage convention, hailed the resolution with glee and spread it broadcast, arousing the wrath of the clergy. As a result, Dr. W. W.

Patton of Howard University preached the next Sunday in the Congregational Church of Washington on "Woman and Skepticism," declaring that freedom for women led to skepticism and immorality, citing as examples, Hypatia, Mary Wollstonecraft, Frances Wright, George Eliot, and so on. Elizabeth and Susan occupied front seats, and at the close of the sermon went directly up to Dr. Patton to remonstrate with him. "Doctor," ejaculated Susan with cutting bluntness, "Your mother, if you have one, should lay you across her knee and give you a good spanking for that sermon."

"Oh no," interposed Elizabeth realizing at once how Susan's remark would be quoted and misinterpreted, "allow me to congratulate you. I have been trying for years to make women understand that the worst enemy they have is in the pulpit, and you have illustrated the truth of it." Then, while Doctor Patton was recovering from his astonishment at being so rebuked, these two indomitable veterans marched out of the church.

It was as Elizabeth had surmised. The press gloated over Susan's remark and spread it in glaring headlines far and wide. Some papers even reported that Susan had interrupted the services. Elizabeth, who left for New York almost immediately after the sermon, read the reports with amusement, but realizing how troubled Susan would be over the tempest which her impulsive words had stirred up, wrote at once:

> The more I think of your Patton volley, the better I like it, for it was the most contemptuous thing that could have been said. It was an attack, a defiance, an argument all in one. Like that shot at Lexington, it ought to go round the world. It is done. Don't regret it. By the way, did you see the "funnyman" of one of the papers said we were "a spanking team?" That's not bad.

While Elizabeth was in Europe, she had not let herself get out of touch with her suffrage organization. She kept her eye on the conventions and criticized them mercilessly when they did not come up to her standards. To Clara Colby, who appealed to her particularly because of her liberal attitude toward religion, she had written a scathing criticism of the convention of 1887:

I am so sorry I was not there to maintain the dignity of our platform. I never did hear such twaddle. Where were you and Miss
Anthony that you did not inject a little common sense into that one-
sided discussion? Who composed the committee on resolutions? The
resolutions read as if they had been thrown together on the way to
the hall. That twaddle about Christ sounds as though it came from
a certain rattle-brained person whom I have in view. I should think
you and Miss Anthony would feel ashamed of the resolutions and
that discussion. I am, I assure you. Fortunately, but few people will
read either resolutions or discussions.

By 1887 members of the Women's Christian Temperance Union
had become a real force in the ranks of the suffragists, realizing,
under the leadership of Frances Willard, how necessary the ballot
was for the success of their particular reforms. They introduced
into the woman suffrage conventions not only the subject of temperance but topics of a distinctly religious cast. At this time they were
advocating the passage of a bill in Congress, declaring Christ the
author and head of the government, and were proposing Puritanical observation of the Sabbath. The more liberal suffragists were
out of sympathy with these reforms and cringed whenever they
were advanced in woman suffrage conventions. Matilda Joslyn
Gage felt very strongly about it and wrote Elizabeth:

> Frances Willard, with her magnetic force, her power of leadership,
> her desire to introduce religious tenets into the government, is the
> most dangerous person on the American continent today.

And Elizabeth in turn wrote Clara Colby:

> We who understand the dangers threatened in the Prohibition
> movement—the rock ahead for woman suffrage—must not be dazzled
> by the promise of a sudden acquisition of numbers to our platform
> with the wide-spread influence of the Church behind them, if with
> all this is coming a religious proscription that will undermine the
> secular nature of our government.

She saw clearly the havoc a group of fanatical prohibitionists
and religionists could work if their reform measures materialized
into laws. She wanted suffragists to be clear on the matter and to
lend no encouragement which might be construed as support of
these measures. Therefore she proposed to Susan a thorough discus-

sion of the subject at the next woman suffrage convention. She
outlined her views:

> An effort should be made to accomplish three things. 1. To keep
> the Federal Constitution as it is—the rights of man recognized.
> 2. To keep our public schools free from all sectarian teachings. 3. To
> keep the seventh day holy for the happiness and improvement of
> the masses by opening all libraries, picture galleries, and places of
> amusement on that day. These women do not seem to see that all
> this special legislation about faith, Sabbaths, drinking, etc., etc., is
> the entering wedge to general governmental interference which
> would eventually subject us to an espionage that would soon become
> tyrannical in the extreme.

She had seen, before most of her colleagues, that any close affiliation of woman suffrage with temperance or puritanical legislation
would rouse powerful opposition throughout the country against
votes for women.

For twenty years the National and American Woman Suffrage
Associations had been functioning independently, both waging admirable campaigns for their common object. Since Theodore Tilton
had made his futile efforts at union in 1870, nothing more had
been attempted in this direction, although the younger suffragists,
who were joining the ranks, repeatedly discussed the need and
possibilities of union. Nothing definite was done, however, until
plans were being made for the meetings of the International Council
of Women. Then, as women of the world were gathering, it seemed
more and more imperative for the women of this country to work
together harmoniously in one organization. The first overture was
made by the American Association in 1887 when in convention it
adopted a resolution proposing that Lucy Stone and Susan B. Anthony confer regarding union. As their conference was successful,
committees were chosen from both Associations to draw up a constitution and to iron out whatever complications might arise. To
two younger suffragists, Alice Stone Blackwell and Rachel Foster
Avery, both secretaries of their respective organizations, goes the
credit of effecting the union. Late in 1887 Miss Blackwell sent
Mrs. Avery her plans, making this suggestion:

Since many members of the National Society regard Mrs. Stone as the cause of the division, and many members of the American regard Mrs. Stanton and Miss Anthony as the cause of it, Mrs. Stone suggested that it would greatly promote harmonious union, for those three ladies to agree in advance that none of them take the presidency of the united association.

Both Elizabeth and Susan had been willing for years to step aside and let others take the helm if thereby harmony could be assumed. They were both eager for union and hopeful that the younger suffragists could build up one strong organization which would hammer down the indifference and prejudice of Congress.

Elizabeth had written Isabella Beecher Hooker as early as 1880:

I feel with you, in spite of all minor drawbacks, the union of the suffrage forces would be a move in the right direction. But our cause is too great to be hurt permanently by what any one individual or group of individuals may do. For over thirty years some people have said from time to time that I have injured the suffrage movement beyond redemption; but it still lives. Train killed it, Victoria Woodhull killed it, the *Revolution* killed it. But with each death, it put on new life. Boston thought that Paulina Davis impaired our best interests; that you did the same; that Susan dealt us a death blow at various times. But every time it is stricken to earth it comes up again with fresh power.

Later, in 1889, she wrote to the Wisconsin Woman Suffrage Association:

Two associations advocating precisely the same measures, yet seemingly in antagonism have been distracting forces in our cause for the last twenty years. Hence, when the proposition from the party that seceded came for union, I readily assented, because in union I saw added strength as well as an immense saving in money and force. As many who took part in the division have passed to another sphere of action and the work is gradually slipping from the hands of those who remain, it is a pity to hand down a heritage of discord to the brave young women on whose shoulders the future labors are to rest.

Henry Blackwell objected to her reference to the American Association, as "the party that seceded," and in the *Woman's Journal* under the heading, "A Correction," gave his version of the formation of the two societies. It was very difficult for the old workers to refrain from blaming each other for the division.

Negotiations continued for two years. The majority of details were easily arranged. The name would be National American Woman Suffrage Association. The National consented to the delegate system of representation and agreed to undertake state work as well as national. Conventions would be held annually in Washington. Two points, however, were difficult to settle—the part men were to play in the organization, and who would be the first president. The American had always insisted on equal rights for men. Henry Ward Beecher had been its first president. Now William Dudley Foulke held that office. The National, on the other hand, was convinced that in order to keep an organization alert to the best interests of women, women must take full charge. This had always been Elizabeth's policy. She tried to keep herself aloof from the negotiations as much as possible but could not refrain from voicing her opinions to her friends. She wrote in her diary:

> I especially do not like Article 12 in the proposed constitution which makes possible the election of a man to the presidency of the organization. I would never vote for a man to any office in our societies, not, however, because I am down on men per se. Think of an association of black men officered by slave-holders! Having men pray or preside for us at our meetings has always seemed to me a tacit admission that we haven't the brains to do these things ourselves. . . . So I have written Susan suggesting that this article might be dropped out. . . . On the whole, I find the suggested constitution very wordy and obscure. It is a very mannish document. It makes my head whirl to read it. One would think it was written to hedge in a pair of foxes. I ask Susan what is the matter with our little old constitution, which we simple-minded women drew up back I do not know when? I tell her that I get more radical as I grow older, while she seems to get more conservative.

Elizabeth's warnings were not heeded. The new constitution placed no disabilities upon men, but in spite of this they gradually retired from active service in the Association.

The question of the presidency was a very delicate one. Lucy Stone had forbidden her name to be used. Susan and Elizabeth were also willing to remain in the background, but the women of the country would not let them stay there. Letters poured in insisting that, as they had led the movement thus far, doing the difficult pioneer work, one or the other must be honored by election to the presidency. Because of her seniority and her unusual ability as presiding officer, the majority of the Nationals favored Mrs. Stanton. A group, however, preferred Miss Anthony, arguing that Mrs. Stanton was too old and spent most of her time in Europe. If it must be one of the two, the American would support Miss Anthony. Mrs. Stanton was too radical. She would embarrass them again with divorce and the Church. Miss Anthony at least could be depended upon to stick to woman suffrage.

The first union meeting was held in Washington in February, 1890. Before the formal organization and election of officers, each organization held a separate executive session. Henry Blackwell addressed the American Association, recommending that if the choice for president lay between Susan B. Anthony and Elizabeth Cady Stanton, they cast their votes for Miss Anthony.

Susan did not want the presidency. She wanted it for Elizabeth. She was incensed at the false rumors that were circulating—that she had made a bargain with the American for the presidency, that she was trying to oust Mrs. Stanton.

At the executive session of the National Association, her voice vibrant with emotion, she pleaded earnestly with the delegates: "I will say to every woman who is a National, and who has any love for the old Association, or for Susan B. Anthony, that I hope you will not vote for her for President. I stand in a delicate position. I have letters which accuse me of having favored the union solely from personal and selfish considerations. I have letters accusing me of trying to put Mrs. Stanton out. Now what I want to say is, don't you vote for any human being but Mrs. Stanton. There are other reasons why I want her elected, but I have these personal ones. When the division was made 22 years ago, it was because our platform was too broad, because Mrs. Stanton was too radical. A more conservative association was wanted. And now if we divide and Mrs. Stanton shall be deposed from the presidency you virtually degrade her. If you have any regard for the National from the beginning, that has stood like a rock without regard to creed or politics, without regard to any possible consideration, that every woman should be allowed to come on our platform to plead for her freedom; if you have any regard for that grand old principle, vote for Mrs. Stanton....

"Our association has always allowed the utmost freedom to vote against everything that would block our way, no matter whether it was the Church, or what it was. Anything and everything that stood in the way of progress was always likely to get its head knocked off on the platform of the National Woman Suffrage Association. I want everyone who claims to be a National to stand for this broad principle. I want our platform to be kept broad enough for the infidel, the atheist, the Mohammedan, or the Christian. I remember thirty years ago George William Curtis said to me: 'If you want your platform to succeed you must not allow Mrs. Ernestine L. Rose to stand upon it; she's a pronounced atheist.' I said: 'We shall never turn her out.' Now we have come to another phase of the fight, and if it is necessary, will fight another forty years to make it broad enough for the Christian to stand upon, whether she be a Catholic, and counts her beads, or a Protestant of the straitest orthodox creed. I shall fight for the rights of the Christians today, as for the rights of the infidels forty years ago. We have also delegates from Utah on our platform. Let not the Nationals go back on their record. Every woman, whether she be Mormon or Gentile, has the right to vote. It was a dastardly act of Congress in disfranchising the women of Utah. They are here today with a magnificent delegation.

"These are the broad principles I want you to stand upon, that our platform may be kept as broad as the universe, that upon it may stand the representatives of all creeds and no creeds—Pagan, Jew, Gentile, Christian, Protestant or Catholic."

The executive session of the National was stormy. Aside from their divided allegiance to Mrs. Stanton and Miss Anthony, the delegates were not wholeheartedly in favor of union. Some were ready to form a new organization of their own. But May Wright Sewall as chairman held the reins firmly, and Susan, with her reputation of always doing what was best for the cause, won over the warring factions.

Union was finally effected. Mrs. Stanton was elected president, receiving 41 more votes than Susan B. Anthony, who then was unanimously chosen vice-president-at-large. Lucy Stone was the unanimous choice for chairman of the executive committee. Rachel Foster Avery was made corresponding secretary, Alice Stone Blackwell, recording secretary, and Jane H. Spofford, treasurer.

Deeply moved by the honor conferred upon her, Mrs. Stanton made the opening speech. "I consider it a greater honor," she said, "to go to England as President of this Association than would be the case if I were sent as Minister Plenipotentiary to any court in Europe." She reviewed briefly the history of the movement for woman's rights, naming its brilliant leaders whose work had blazed the way for this vigorous organization. She paid special tribute to Lucy Stone, whose illness had kept her from the convention.

"For fifty years," she continued, "we have been plaintiffs in the court of justice, but as the bench, the bar, and the jury are all men, we are non-suited every time. Some men tell us we must be patient and persuasive; that we must be womanly. My friends, what is man's idea of womanliness? It is to have a manner which pleases him—quiet, deferential, submissive, approaching him as a subject does a master. He wants no self-assertion on our part, no defiance. . . . What do we know as yet of the womanly? The women we have seen thus far have been with rare exceptions, the mere echoes of men. Man has spoken in the State, the Church, and the Home, and made the codes, creeds, and customs which govern every relation in life, and women have simply walked in the paths he prescribed. And this they call womanly!"

Undaunted by the fact that she was addressing not only her National Association, but also the more critical and conservative members of the American, she touched on several of her favorite controversial subjects. She pleaded for equality for women in the Church, and that there be no further legislation on marriage and divorce until women had a voice in making the laws. She cared not whether this made members of the American cringe or not. These were facts that had to be faced.

Then she leveled her guns at the Women's Christian Temperance

Union. "As women," she continued, "are taking an active part in pressing on the consideration of Congress, many narrow sectarian measures, such as more rigid Sunday laws to stop travel and the distribution of mail on that day and to introduce the name of God in the Constitution—as this action on the part of some women is used as an argument for the disfranchisement of all, I hope this convention will declare that the Woman Suffrage Association is opposed to all union of Church and State and pledges itself so far as possible to maintain the secular nature of our Government."

She concluded with this appeal for free speech: "I think we should keep our platform as broad as Mrs. Gage and myself desire. It has always been broad. We have discussed upon it everything, and I suppose we always shall. At least I shall, and I suppose Miss Anthony will. My idea of that platform is that every woman shall have a perfect right there; that she and her wrongs shall be represented in our conventions. We do not want to limit our platform to bare suffrage and nothing more. We must demand equality everywhere in Church and State. Wherever a woman is wronged, her voice should be heard on our platform. We want all types and classes to come. We want all races as well as all creeds and no creeds, including the Mormon, Indian and black women...."

When she had finished, she proudly introduced her daughter, Harriot Stanton Blatch. Lucy Stone and Elizabeth Cady Stanton had each brought a capable daughter into the suffrage fold. Alice Stone Blackwell like Harriot Stanton Blatch gave every evidence of carrying on this beloved cause with the devotion and ability of the pioneers.

The retiring president of the American Association, William Dudley Foulke, then made a scholarly address, but it was theoretical and cold compared to Mrs. Stanton's vigorous speech, which so courageously brought out concrete facts that needed to be handled. After his address, she and Harriot were obliged to leave immediately for New York to catch their steamer for England, and as they left the platform the entire audience rose, and waving their handkerchiefs, gave their beloved president three farewell cheers.

XXIV

WRITING AND THINKING

ELIZABETH left for England with three very happy memories. Her election as president of the united suffrage organization was an honor and a satisfaction, an expression of confidence and gratitude from the majority of American suffragists. The Congressional hearings at which she had spoken were a great success in that they resulted in a majority report favoring an amendment to the Constitution granting woman suffrage. This was the first time such a victory had been won. She had also been the principal speaker at a dinner at the Riggs House to celebrate Susan's seventieth birthday. To the two hundred men and women assembled to pay tribute to Susan she had said: "If there is one part of my life that gives me more intense satisfaction than another, it is my friendship of forty years standing with Susan B. Anthony. Her heroism, her faithfulness and conscientious devotion to what she thinks is her duty, has been a constant stimulation to me to thought and action." Deeply moved, Miss Anthony had responded, "If I have ever had any inspiration, she has given it to me. I want you to understand that I never could have done the work I have if I had not had this woman at my right hand."

This last visit which Elizabeth had with Harriot in England in 1890 was a very happy one, watching Nora grow up. Theodore's daughter, Lizette, came from France, and the two children found a perfect companion in their Queen Mother, as they called her. She loved to tell them stories with little girls as heroines and they listened spellbound. No one else could tell such stories and no one understood little girls so well.

She spent a great deal of time writing provocative articles for the *Westminster Review*, the *Arena*, the *Forum*, and the *North American Review*. Almost every week she sent an installment of her "Reminiscences" to Mrs. Colby to be published in the *Woman's*

Tribune, which had now moved its office to Washington. Occasionally she made speeches for the English suffragists, visited in their homes, and met their interesting friends. A few days in London and an evening at the theater were a real treat. She wrote in her diary:

> How I do enjoy going to the theatre! But I am probably in my dotage, for I see few people on the shady side of seventy drinking in these worldly joys at the midnight hour especially in rainy, foggy London.

There were many visitors at the Blatch home in Basingstoke who came especially to see Elizabeth, among them Emmeline Pankhurst, Priscilla McLaren, Mrs. Jacob Bright, and Annie Besant.

Annie Besant was associated with Bradlaugh, fighting for free thought and Malthusianism, when Elizabeth first met her, and was being persecuted for advocating birth control as a solution for poverty and misery among the masses. Elizabeth had admired her courage and regarded her as the greatest woman in England. Now Annie Besant was deep in Theosophy—a disciple of Madame Blavatsky.

Always irresistibly attracted by a fellow explorer, Elizabeth listened at first with interest to Annie Besant's presentation of Theosophy.

Harriot remonstrated with her mother, questioning in this instance as in others whether she, as an accepted leader among women, was justified in marching up to a precipice to look into its depths when she herself never grew dizzy. A light-headed admirer, she warned, following her example might plunge over the edge to destruction. But Elizabeth with a laugh answered her troubled daughter, "How can I warn of the dangers of a seething caldron if I do not take even a peep in myself?"

Annie Besant and Elizabeth Cady Stanton stood out in sharp contrast. Elizabeth clung with every fiber to feminism and free thought. Annie Besant had deserted old loyalties and served just one master, Theosophy. Her emotions revolved around a philosophy; Elizabeth's were centered on human beings. Elizabeth argued that Fabianism could do more for humanity than Theosophy;

Annie Besant could see nothing but Theosophy as the solution of every problem.

But in spite of her disappointment in this interesting woman, Elizabeth still regarded her as the greatest woman in England.

At this time the O'Shea divorce suit, involving Charles Stewart Parnell, was causing a great stir in English society. Such a determined drive was made to force Parnell to retire and such intolerance was manifested that Elizabeth could not keep silent. She sent off an article to the *Westminster Review* called "Patriotism and Chastity" in which she spoke her mind freely. It too caused a stir not only in England but among the suffragists in America.

Of her English critics, she wrote:

> The little set of Social Purity people who are down on my *Westminster* article, do not choose to understand it. I simply state facts when I say that men are not educated to consider chastity an imperative virtue for them, and that they are educated to practice patriotism; hence they may fulfill the duties of one virtue without fulfilling those of the other. There have been statesmen, soldiers, poets, scientists, philosophers, and even clergymen who were not chaste according to the standard of the nineteenth century. I do not apologize for Parnell, I only show how our civil and canon law, Blackstone and the Bible, educate men. The sole remedy for our present chaos is the mental development and the political emancipation of the great factor in social life, namely, woman. The papers that represent me as an apologist for immorality, do so willfully; no such conclusion can be fairly drawn from my words.

Frances Willard took up the cudgels for morality in the National American Woman Suffrage Convention. Regarding this, Elizabeth wrote to Mrs. Colby, whom she now felt was one of her most understanding friends:

> How is it that not one word of the convention reaches this side, except sixteen lines of Miss Willard's opening speech condemning Parnell? Is it Miss Willard's policy to make people think this side of the ocean that that great convention of women endorsed her silly view of that case? Is the Irish cause nearer her heart than it was to Parnell's? By the way, you remember she presented a resolution at the International Council to make us all endorse her temperance policy. But I defeated it on the spot. Miss Anthony did not see the drift of the resolution and let it pass. Frances Willard needs watching. She is a politician.

When the news reached her that Wyoming had been admitted into the Union as a woman suffrage state, the very first, she wrote in her diary:

> I cannot express the joy that this victory has brought to my soul. This triumph is enough for one year. The last number of the *Westminster Review* contains an article by me, my formal rejoicing on the subject. This paper has served me in several ways. First as a tract which has been scattered throughout Dakota; secondly as a speech at two meetings over here.

She did not fail to send a speech to be read or a letter to each important suffrage meeting in the United States. To Lucy Stone for the commemoration of the first National Woman Suffrage Convention held in Worcester, Massachusetts, in 1850, she sent a plea for militancy:

> I cannot say that my heart is overflowing with gratitude when I consider the prolonged struggle we have made, the petitions we have rolled up, the appeals written, the conventions held, the legislatures besieged, the ecclesiastical councils invaded, the hand to hand fight. They tell us to be patient, persuasive, unaggressive, and work along the same lines for perchance, forty years longer!... To talk to us today after years of persistent effort, of patience, philosophy, and gratitude for privileges conceded to us is down right mockery.... Never was there a class battling for their rights thrown so wholly on their own resources or counseled to such suicidal measures. While in fighting their own battles, men use their sharpest weapons and most pungent language, and attack the enemy at every turn, no one regards our demands as requiring prompt action. Our best friends seem to regard our reform as kind of a sentimental question to be referred to the limbo of romance, of no greater importance than who wrote Junius or whether Bacon wrote Shakespeare.

She had been reading for six months to collect data for a paper for the National Council of Women on the matriarchate, and was most enthusiastic. She wrote in her diary:

> I am amazed to find how much more we are indebted to woman than to man for not only the intelligence and morality of the race, but for many of the greatest steps in material progress. Two things are strikingly evident—that woman has not always been the slave of man, nor has she always been his inferior in physical strength. In early savagery he looked out for himself alone, while she looked out for herself and her children. ... Maternity was the source and center of all

the first steps in civilization. Because of the variety of things she was forced to do, woman necessarily cultivated many faculties; hence she was better developed physically than the man by her side; and forced to provide for others, her moral sentiments were roused long before his were.

When she sent her paper, "The Matriarchate, or the Mother Age," to Susan and with it one from Harriot on "Voluntary Motherhood," she wrote Mrs. Colby:

> I fear my beloved Susan will not appreciate either, as the word suffrage does not come in. But they are alike valuable documents.... I hope you and Miss Anthony will get up some decent resolutions this time and not publish such trash as you did last year. I will try to grind out some resolutions; but do not let it be known that they are mine.

Susan was better satisfied with the address she wrote in 1891 for the convention of the National American Suffrage Association, "The Degradation of Disfranchisement." But at all these gatherings she read everything that Elizabeth sent, with reverence and pride.

Elizabeth returned to New York in August 1891 to a still smaller family circle. Daniel, her oldest son, her sister, Tryphena, and Margaret's husband had passed away. Margaret had come to New York from the West where she had been living and was taking a course in physical training with a view to teaching. Subsequently she was appointed Director of Physical Training at Teachers College, Columbia University. Elizabeth had sold her house at Tenafly, and now had no home to go to. With Margaret and her youngest son, Robert, she rented an eight-room apartment at 26 East Sixty-first Street. This was a great disappointment to Susan, who had settled down with her sister, Mary, in the old family home in Rochester, and had hoped that Elizabeth would live with them and that together they might finish up the writing that she thought ought to be done. She wrote Elizabeth:

> We have just returned from the Unitarian Church where we listened to Mr. Gannett's rare dissertation on the religion of Lowell; but all the time there was an inner wail in my soul, that by your fastening yourself in New York City I couldn't help you carry out the dream of my life—which is that you should take all of your

speeches and articles, carefully dissect them, and put your best utterances on each point into one essay or lecture; first deliver them in the Unitarian Church on Sunday afternoon, and then publish in a nice volume, just as Phillips culled out his best. Your *Reminiscences* give only light and incidental bits of your life—all good but not the greatest of yourself. This is the first time since 1850 that I have anchored myself to any particular spot, and in doing it my constant thought was that you would come here, where are the documents necessary to our work, and stay for as long, at least, as we must be together to put your writings into systematic shape to go down to posterity. I have no writings to go down, so my ambition is not for myself, but it is for one by the side of whom I have wrought these forty years, and to get whose speeches before audiences and committees has been the delight of my life. Well, I hope you will do and be as seemeth best unto yourself, still I cannot help sending you this inner groan of my soul, lest you are not going to make it possible that the thing shall be done first which seems most important to me. Then, too, I have never ceased to hope that we could finish the *History of Woman Suffrage* at least to the end of the life of the dear old National.

Elizabeth's children would not consent to this plan. However, in September, she left for a month's visit with Susan. The time was not to be spent in writing, however, but in sitting for a talented young sculptor, Adelaide Johnson, who had already made busts of Susan and Lucretia Mott for the World's Fair.

Those were happy, homey days in Rochester with Susan, with opportunities to talk and laugh with an all-satisfying companion. Prominent suffragists always stopped over in Rochester to confer with Susan, and there was a visit with Elizabeth Smith Miller in Geneva, and with Martha Wright's daughter, Eliza Wright Osborne in Auburn. The visits to Geneva and Auburn were repeated through the years. Often Anna Howard Shaw and other younger suffragists joined them and listened with delight to the conversation of the pioneers. Anna Howard Shaw said of these visits:

> Mrs. Stanton was the most brilliant conversationalist I have ever known and the best talk I ever heard anywhere was that to which I used to listen in the home of Mrs. Eliza Wright Osborne in Auburn, New York, when Mrs. Stanton, Susan B. Anthony, Emily Howland, Elizabeth Smith Miller, Ida Husted Harper, Miss Mills, and I were gathered there for our occasional week-end visits. . . . Most of the conversation . . . was contributed by Mrs. Stanton and Miss Anthony,

while the rest of us, as it were, sat at their feet. . . . Mrs. Stanton, for example, was rarely accurate in giving figures and dates, while Miss Anthony was always very exact in such matters She frequently corrected Mrs. Stanton's statements, and Mrs. Stanton usually took the interruption in the best possible spirit, promptly admitting that "Aunt Susan" knew best.

When the National American Woman Suffrage Association convened in Washington in January 1892, Elizabeth, then seventy-seven years old was determined to retire as president, and asked that Susan be elected to take her place. Lucy Stone also wished to be relieved of her duties as chairman of the executive committee. The result was that Susan was elected president, Elizabeth and Lucy were made honorary presidents, and Anna Howard Shaw took Susan's place as vice-president-at-large, and from that time on was her able and dependable assistant. When Elizabeth, Susan, and Lucy, the three pioneers, appeared on the platform the first evening of the convention, they were greeted by a storm of applause. It was the last convention that Lucy and Elizabeth attended. Lucy passed away the next year, and Elizabeth quietly retired from active work in the suffrage cause.

The speech which Elizabeth delivered at this convention, and before the House and Senate Judiciary Committees made a tremendous impression. "The Solitude of Self" was not the usual argument for woman suffrage Original, philosophical, basic, it was the culmination of all the pleas that she had made before Congressional committees for the past twenty years. "The point I wish plainly to bring before you on this occasion," she said, "is the individuality of each human soul; our Protestant idea, the right of individual conscience and judgment—our republican idea, individual citizenship. In discussing the rights of woman, we are to consider, first, what belongs to her as an individual, in a world of her own, the arbiter of her own destiny. . . . Secondly, if we consider her as a citizen, as a member of a great nation, she must have the same rights as all other members, according to the fundamental principles of our Government. Thirdly, viewed as a woman, an equal factor in civilization, her rights and duties are still the same—individual happiness and development. Fourthly, it is only the incidental relations of life, such as mother, wife, sister, daughter, that may involve some special duties and training. . . . In discussing the sphere of men we do not decide his rights as an individual, as a citizen, as a man, by his duties as a father, husband, brother or son, relations some of which he may never fill. Moreover, he would be better fitted for these very relations, and whatever special work he might choose to do to earn his bread, by the complete development of all his faculties as an individual. Just so with woman. . . ."

She closed her masterful address with this searching question, "Who, I ask you, can take, dare take, on himself, the rights, the duties, the responsibilities of another human soul?"

The Senate Committee made a favorable majority report. The House Committee were so impressed by her speech that they had 10,000 copies reprinted from the Congressional Record and sent throughout the country. On a copy which Susan presented to Elizabeth, she wrote, "To Elizabeth Cady Stanton—This is pronounced the strongest and most unanswerable argument and appeal ever made by mortal pen or tongue for the full freedom and franchise of women."

Anna Howard Shaw said: "It is one of the finest pieces of literature in our language. It is an English classic."

Although Elizabeth had severed her connections officially with the National American Woman Suffrage Association, her mind and her pen were still busy for her beloved Susan. In July she confided to her diary:

> Susan is still on the war-path. All through this hot weather she has been following the political conventions. I wrote the addresses to all, and she read them all and signed them as President of the Woman Suffrage Association. By resigning that office, I hoped to have done with all "State Papers." But I am at it still.

For meetings to be held during the World's Fair in Chicago in 1893, she wrote five addresses for Susan to read. She felt she could not undertake the journey, nor endure the heat and the crowds. At Susan's instigation and under the leadership of Bertha Honoré Palmer of Chicago, women were playing an important part in the World's Fair. The outstanding event for them was the World's

Congress of Representative Women for which Elizabeth wrote "The Antagonism of Sex." For the Congress of Religions she wrote "The Worship of God in Man," and at the earnest request of Mrs. Russell Sage she prepared an address for the meeting of the Emma Willard Association in Chicago, "Emma Willard, The Pioneer in the Higher Education of Woman." They were all sympathetically delivered by Susan.

For some time previous to the opening of the World's Fair, she was busy combating the religious zealots who insisted that the Fair be closed on Sunday. In an article in the *North American Review* entitled "Opening the Chicago Exposition on Sunday" she began her campaign and continued it in other newspapers and magazines. She had 10,000 leaflets printed and scattered broadcast. Her main point was that working people had no other day in which to see the Fair and that they, more than anyone else, needed its educational advantages and inspiration. She wrote:

> All great national celebrations in a republic should be arranged for the benefit of those who do the paid work of the world and most need the inspiration and enlightenment of all that is beautiful in nature and wonderful in art.

In 1894, New York State held a Constitutional Convention and she and Susan, as in 1867, prepared for the event, urging once again that the word "male" be struck out of Article 2 Section 1 of the constitution. Together they planned a campaign and drafted resolutions which were printed as leaflets. Unlike 1867 they were supported by a strong organization of women. Even society was endorsing woman suffrage, and large meetings were held at Sherry's and Delmonico's. All over the state women were busy holding meetings, distributing literature, and circulating petitions. Elizabeth spoke frequently in New York City and sent many forceful articles to the newspapers. In the midst of the campaign Harriot arrived from England, and as her mother had had a bad fall and was doubtful of attending the mass meeting at Cooper Union, she took her place on the program. But Elizabeth was there on the platform, listening with pride to Harriot's eloquent speech. When Harriot had finished, Elizabeth rose, walked to the front of the platform, and leaned on the reading desk for support until the deafening cheers and hand clapping ceased. Then in a clear voice which could be heard throughout the hall, she said she was more convinced than ever that a person could not represent another no matter how good his intentions were. She spoke for forty-five minutes, rousing enthusiasm like that at the famous Cooper Union meetings of anti-slavery days. Frank Carpenter, the portrait painter, was so impressed by the meeting that he wished to paint a picture of it with Mrs. Stanton as the central figure.

Like the Constitutional Convention of 1867, that of 1894 also ignored the demands of women. Commenting on this defeat, Elizabeth wrote Mrs. Colby:

> Well, you see, we were defeated in the convention. The point made by our opponents is that a majority of women do not ask for the vote. What step in progress was ever asked for by a majority? If in 1776, we had waited for a majority to assert our national independence, we should still be under the British yoke. If Luther had waited for the majority to protest against the tyranny of the Church, we should all be subjects of the Pope today. Luther's coadjutors were few indeed. Jesus had fewer still. The grand principles of human brotherhood he annunciated two thousand years ago are not accepted throughout the globe by a majority. Why should the indifference of the majority of women handicap the intelligent minority? Alas, how little logic men use in their reason! I am heart-sick and disappointed that half a century of education on this question has not at least aroused women to their public interests and duties.

"This is Stanton Day in New York," read an editorial in the *New York Sun* on November 12, 1895, Elizabeth Cady Stanton's eightieth birthday. Even the antisuffrage paper, the *Boston Herald,* commented editorially, "Congratulations on Elizabeth Cady Stanton's beautiful white head and to its owner at eighty."

In all parts of the country men and women gathered on November 12 to honor her. In New York an audience of 6000 filled the Metropolitan Opera House. Representatives from women's organizations occupied the boxes and balconies, which were elaborately decorated with their colors and emblems. On the stage against a background of white chrysanthemums in which Stanton was written in red carnations, Elizabeth sat in a high-backed red plush chair festooned with roses. In her long black satin gown with rare old lace at the neck and wrists, with her glorious white hair fluffed about her face, her cheeks rosy as in her youth and her blue eyes glowing, she made a never-to-be-forgotten picture. On either side of her in the center of the stage sat Susan and Mary Lowe Dickinson, President of the National Council of Women, and all about her were her coworkers and members of her family. The event of the evening was her speech, and as she walked to the front of the stage leaning on her cane, the audience rose and a roar of applause burst forth. As she looked out over this vast audience, she trembled with emotion. Again and again she had faced such audiences with a message of freedom for women, but tonight was more personal. It was a tribute to her—such a tribute as she had never imagined possible.

"I thank you all very much," she began, "for the tributes of love, respect, and gratitude which have been sent to me in telegrams, and letters, and expressed in the presence of this great audience.... I am well aware that all these public demonstrations are not so much tributes to me as an individual as to the great idea I represent—the enfranchisement of women...."

Then she added, "As I am not able to stand very long, nor to talk loud enough, I have invited Miss Helen Potter to read what I have to say to you." Miss Potter delivered Elizabeth's message forcefully and sympathetically but no one could adequately fill her place.

While Elizabeth was writing her speech, she had realized that this was probably the last time she would speak to such a large representative group of people and that she must leave with them something constructive, something to think about, truths that would free women. She decided to emphasize two points, woman's sphere and woman's bondage under theological dogma. The first she summed up in these words, "The spheres of man and woman are the same, with different duties according to the capacity of the individual." The second she dealt with specifically. "We must demand an equal place in the offices of the Church," she declared, "as pastors, elders, deacons; an equal voice in the creeds, discipline, and all business matters in synods, conferences, and general assemblies. ... Women must demand that all unworthy reflections on the dignity and sacred office of the mother of the race be expunged from religious literature, such as the allegory as to the creation of woman, and Paul's assumptions as to her social status. These ideas conflict with the Golden Rule and the fifth commandment, 'Honor thy mother,' and should no longer be rehearsed in the pulpit."

Having delivered this message, she was content, although Susan, when she read over the speech previous to its public delivery, had questioned her singling out the Church, for Susan believed that the Church had advanced as rapidly as other fields. Here they continued to differ, for Elizabeth was convinced that she was pointing the way to women as she had in 1848 when in the face of the protests of her most liberal friends she had proposed woman suffrage. Then she had been ridiculed and denounced, but now conventions demanding woman suffrage were held every year; school suffrage had been granted to women in half of the states, municipal suffrage in Kansas, and full suffrage in three states, Wyoming, Utah, and Colorado. Some day, she was sure, her attack on the Church would be equally appreciated.

XXV

"THE WOMAN'S BIBLE"

ELIZABETH was not allowed to bask for long in the praise and adulation of her birthday celebration. A storm of ridicule and abuse burst forth when, later in November 1895, she published Volume I of *The Woman's Bible.*

She had begun work on *The Woman's Bible* in England in 1887. It was her object to make women question the theological doctrines, so derogatory to them, which had been evolved by the clergy in past ages and were still being preached from the pulpit. That women could go to church and listen docilely to sermons on texts which declared they were inferior beings and the cause of man's downfall was incomprehensible to her. This was possible only because women had been taught and still believed implicitly that the Bible was the direct word of God. It was time, she felt, that women themselves sift the matter to the bottom, find out what the Bible actually said about them, and test its validity in the light of nineteenth-century knowledge.

Therefore she proposed that a committee of competent women, among them Latin, Greek, and Hebrew scholars, make a thorough revision of the Bible and ascertain what woman's status really was under the Hebrew and Christian religions. Commentaries on and revised versions of the Bible were being issued by men scholars. It was only fitting that women should advance their own findings on the book that heretofore had always been interpreted for them.

She had talked the matter over with Harriot, with Frances Lord, with Clara Colby and Matilda Joslyn Gage. All were heartily in favor. She wrote to a picked list of women explaining her plan, asking their co-operation. Many were interested but few were willing to share in the work. A larger group, however, considered any revision of the Bible a sacrilege and entreated her to refrain from doing anything which would weaken the faith of the people.

What was hardest to bear was Susan's lack of interest in this subject which seemed of such tremendous importance. Susan wrote that she thought *The Woman's Bible* a work of supererogation, that when women's political equality was recognized the Church would hasten to bring her Bibles, prayer books, creeds, and discipline up to the same high water mark of liberty. Religion presented no problem to Susan. Brought up as a liberal Quaker, she had little to unlearn when she began to test her religious beliefs with her intelligence. Her church more than any other accorded women equal rights, an opportunity to preach, and a voice in the government. The shadow of theological dogma had not fallen across her life. There had been no struggle, no rebellion in her religious development. Elizabeth, on the other hand, knew how orthodox theology could blight one's life. She remembered how she had struggled to free herself. She understood well how women were kept subservient through fear and superstition and longed to enlighten them and free them as she had been freed.

So here she went counter to Susan's judgment. She bought some cheap Bibles, cut out the parts referring to women, pasted them on blank pages, and underneath wrote her commentaries as clearly and concisely as possible. Clara Colby published them in the *Woman's Tribune*. She explained Elizabeth's purpose in her paper, asked women to co-operate, and gave minute instructions to those wishing to take part in this work. In fact she was Elizabeth's mainstay during this period, and Elizabeth wrote her frankly of her hopes, of her ups and downs, and her disappointment in Susan's attitude.

So useful, so imperative did work along this line seem to her that Susan's indifference rankled more and more. "Miss Anthony," she confided to Mrs. Colby, "has one idea and she has no patience with anyone who has two. I cannot sit on the door just like Poe's raven, and sing suffrage evermore. I am deeply interested in all the live questions of the day."

As time went on she saw that the burden of compiling *The Woman's Bible* would rest wholly on her shoulders. Those who she hoped would help her put off the work. Many who were willing were incapable. She herself was no scholar of Greek, Hebrew, or Latin, but she made a thorough study of English commentaries and the higher criticism. The prospect of completing the book un-aided was so overpowering that again and again she thought she must give it up.

In one of these moods of abandoning the project, she wrote Mrs. Colby:

> My life has been a busy one with all my family cares and the suffrage movement, and now I want to give my time to general reading and thinking, to music, poetry, and novels. I cannot work in the old ruts any longer. I have said all I have to say on the subject of suffrage. As to the Bible, I thought the moral effect of a committee of women revising the Scriptures would be very great. But I could not get together a committee of leading English and American women. For me, as an individual to do this revising would not have the same effect nor be so dignified. So now I prefer to use my eyes for more pleasant occupations. There is such a thing as being too active, living too outward a life. Most reformers fail at this point. I cannot find an article on meditation which I intended to send you. But the gist of it was that, in order to develop our real selves, we need time to be alone for thought. To be always giving out and never pumping in, the well runs dry too soon.

But so convinced was Elizabeth that she must rouse women out of their theological bondage that she kept at work in spite of ob-stacles and discouragement. Mrs. Colby proved to be a great help. She contributed many comments on the Scriptures, wrote editorials in her paper in praise of the undertaking, and reprinted the opinions of the clergy and the press. Lillie Devereux Blake, a popular au-thor, who for eleven years had been president of the New York State Woman Suffrage Association and now was president of the New York City Woman Suffrage League, wrote some of the com-mentaries. Other contributors whose names also appeared on the title page were the Reverend Phebe Hanaford, Ellen Battelle Diet-rich, Ursala Gestafield, Louisa Southworth, and Frances Ellen Burr. But the major part of the work was Elizabeth's.

In the excellent introduction explaining the purpose of *The Woman's Bible,* Elizabeth wrote:

> The canon and civil law, church and state, priests and legislators, all political parties and religious denominations have alike taught

that woman was made after man, of man, and for man, an inferior being, subject to man. Creeds, codes, Scriptures, and statutes are all based on this idea. The fashions, forms, ceremonies and customs of society, church ordinances and discipline all grow out of this idea.

Such a doctrine, she believed, was not in harmony with our ideal first great Cause, "the spirit of all good."

Woman's religious sense, she continued, has been so perverted that she has been the chief support of the Church and clergy "the very powers that make her emancipation impossible." To free her from this man-made fallacy, to examine the Bible as regards the position of women in the light of reason and common sense is the object of *The Woman's Bible*.

She explained carefully that she was not irreligious, that she differed from ecclesiastical teaching only on a few points. She did not believe any man had ever seen or talked with God, that God had inspired the Mosaic code, or that He had told historians what they said He did about women. She objected seriously to the phrase, "Thus saith the Lord," which men had so smugly taken unto themselves to bolster up their own theories. She acknowledged that there are "many grand and beautiful passages" in the Bible and "many lofty examples of good and true men and women, all worthy of our acceptance and imitation."

Her comments on the Bible were intelligent and keen, sarcastic, biting, and humorous. She did not sugar-coat them with reverence. Only the brutal, naked truth she felt would startle women out of their sanctimonious attitude toward the Bible and the Church. Occasionally her collaborators had suggested that she approach the subject more reverently, but she did not, and they tried to make up for her lack of it. The more that she read and studied the Bible the more she was impressed with the absurdity of regarding it as anything but the legend and history of a people searching for God.

The well-known stories of creation, of Cain and Abel, Abraham, Sarah, and Hagar, of Isaac and Rebecca, Jacob and Rachel, Moses, Miriam, Deborah, Hilda, and Vashti were all examined critically and held up to the light. The first account of creation in the first chapter of Genesis, she used as a working principle for analysis:

So God created man in his own image, in the image of God created he him; male and female created he them. [Genesis 1:27]

She commented:

If language has any meaning, we have in these texts a plain declaration of the existence of the feminine element in the Godhead, equal in power and glory with the masculine. The Heavenly Mother and Father. . . . The first step in the elevation of woman to her true position, as an equal factor in human progress, is the cultivation of the religious sentiment in regard to her dignity and equality, the recognition by the rising generation of an ideal Heavenly Mother, to whom their prayers should be addressed, as well as to a Father.

The idea of a Father-Mother God was not original with her. She had heard both William Henry Channing and Theodore Parker use it. Mary Baker Eddy had made it one of the basic teachings of Christian Science. Elizabeth Cady Stanton used it as the unanswerable argument for woman's equality with man, discrediting that old theological stumbling block, the fable of Adam and Eve.

To a generation brought up to believe that the Bible was the direct word of God and must not be questioned, *The Woman's Bible* was the work of Satan. To be sure the Bible had been questioned in this way before. The French Revolution and the works of Thomas Paine had inaugurated an era of doubt. The discoveries of science and Darwin's theory of evolution had upset many preconceived ideas. But never before had such an appeal to reason been made to the more docile Church members—to women, the backbone of the Church. It was greeted with dismay.

New York newspapers give it thorough reviews, and papers throughout the country and England commented freely. Only a few dared to praise, for an army of virtuous womanhood which would not countenance any deviation from orthodoxy or a strict moral code had become articulate and were a power to be reckoned with. This guardian of the nation's morals threatened editors and made them watchful.

The *New York Sun* commented editorially: "We have read some of the passages of the commentary prepared for *The Woman's Bible* by that very accomplished American woman and Biblical student, Elizabeth Cady Stanton. They are a great deal more satisfactory than many of the comments upon the same texts that we have read in other and more pretentious commentaries. Mrs. Stanton's interpretive remarks are shrewd and sensible."

"Robert Ingersoll," said the *Chicago Times-Herald*, "is the only person on earth capable of a work equal to Mrs. Stanton's sensation, *The Woman's Bible.*"

"The attack of the new woman on the King James Bible," said the *Chicago Post*, "will be observed with interest where it does not alarm. But let *The Woman's Bible* and the truth prevail."

The title was widely criticized because it gave the impression that the good old Bible of the Fathers was being given up by feminists for a wholly inadequate substitute. Even Elizabeth's collaborators had frequently suggested that it be changed. But she fought for it and meant to keep it. She wrote Mrs. Colby:

> The *Woman's Bible* is the most happy title that I could have selected. I am sure of that. *Women's Commentaries on what the Bible says of Woman* would have been too lumbering. When John Stuart Mill gave his little book the title of *The Subjection of Women* everybody carped at it. Men said it made them appear like tyrants and suggested to women that they were victims. They did not like to be published as such. Mill, on his side, said he knew he had hit the right title because everybody had criticized it. I am sure, for the same reason, that our title is the true one.

Clergymen preached sermons against *The Woman's Bible*. Church book concerns refused to handle it, regarding it as a travesty on the Scriptures. Trustees of libraries announced that it would be kept on their shelves for reference only and would not be allowed to circulate. Occasionally a clergyman was open-minded enough to understand what *The Woman's Bible* actually was—not an attack on religion, but on false teachings about women. Such a man was the Reverend Alexander Kent of Washington, D. C. He thought the title unfortunate, as it needlessly offended many, but he welcomed the book, believing that intelligent women should deal with the whole Bible as Jesus did with the Scriptures of his time. In his judgment the book contained more common sense and was more in accordance with the teachings of Jesus than any other commentary dealing with the same passages. Of all the col-

laborators of *The Woman's Bible* he found Mrs. Stanton the least
reverent and tolerant, but he regarded her as the best critic, the
most logical and consistent.

Reading of his sermon, Elizabeth wrote in her diary:

> A Washington clergyman, named Kent, has been preaching a
> sermon on *The Woman's Bible*. It is admirable. I was filled with
> surprise and gratitude as I read line by line, so fair, so clear, and so
> appreciative.

Praise was very sweet in the midst of the barrage of criticism.

A delegation of Jewish women called on her to protest against
The Woman's Bible, maintaining that their religion exalted women
as wives and mothers. In answer, she asked them why, if this were
so, one heard, in the synagogue service every week, men chanting
"I thank thee, O Lord, that I was not born a woman." This, they
insisted, was not meant in an unfriendly spirit or to degrade or
humiliate women. "But it does, nevertheless," she declared. "Suppose the service read, 'I thank thee, O Lord, that I was not born
a jackass.' Could that be twisted in any way into a compliment
to the jackass? Oh no, ladies, the Jews accord us women no more
honor than do the Gentiles."

The Woman's Bible of course caused a furor in the W.C.T.U.
and in woman suffrage ranks. There had been protests while extracts were being published in the *Woman's Tribune*. Frances Willard and her coworkers were up in arms. Correspondence ensued
which ended with this conciliatory letter from Miss Willard:

> We have taken your advice and "dropped the subject." You have
> shown us your large heartedness in appreciating the difficulty of our
> position, and we have never mentioned you except in terms of reverence and affection, but as we certainly do differ on the question of
> the Bible, it is better that we do not try to work together on that
> one subject. Miss Greenwood wrote me that she thought everything
> was now satisfactory between us, and we are rejoiced to think so.
> Believe me, dear friend, it has been Lady Henry's purpose and mine
> from the first to manifest to all concerned the affection and regard
> we feel for you as a mighty pioneer in the work of uplift for one
> half the human race.

Carrie Chapman Catt, a young suffragist from Iowa who had become one of Susan's able organizers, wrote Elizabeth frankly before the book was published:

I find every one seems to have a misconception about it. Some think the women are to write an entirely new Bible, giving their own revelations; others think women are going to put forth a new translation of the holy book, while still others announce that agnostics are banding together to ridicule the Scriptures. For the moment, the affair is doing us great harm. Some persons who had agreed to give money to suffrage now refuse on the ground that they cannot support an association whose aim is to break down the Bible, while others threaten to resign. I must confess that I am somewhat alarmed at the outlook. Some women who are known to be thoroughly orthodox and whose names carry weight should also comment and their comments should appear with those of yourself and friends. That would remove the present difficulty and straighten out the whole trouble. I see no harm in discussing this Bible question or in the anger of clergymen, but I do fear a malicious press using the wrong conception of the plan. I fear the bad effect of this....

This was the feeling of all of the more conservative members of the National American Woman Suffrage Association. With the publication of the book and the wide publicity given it by the clergy and the press, their opposition grew. Those closest to Susan in the work, Rachel Foster Avery and Anna Howard Shaw, as well as Carrie Chapman Catt, heartily disapproved. Henry Blackwell and Alice Stone Blackwell had always resented what they had considered Mrs. Stanton's introduction of extraneous subjects into the suffrage movement. Trouble was brewing. The book was bound to be discussed at the next convention. Elizabeth wrote Mrs. Colby just prior to the convention in January 1896:

Do your best not to allow the association as such to take any action on *The Woman's Bible*. It would be a great pity for the only liberal association of women we have to cater to the religious bigotry of the age.... A resolution denouncing *The Woman's Bible* with Susan B. Anthony in the chair, would be a stain on Susan's honesty that would never be forgotten. Everyone who knows her knows that she is at heart as liberal as I am and that any action looking in the other direction is simply policy. If I were Susan, I would resign rather than endorse any such proceeding. I have just written her a strong letter. ...I trust Susan after fifty years of education will be able to stand

firmly for religious equality. . . . Make the speech of your life in favor
of religious freedom.

There was no reason why the National American Suffrage Association should pay any attention to or take any action on *The Woman's
Bible*. Mrs. Stanton had compiled it as an individual and it had
no connection whatever with the Association. She was no longer
an active member and had not attended a convention since 1892. A
group, however, led by Rachel Foster Avery, were so obsessed with
the idea that *The Woman's Bible* was ruining the suffrage movement that they made up their minds to repudiate it in the convention. In her report as corresponding secretary, Rachel Foster
Avery read a paragraph condemning the book. Susan was aghast.
Mrs. Colby, alert to the situation, managed after a spirited discussion, to have the paragraph deleted, but her opponents were
determined, and later offered the following resolution:

> This association is non-sectarian, being composed of persons of all
> shades of religious opinions, and has no official connection with the
> so-called Woman's Bible, or any theological publication.

For an hour the resolution was hotly debated. Susan was presiding.
She listened in real anguish of soul to the attacks on her beloved
"Mrs. Stanton" by the most trusted and active members of the
movement. How could these young, self-righteous workers presume
to attack the mother of the woman suffrage movement! She sensed
with alarm the narrowness and intolerance which had developed
in the movement. Clara Colby, Lillie Devereux Blake, Charlotte
Perkins Stetson, and Mary Anthony, among others, were fighting
the resolution. Susan, leaving the chair, entered her plea against it:

> The one distinct feature of our Association has been the right of
> individual opinion for every member. We have been beset at every
> step with the cry that somebody was injuring the cause. . . . All the
> way down the history of our movement there has been the same
> contest on account of religious belief. Just forty years ago one of the
> most beautiful-spirited men on our platform said, "You had better
> never hold another convention than let Ernestine L. Rose stand on
> your platform," because that Polish woman who always stood for
> justice and freedom did not believe in the verbal inspiration of the
> Bible. Did we banish Mrs. Rose? Now a lot of new people come up

and go over the same old ground. The question is whether you will sit in judgment on a woman that has written views different from yours. If she had written your views you would not object. There was a person once, in the early days, who wanted us to pass a resolution that we were not free lovers, and I was not more shocked then than I am today at this. It looks like the reviving of the old censorship. We have been growing larger and broader and I thought we had got away from this. When Lucy Stone did not take the name of her husband, many claimed it injured the cause and Olympia Brown said once, she had to spend much of her time in explaining that she was legally married. Suppose we had passed resolutions against a woman not taking her husband's name. Thank God! we had strength not to do it. To pass such a resolution is to set back the hands on the dial of reform. I would say to the organizers, tell them we have all sorts of people in the Association and that a Christian has no more right on our platform than an atheist. When this platform is too narrow for all to stand on, I shall not be on it. I have endured many things in the convention that I thought would harm the cause. Who is to set up a line? Neither you nor I can tell but Mrs. Stanton will come out triumphant and that this will be the greatest thing ever done in woman's cause. Lucretia Mott at first thought Mrs. Stanton had injured the cause of woman's rights by insisting on the demand for woman suffrage, but she had sense enough not to pass a resolution about it. When in 1860 Mrs. Stanton made a speech before the committee in favor of a bill making drunkenness a cause for divorce, many people thought she had killed our cause. Just think of it. You ought to be able, girls, to stand this and go on with your work and say this has nothing to do with Mrs. Stanton's views on the Bible. I should be pained beyond expression if we are not broad enough to drop this. We need not mind what the newspapers say about it. They are only talking to say something, and not because they care about the Bible. I have yet to see the first editorial word from an honest soul that takes the position that the Bible was directly inspired. You might just as well give up resolving or your hands will be full. Are you going to cater to the whims and prejudices of people that don't like this or that? The two women that stood by Lucy Stone in keeping her own name were Mrs. Stanton and myself. Who are these people who are troubled about this? They are people that have not thought. If you fail to teach women a broad Catholic spirit, I would not give much for them after they are enfranchised. If they are going to do without thinking, they had better do without voting. They are not yet indoctrinated in the broad principles of this Association that knows no creed line. We draw out from other people our own thought. If when you go out to organize, you go with a broad spirit you will create and call out breadth and toleration. You had better organize one woman on a broad platform than 10,000 on a narrow platform of intolerance and bigotry....

She warned in conclusion:

This resolution adopted will be a vote of censure upon a woman who is without a peer in intellectual and statesmanlike ability; one who has stood for half a century the acknowledged leader of progressive thought and demand in regard to all matters pertaining to the absolute freedom of woman.

But even Susan's impassioned appeal did not save the day. The resolution was passed 53 to 41.

It was a bitter disappointment. Her own organization, which she had always been able to guide, refused to heed her warning. Her dearest, most respected friend had been publicly censured by the organization which should always honor her. But worse even than that was the precedent established. The young workers, feeling their power, were rushing headlong down the wrong road. Could she save them from their folly?

At first she thought she must resign. Elizabeth insisted that they both resign, for she was hurt and indignant. But Susan could not leave her Association. She must make one more effort to guide it aright. She wrote Elizabeth:

During three weeks of agony of soul, with scarcely a night of sleep, I have felt I must resign my presidency, but then the rights of the minority are to be respected and protected by me quite as much as the action of the majority is to be resented; and it is even more my duty to stand firmly with the minority because principle is well there.... No my dear, instead of my resigning and leaving those half-fledged chickens without any mother, I think it my duty, and the duty of yourself and all the liberals to be at the next convention and try to reverse this miserable narrow action.

Although Elizabeth appreciated Susan's earnest defense of her at the convention, she knew that Susan at heart did not approve of the time she spent on *The Woman's Bible*. She knew Susan had made this plain to Anna Howard Shaw, Rachel Foster Avery, and Carrie Chapman Catt long before the resolution had been contemplated, and so in a small measure she blamed Susan for the state of thought which produced the resolution. It was hard to forgive Susan for not coming wholly over to her side. She knew that

Susan's new friends were bringing pressure to bear to make her impatient with *The Woman's Bible*. She recognized, when she stopped to think about it, the efforts of the liberals to make her impatient with Susan's continual harping on suffrage. All through the years people had tried to make trouble between her and Susan, but they had always understood each other so well and trusted each other so implicitly that even the most subtle machinations were unavailing. Both were frank and outspoken, and occasionally in moments of impatience said severe things about each other, but as Elizabeth often remarked: "We have said worse things to each other face to face, than we have ever said about each other. Nothing Susan could say or do could break my friendship with her, and I know nothing could uproot her affection for me."

Therefore even at this time when feelings ran high, their friendship was able to weather the storm. But for work nearest her heart —woman suffrage—Susan turned more and more to Anna Howard Shaw for the support Elizabeth had given her in the past, while Elizabeth turned to Clara Colby and Lillie Devereux Blake for sympathy and understanding in her campaign for religious freedom for women.

In the summer of 1896, Susan went to California to take part in the strenuous campaign for an amendment to the state constitution, enfranchising women. Elizabeth was disappointed because Susan was not eager to circulate her birthday speech as a tract. From California, Susan wrote Elizabeth:

> In this California campaign, I shall no more thrust into the discussions the question of the Bible than the manufacture of wine. What I want is for the men to vote "Yes" on the suffrage amendment....I have your grand addresses before Congress and enclose one in nearly every letter I write. I have scattered all your "celebration" speeches that I had, but I shall not circulate your "Bible" literature a particle more than Frances Willard's prohibition literature....I have been pleading with Miss Willard for the last three months to withdraw her threatened W.C.T.U. invasion of California this year, and at last she has done it; now, for heaven's sake, don't you propose a "Bible" invasion. It is not because I hate religious bigotry less than you do, or because I love prohibition less than Frances Willard, but because I consider suffrage more important just now.

Because she loved Elizabeth and did not want misunderstanding between them, she explained further:

> You say "women must be emancipated from their superstitions before enfranchisement will be of any benefit," and I say just the reverse, that women must be enfranchised before they can be emancipated from their superstitions. Women would be no more superstitious today than men, if they had been men's political and business equals and gone outside the four walls of home and the other four of the church into the great world, and come in contact with and discussed men and measures on the plane of this mundane sphere, instead of living in the air with Jesus and the angels. So you will have to keep pegging away, saying, "Get rid of religious bigotry and then get political rights"; while I shall keep pegging away, saying, "Get political rights first and religious bigotry will melt like dew before the morning sun"; and each will continue still to believe in and defend the other.

In spite of this difference of opinion they both still felt a great need of each other in their work. Again and again Susan wrote Elizabeth from California, "Oh, that I had you by my side; what a team we would make!" And she wrote Susan: "I read all the papers you send and watch closely the progress of the campaign. I feel at times as if I should fly to your help."

While Susan campaigned in California and wherever else there was a need for her, Elizabeth worked on the second volume of *The Woman's Bible*. This was published in 1898 and continued the commentary through Judges, Kings, the Prophets, and Apostles. In preparing this volume, Elizabeth was obliged to change her collaborators somewhat. Lucinda B. Chandler, Matilda Joslyn Gage, and Clara B. Neyman took the places of Mrs. Colby and Mrs. Blake, who were too busy to give more time, and of Mrs. Dietrich, who passed on before the work was completed.

Both volumes sold well, and stirred up so much comment in the press and among women that people were forced to think on the subject. This was all that Elizabeth asked. She had learned in her long and active life that when people were thinking on a subject half the battle was won. *The Woman's Bible* was soon forgotten, but by calling attention to a false outworn doctrine, it contributed in some measure to the search for Truth.

XXVI

"THE GRAND OLD WOMAN OF AMERICA"

IN 1898, when Elizabeth was eighty-three years old, she published her reminiscences under the title, *Eighty Years and More.* She dedicated this story of her life to Susan B. Anthony with the tribute, "my steadfast friend for half a century." She wrote Susan, "The current of our lives has run in the same channel so long it cannot be separated, and my book is as much your story, as I doubt not, yours is mine." Susan's life story was also being written by a capable newspaper woman and suffragist, from Indiana, Ida Husted Harper.

Eighty Years and More was a chatty, readable account of Mrs. Stanton's private life. Her public career had been recorded in *The History of Woman Suffrage.* It was well reviewed in the principal newspapers and magazines in the United States and in England. The *New York Times* said:

> Elizabeth Cady Stanton's recollections, covering eighty years, easily comes first in the array of new noteworthy books ... because of the impressive and protracted public career of the author; because of her inflexible devotion to and sincerity in a cause long unpopular, and because, moreover, Mrs. Stanton is an American. This is a most interesting volume.

Even the *Nation,* opposed to woman suffrage, gave it a friendly review.

Elizabeth was now continually busy with magazine and newspaper articles. Editors regarded her as an interesting personality with something worth-while to say, and sought her comments on various subjects. Her views were always original and touched with humor. Somehow or other, no matter what her subject, she always smuggled in a word or two on woman's emancipation. Practical, sensible clothing for women was still one of her hobbies. On this subject she wrote, "Trailing Skirts and No Pockets" and "A Word about Dust," a plea for short skirts. She said:

> Imagine our beloved lords of creation rushing to and fro in the busy marts of trade, with their hands behind them holding up their trousers to prevent the "bottoms" from trailing in the mud and dust, with no pockets for purse or bunch of keys. What a picture this would be! Women with trains always make me think of peacocks strutting around the barnyard.

When the bicycle craze was at its height, she was besieged by editors for her opinions on the propriety of women taking up the sport. For the *Wheelman* she wrote an article dealing with the questions, "Should women ride the bicycle? What should they wear when riding the bicycle? Should they ride on Sunday?" In her pithy style she answered:

> If women can ride, God intended they should do so.... They should wear what they find most convenient and comfortable.... I believe that if women prefer a run in the open air on Sunday to a prosy sermon in a close church they should ride by all means. With the soft changing clouds before their eyes, and the balmy air in their lungs, moving among hills, rivers, trees, and flowers, singing with the birds the praises of the Lord in that temple not builded with human hands, but standing eternal under the blue heavens—this worship is far preferable to playing the role of "miserable sinners" in the church service, and listening to that sanctimonious wail, "Good Lord deliver us."

She was heartily in favor of bicycle riding for women because it would entice them to take wholesome exercise in the fresh air; because it would necessitate a more sensible dress, and big hats and sleeves and trailing skirts would have to be discarded; and because it would inspire women with more courage, self-respect, and self-reliance.

She wrote a great deal about keeping American cities clean and recommended city house cleaning. She urged that Sunday be a day of joy and rest and suggested how people could spend it properly. She still wrote frequently on the subject of divorce. She was a steady contributor to the Sunday edition of the *New York Journal* and *American*. She was featured as "the grand old woman of America."

Her interest in public affairs never waned. As the country developed industrially and she saw the contrast between the lot of the working man and his wealthy employer, she became more and more socialistic in her views. "My motto is," she wrote for the *New York Journal,* "the few have no right to the luxuries of life while the many are denied its necessities." When labor troubles were flaring up throughout the country and the Pullman strike led by Eugene Debs spread through the West, she wrote in her diary:

> Well, these things must needs be until all the human race enjoy alike the fruits of their labor. We are perhaps in the midst of an industrial revolution. And see those stupid men in Congress talking against the income tax, one of the most just measures passed in a long time. Well, the time has come for labor to assert its rights. It is good that the working masses should now and then show their power and our dependence.

Her sympathies were with the liberals in politics. In letters to the press, she advocated that the Prohibitionists, Populists, labor organizations, and women join hands and show their power. She was up in arms against the Chinese exclusion bill, and wrote in her diary:

> I am much worked up over the infamous Geary bill against the admission of the Chinese into the United States. How my blood boils over these persecutions of the Africans, the Jews, the Indians, and the Chinese. I suppose the Japanese will come next. I wonder if these fanatical Christians think that Christ died for these peoples, or confined his self-sacrifice to Saxons, French, Germans, and Italians.

She was no pacifist in the war with Spain:

> Though I hate war per se, I am glad it has come in this instance. I would like to see Spain and Turkey swept from the face of the earth. They are a disgrace to the civilization of the nineteenth century.

She was a great favorite with reporters. She was always willing to grant them interviews and expressed herself freely on all subjects; for how better could she get her ideas on feminism before the public? One afternoon two young reporters from the *Sun* and the *Tribune* called while she was baking an orange cake. When she sent word to them that she could not leave it until it was finished, they replied that there was nothing they would like better than to see Elizabeth Cady Stanton bake a cake. They hadn't dreamed she could.

They were ushered into the dining room, where, in a black satin dress covered with a big white apron, she sat at the table like a queen, stirring her cake. All the ingredients were arrayed in front of her on a large sheet of brown paper. They sat down beside her and at once felt perfectly at home. It was more like a visit with a favorite relative than an interview. They scraped the bowl and licked the spoon just as they had years ago when they were boys at home, and before they left she presented each one with two freshly baked little cakes thickly spread with orange frosting.

She was now living at 250 West 94th Street, and Nora, who had come from England to prepare to enter Cornell University, was one of the family. Nora had her mother's flare for mathematics and was looking forward to a course in architecture and engineering. How proud Elizabeth was of her granddaughter's ambition to pioneer in this new field, and how happy as she saw the interests and opportunities of the younger generation of women widen!

As the years went by she was obliged to acknowledge that she was growing weaker physically and that her eyesight was failing. So she stayed quietly at home and conserved her energies. Her failing eyesight was a real trial. She so dearly loved to read and now she must be read to. The newspapers were thoroughly read to her every day by her secretary and blue-penciled to remind her to answer certain articles. She would not be kept from taking part in world affairs nor from enjoying new books or scholarly volumes. She wrote in her diary:

> My eyes grow dimmer and dimmer. Oh, what a privation! I say nothing to my children of this great grief, but it is a sore trial, with prospective total blindness!! I will then be able to do nothing but think. However, I can still write without spectacles, though I cannot read my own writing. But my hearing is as good as ever, and I am perfectly well otherwise. As Stevenson says, "No man lives in the external truth, among salts and acids, but in the warm, phantasmagoric chamber of his brain, with the painted windows and storied walls."

Her mind was as active as ever, and she felt she still had a great deal of work to do. She planned her days accordingly. Every day she was up for an eight o'clock breakfast, faultlessly gowned. She spent many hours at her desk. When she was eighty-five, she wrote in her diary:

> I am writing articles long and short, all the time. Last week I had something in seven different papers. The December number of the *North American Review* contains an article of mine, and so does the *Cosmopolitan*. In a word, I am always busy, which is perhaps the chief reason I am always well.

When she had done her quota of work for the day, she took a nap, played the piano and sang songs of her youth, baked her favorite cakes, or drove in Central Park or up Riverside Drive. She still loved her games and spent many evenings playing backgammon with Robert. Friends and suffrage workers, old and young, called frequently. She was a delightful companion, full of fun and interested in everything. She did not live in the past nor long for the good old days, nor wonder what the world was coming to. She expected much of the future and greeted each invention and each new thought with enthusiasm. Life was still an adventure to her, and she enjoyed it to the full. Every birthday she recorded some such sentiment in her diary:

> I do enjoy life more and more every hour, and am truly thankful that I have so few annoyances and so few pains and aches to rob me of the satisfaction.

or:

> This is my birthday. Well, I am glad I was born. I feel that I have done something to make the world better, especially to render it a more endurable sphere for women.

She had been so criticized for writing *The Woman's Bible,* had been accused of being irreligious and a heretic, and had so often been asked to state her religious views that in these last years she wrote out her creed in a large faltering hand. In answer to the question, Do you believe in God? she wrote:

Yes, as I look about I see law everywhere; the sun, moon and stars, the constellations, the days, and nights, the seasons at regular intervals all come and go. The centrifugal and centripetal forces, positive and negative, magnetism, the laws of gravitation, cohesion, attraction are all immutable and unchangeable, one and all moving in harmony together. Hence behind all this, I argue, intelligence, a supreme law, Nature, God, or whatever one may choose to call the eternal forces that set all in motion. As we learn these laws that govern the universe of mind and matter alike in the moral and material world and walk in line with them, we secure health, comfort, happiness, harmony and that peace that passeth all understanding.

She believed that the supreme law of the universe was beneficent:

Our sorrows in life are not caused by the direct fiat of a malevolent Being, but by our own ignorance and indifference to the laws of our being. . . . Man has been so sedulously educated with the belief of evil as a supreme force, the total depravity of the race, a stern God punishing us by direct fiat for our violations of law that justice, love, mercy, and happiness have been eliminated in a large measure from this life and the life to come.

I see inexorable law everywhere, cause and effect. Our sufferings and prayers do not mitigate one iota the effect of violated law either in the moral or material world. If we defy the law of gravitation, a broken neck or leg will be the penalty. If we do not exercise the tender emotions of love, friendship, sympathy, and charity, we blunt the moral sense and isolate ourselves from all that is best in human companionship. . . .

She said she believed in immortality, but added:

What lies beyond the veil that now separates us from the next sphere of action, we know nothing. We have no facts on which to predicate our next form of existence. We may logically infer that the same laws will govern eternity and that the next life will be a continued progression and development.

Although she and Susan rarely saw each other now, they corresponded regularly. Susan too had grown less active, but was unwilling to stay quietly at home. She still made speeches here and there and attended all the woman suffrage conventions. Whenever she was near New York, she had a visit with Elizabeth. Elizabeth still helped her with important letters, speeches, and resolutions. Susan and Ida Husted Harper were working on the fourth volume of the *History of Woman Suffrage* which Susan had hoped she and

Elizabeth would undertake together. But although Elizabeth had not felt equal to the task, she took a keen interest in it and wrote weekly letters filled with excellent suggestions regarding material and arrangement. Susan kept her informed of the progress of the work. She also still sent her speeches to all the suffrage conventions, and although occasionally the younger suffragists protested at the subject matter, Susan insisted that they be read. Often she herself was not in sympathy with the subjects Elizabeth chose, especially when they dealt with the Church or educated suffrage.

On the question of educated suffrage they could not agree. Elizabeth was appalled by the numbers of ignorant immigrants who almost immediately became voting citizens. They had no sympathy with democratic institutions, and hence their vote hindered the proper development of the country. As she pondered the matter, it became clearer and clearer to her that an educational qualification should be required of voters. She wrote:

> The greatest block today in the way of granting woman suffrage is fear of the ignorant vote. Our opponents say that to extend the suffrage to women would be doubling this ignorant vote, which is already so large that it threatens to swamp our free institutions. The most speedy way to limit this ignorant vote is to require an educational qualification. To this end, we should demand that after the dawn of the next century no one shall be permitted to exercise the right of the elective franchise unless he can read and write the English language intelligently.

Elizabeth and Susan thrashed out the question of educated suffrage with the utmost frankness. Each accused the other of growing conservative. Susan wrote her:

> Now my dear, it is you who are becoming conservative when you take up the fad of restricting suffrage. There is not a man or woman opposed to woman suffrage whose first proposition is not to restrict the suffrage in one way or another.... The difference between you and me has always been that you are ready to switch off on some side track—the settlement of the social, the theological, and last autumn, the money questions. I shall not stop or try to settle any possible question except that of our right to vote on equal terms with men; and whatever changes ought or ought not to be made on the basis of suffrage or in the conditions of the world socially, religiously or politically, I shall let entirely alone until I get the right

to have woman's opinion counted at the ballot box. There is not the slightest pleasure to me in pushing my opinions on these questions so long as that opinion is counted of no more value than that of the idiot, the lunatic or the convict.... I had hoped that you would make a comprehensive survey of the great work you, yourself, and all the progressive women of the nation have done in the last fifty years and give to the world a summing up of the results, such as no other human being has the capacity to do; but if you can't and won't do that, but prefer to narrow down yourself and your subject to "educated suffrage," that is your business not mine; and if it comes into my hands, I shall religiously see that your thought goes before the Convention. But it will go there as your thought, not mine.... Do try to get your mind off that old, old fad of "limiting the suffrage" and on the great broad question.

Elizabeth had not grown conservative. Nor was her interest in an educational qualification for voters out of line. Many states have imposed that qualification on their voters to good advantage. She was by far the most liberal and farseeing of all the suffragists. Susan's steadfast adherence to her one object, woman suffrage, was highly commendable and necessary. Elizabeth's interest in related fields was also essential. She was convinced that even if women did win the ballot, they would not accomplish much with it as long as their minds were closed. If they continued to concentrate only on winning woman suffrage and refused to think about or discuss any other social or governmental questions, they would be sadly unfitted to use the ballot. So, when in 1899 Susan asked her to write out her suggestions for the next convention, she outlined an admirable plan:

1. A resolution should be passed in favor of establishing a new government in Hawaii. It is a disgrace to the civilization of the nineteenth century to make that island a male oligarchy.
2. We should protest in clarion notes against the proposal by railroad kings to turn women out of all the positions which they hold in the Northwestern Railroad, especially as it is generally admitted that they have given faithful service.
3. We should discuss and pass a resolution against the proposition of the Knights of Labor to remove women from all factories and industries which take them from home. If these gentlemen propose to provide every woman with a strong right arm on which she may lean until she reaches the other side of Jordan; a robust generous man pledged to feed, clothe, and shelter the woman and her children

to the end of life; a husband or brother sure not to die or default on the way—why then this proposal might be worthy of woman's consideration. But as long as she is often forced to be the breadwinner for herself, husband, and children, it would be suicidal for her to retire to the privacy of home and with folded hands wait for the salvation of the Lord. . . .

4. To my mind our Association cannot be too broad. Suffrage involves every basic principle of republican government, all our social, civil, religious, educational and political rights. It is therefore germane to our platform to discuss every invidious distinction of sex in the college, home, trades, and professions, in literature, sacred and profane, in the canon as well as in the civil law. At the inauguration of our movement, we numbered in our Declaration of Rights eighteen grievances covering the whole range of human experience. On none of these did we talk with bated breath. Note the radical claims we made, and think how the world responded. . . . In short, in response to our radicalism, the bulwarks of the enemy fell as never since. . . . But at present our association has so narrowed its platform for reasons of policy and propriety that our conventions have ceased to point the way.

5. Our national convention should always be held in Washington, where we could examine intelligently the bills before Congress which nearly or remotely affect the women of the nation. We should have a sort of Woman's Congress, if we can afford it, which should sit at the federal capital for a longer or a shorter period every year.

The younger suffragists did not feel the need of Elizabeth's advice. They knew how they wanted their organization run. They had their own plans and made their own programs. They still listened to Susan but she had become more of a symbol and saint of woman suffrage during these last years than an actual director of policy. In 1900 she retired as president of the National American Woman Suffrage Association, and on her recommendation Carrie Chapman Catt was elected to take her place.

As the general tenor of the Association was toward conservatism, Elizabeth's liberalism was anathema to the majority, a younger generation, who had entered the fight when woman suffrage had become respectable. They were capable, consecrated workers, with remarkable executive ability, and Susan felt that with this equipment they could win the suffrage victory. Liberalism could wait, or perhaps they would learn it on the way.

Occasionally there were gleams of vitality in the Association which encouraged Elizabeth, and she knew that some day someone must arise to lead women out of their apathetic, academic methods of working for woman suffrage. She was completely out of patience with continuing the same old tactics year after year. "Our movement is belated," she said, "and like all things too long postponed now gets on everybody's nerves." She grew tired of hearing the suffragists congratulate themselves on what had been accomplished. The accomplishments were so meager compared to the years of effort expended. What energy women could put into the business of good government if they did not have to wear themselves out fighting for their citizenship rights!

Some years before, Frances Ellen Burr had suggested a militant plan of which she highly approved—a march on the state legislatures and the national Capitol by hundreds of women demanding their rights. Now in 1900, she wrote in her diary:

> What can be done to strike these dull minds and awaken them to the deep significance of our agitation? Something sensational should be done, like Miss Burr's march on the capitals. Once set a woman to thinking, and she thinks faster and often better than a man. But she has been kept under so long that she must be given the necessary momentum, and then how she will go!

How she would have rejoiced in the militant campaigns of Emmeline Pankhurst and Alice Paul, and of her own daughter, Harriot Stanton Blatch!

Susan spent a week with her in May 1902, and recorded in her diary:

> It seems good to be here though Mrs. Stanton does not feel quite as she used to. We have grown a little apart since not so closely associated as of old. She thinks the Church is now the enemy to fight and feels worried that I stay back with the children—as she says—instead of going ahead with her.

In June Susan spent another day with Elizabeth. She said goodby with tears in her eyes, sensing that it might be the last time she would see her beloved friend. "Shall I see you again?" she asked.

"Oh yes," replied Elizabeth with her characteristic bravado, "if not here, then in the hereafter, if there is one, and if there isn't we shall never know it."

In October the children gathered to be near their mother and possibly to celebrate her eighty-seventh birthday. Harriot came from England, and Theodore from France. Harriot wrote Susan, "I wish you could be in New York at the time of the eighty-seventh birthday, as I'm sure there won't be another."

But Elizabeth continued at her work. Her mind was still keen and there was much to be written. A long article of hers on divorce appeared in the *New York American,* October 12. It gave her great satisfaction, and she was deeply touched when a few days later a postcard came from an unknown woman in Chicago saying:

> Today's *American* has a half page that should be framed, or better still, writ large or megaphoned everywhere. How many hearts today will thrill in response and how many heads will begin to think. It is by a Grand Old Woman. God bless her! So say all of us.

On October 25 she wrote a letter to President Roosevelt urging him to immortalize himself by bringing about the complete emancipation of his countrywomen. She worked on the letter most of the afternoon. Her children came in one by one to see her. She greeted them and went on with her work, undisturbed by their laughing and talking. When the letter was finished, she was satisfied, and joined in the conversation with her old-time merriment and zest.

The next afternoon she passed away quietly in her chair. When the news reached Susan, she sat for hours alone in her room where Elizabeth's portrait looked down upon her. Later when a reporter called, she said, "For fifty years there has been an unbroken friendship between us. . . . I cannot express myself at all as I feel. I am too crushed to speak. If I had died first she would have found beautiful phrases to describe our friendship, but I cannot put it into words."

On her way to the funeral she wrote Ida Husted Harper:

> Well, it is an awful hush—it seems impossible—that the voice is hushed that I have longed to hear for fifty years—longed to get her opinion of things—before I knew exactly where I stood. It is all at sea—but the Laws of Nature are still going on—with no shadow or

turning—what a wonder it is—it goes right on and on—no matter who lives or who dies.

The funeral was private. Only the family and a few intimate friends were present. Antoinette Brown Blackwell, Phebe Hanaford, and Moncure D. Conway conducted the services. Young reporters, men and women, stood in silent tribute with bowed heads and with tears streaming down their cheeks.

For months afterward newspapers and magazines throughout the world paid tribute to this great American woman. People flocked to memorial meetings, eager to show their appreciation of her work and to speak their words of praise. She was called the great statesman of the woman's rights movement, the mother of woman suffrage, the greatest woman the world has ever produced.

She had started a great revolution when she called the first Woman's Rights Convention in 1848. Since then a remarkable change in woman's status had taken place. Women were receiving college educations, entering business and the professions, and growing economically independent. Many legal discriminations had been removed. But after fifty-four years of continuous work for woman suffrage, she had had the satisfaction of seeing only four states, Wyoming, Colorado, Idaho, and Utah, enfranchise women. The Federal Amendment still looked far away, and it was not passed until eighteen years later. "Lifting woman into her proper place in the scale of being," she had said, "is the mightiest revolution the world has yet known, and it may be that more than half a century is needed to accomplish this."

The revolution, she knew, was well started. It would gain momentum as women tasted freedom, lost their psychological handicaps, and sensed their power. Women were now on the road to victory, and she had led the way.

CHRONOLOGY

1815	November 12. Elizabeth Cady born in Johnstown, New York.
1830	Attended the Troy Female Seminary, conducted by Emma Willard.
1840	May 10. Married Henry Brewster Stanton.
1840	June 12. Attended World's Antislavery Convention, Freemasons' Hall, London, to which her husband was a delegate. Met Lucretia Mott.
1841–42	Lived in Johnstown and Albany.
1843–46	Lived in Boston and Chelsea.
1847	Moved to Seneca Falls, New York.
1848	July 19 and 20. Called first Woman's Rights Convention and made first public demand for woman suffrage.
1849	Began writing for the *Lily*.
1851	Adopted the Bloomer Costume. Met Susan B. Anthony and their lifelong friendship began.
1853	Became regular contributor to the *Una*.
1854	President, New York State Woman Suffrage Society. Addressed joint Judiciary Committees of the New York Legislature regarding amendments to Woman's Property Law.
1860	Addressed joint session of the New York Legislature on amendments to Woman's Property Law. Introduced liberal resolutions on divorce at Woman's Rights Convention.
1861	Moved to Brooklyn.
1863	Moved to New York City to 75 West 45th Street With Susan B. Anthony, organized Women's Loyal League to help win the war and free the Negroes.
1865	Moved to 464 West 34th Street, New York City. Circulated petitions for Congressional action on woman suffrage.

1866   Candidate for Congress.

1867   Campaigned with Susan B. Anthony in Kansas for Woman Suffrage Amendment.

1868–70   Editor of the *Revolution*.

Began campaign to enfranchise women and Negroes by one and the same federal amendment and in the New York Constitutional Convention.

1868   Moved to Tenafly, New Jersey.

1869   Elected President of the National Woman Suffrage Association. Held office for twenty-one years until merger with American Woman Suffrage Association.

Began lecture tours for the Lyceum Bureau, which continued for twelve years, to 1881.

1869   March 15. A Sixteenth Amendment to enfranchise women introduced by Congressman Julian of Indiana.

1871   Campaigned in California for woman suffrage with Susan B. Anthony.

1878   Conferred with Senator Sargent of California regarding a Federal Woman Suffrage Amendment which was introduced by Senator Sargent on January 10. Spoke for it before Senate Committee.

1880   Attempted to vote in Tenafly, New Jersey.

1881   Co-author of *The History of Woman Suffrage*. Volume I published in May.

1882   Volume II published.

Trip to France and England.

Harriot Stanton and Henry Blatch married in London on November 12.

1885   Honored by nationwide celebration on her seventieth birthday.

1886   Volume III of *The History of Woman Suffrage* published.

1886–87   Trip to England and France to visit Harriot and Theodore.

1887   January 14. Death of Henry B. Stanton.

1888   Made principal speech at the first meeting of the International Council of Women in Washington.

Spent winter in Omaha, Nebraska, with daughter, Margaret Stanton Lawrence.

1890 First President of the National American Woman Suffrage Association. Held office for two years until 1892 when she resigned.

Last visit with Harriot in England.

Returned to New York to apartment at 26 West 61st Street.

1892 Address before House and Senate Judiciary Committees, "The Solitude of Self."

1895 Honored by celebration of eightieth birthday at Metropolitan Opera House.

Published *The Woman's Bible*. Volume I.

1898 Volume II, published.

Eighty Years and More published.

Moved to 250 West 94th Street, New York.

1902 October 26. Died in New York.

ACKNOWLEDGMENTS

ALL THOSE to whom I have turned in my search for material have been most helpful, and I appreciate their interest and co-operation. I am especially indebted to Harriot Stanton Blatch for permission to quote from her mother's letters and to publish photographs, for all the material she has made available, and for the time she has spent telling me of her mother and her contemporaries.

Ida Husted Harper, Adelaide Johnson, and Katherine Devereux Blake told me some of their personal memories of Elizabeth Cady Stanton.

I am grateful to Alice Stone Blackwell for permission to quote from letters of her mother and father, Lucy Stone and Henry B. Blackwell; to Lucy E. Anthony for permission to quote from letters of Susan B. Anthony; to Carrie Chapman Catt for permission to quote from one of her letters; to the *Christian Science Monitor* for permission to use material which appeared in two articles in the Weekly Magazine Section, "The Bloomer Costume," December 5, 1934, and "Bibles from Feminine Hands," May 13, 1936; and to Harper & Brothers for permission to quote from Mrs. Stanton's letters and diary published in 1922 in *Elizabeth Cady Stanton, As Revealed in Her Reminiscences, Letters, and Diary,* edited by Theodore Stanton and Harriot Stanton Blatch.

The Life of Susan B. Anthony by Ida Husted Harper and *The History of Woman Suffrage* have been invaluable in their preservation of records of this period.

For the use of special collections and original letters I am indebted to the Boston Public Library; the Library of Congress; the Vassar College Library; the Henry E. Huntington Library, San Marino, California; the Gerrit Smith Miller Collection of Syracuse University; the New York Public Library; the Historical Society of Pennsylvania; the New York State Library; and the Buffalo Public Library.   ALMA LUTZ

BIBLIOGRAPHY

MANUSCRIPTS

Anthony: Scrapbook of press comments relating to Elizabeth Cady Stanton collected by Susan B. Anthony. 3 volumes. Congressional Library, Washington.

Garrison: Antislavery letters written to W. L. Garrison and others, 1842-66. Boston Public Library.

Stanton: Elizabeth Cady Stanton Papers, letters, manuscripts, and clippings. 7 volumes. Congressional Library, Washington.

———. MS. Articles on Marriage and Divorce by Elizabeth Cady Stanton. Congressional Library, Washington.

———. MS. Biographical Sketches of Elizabeth Cady Stanton by Margaret Stanton Lawrence. In possession of Harriot Stanton Blatch, New York.

———. MS. First Kansas Speech by Elizabeth Cady Stanton. Kansas Historical Society, Topeka.

———. MS. Letters of Elizabeth Cady Stanton. Buffalo Public Library.

———. MS. Letter of Elizabeth Cady Stanton. New York State Library, Albany.

———. MS. Letters of Elizabeth Cady Stanton. Gerrit Smith Miller Collection, Syracuse University.

———. MS. Letters of Elizabeth Cady Stanton. Historical Society of Pennsylvania, Philadelphia.

———. MS. Letters of Elizabeth Cady Stanton. In possession of Harriot Stanton Blatch, New York.

———. MS. Letters of Elizabeth Cady Stanton. New York Public Library.

———. MS. Letters of Elizabeth Cady Stanton, Susan B. Anthony, Lucy Stone, Frances Willard, and others. Ida Husted Harper Collection. Henry E. Huntington Library, San Marino, California.

———. MS. Letters of Elizabeth Cady Stanton to Clara Colby and articles for the *Woman's Tribune*. Congressional Library, Washington.

———. Papers of Elizabeth Cady Stanton. 3 volumes. Vassar College Library, Poughkeepsie, New York.

———. Scrapbook of clippings of press comments relating to the Woman's Rights Convention, 1848. Congressional Library, Washington.

———. MS. Speeches, 1850-91, by Elizabeth Cady Stanton. Congressional Library, Washington.

Tilton: Scrapbook of clippings relating to the Beecher-Tilton trial, from the office of the *Independent*. New York Public Library.

BOOKS

Albree, John, Editor. *Whittier Correspondence*. From the Oak Knoll Collections, 1830-1892. Salem, Mass., 1911.

Allen, Orrin Peer. *Descendants of Nicholas Cady of Watertown, Mass., 1645-1910*. Palmer, Mass., 1910.

Ames, Mary Clemmer. *A Memorial of Alice and Phoebe Cary*. New York, 1873.

Anthony, Katharine. *Margaret Fuller*. New York, 1920.

Austin, George Lowell. *The Life and Times of Wendell Phillips*. Boston, 1888.

Beard, Charles and Mary. *The Rise of American Civilization*. New York, 1927.

Birney, Catherine H. *The Grimké Sisters*. Boston, 1885.

Birney, William. *James G. Birney and His Times*. New York, 1890.

Blackmar, Frank W. *The Life of Charles Robinson*. Topeka, Kansas, 1902.

Blackwell, Alice Stone. *Lucy Stone*. Boston, 1930.

Blatch, Harriot Stanton. *A Sketch of the Life of Elizabeth Cady Stanton by Her Daughter*. New York, 1915.

Blatch, Harriot Stanton, and Theodore Stanton, Editors. *Elizabeth Cady Stanton as Revealed in Her Letters, Diary, and Reminiscences*. New York, 1922. 2 vols.

Bloomer, D. C. *Life and Writings of Amelia Bloomer*. Boston, 1895.

Browne, Junius Henri. *The Great Metropolis; A Mirror of New York*. Hartford, 1869.

Bullard, Laura Curtis. "Elizabeth Cady Stanton." In *Our Famous Women*. Hartford, 1884.

Catt, Carrie Chapman, and Nettie Rogers Shuler. *Woman Suffrage and Politics*. New York, 1923.

Chadwick, John White. *A Life of Liberty. Anti-slavery and Other Letters of Salley Holley*. New York, 1899.

Channing, William Henry. Review of *The History of Woman Suffrage*. Reprint from the *Inquirer*, London, November 5, 1881.

Clarke, James Freeman. *Anti-Slavery Days*. New York, 1884.

Conway, Moncure D. *Autobiography, Memories and Experiences*. Boston, 1904. 2 vols.

Davis, Paulina W. *A History of the National Woman's Rights Movement*. New York, 1871.

Dorr, Rheta Childe. *Susan B. Anthony*. New York, 1928.

Douglass, Frederick. *Life and Times of Frederick Douglass*. Hartford, Conn., 1882.

Duane, William. *Remarks upon a Speech Delivered by Mrs. E. Cady Stanton during the Summer of 1870*. Philadelphia, 1870.

Eliot, Hugh S. R. *The Letters of John Stuart Mill.* New York, 1910.

Frothingham, Octavius Brooks. *Gerrit Smith.* New York, 1878.

Garrison, Francis Jackson. *Ann Phillips.* Boston, 1886.

Garrison, Francis Jackson, and Wendell Phillips. *William Lloyd Garrison, 1805-1879.* New York, 1889.

Gordon, Anna A. *The Beautiful Life of Frances E. Willard.* Chicago, 1898.

Hallowell, Anna Davis. *James and Lucretia Mott.* Boston, 1884.

Harper, Ida Husted. *Life and Work of Susan B. Anthony.* Indianapolis, 1898. 3 vols.

———. *Story of the National Amendment for Woman Suffrage.* New York, 1919.

Hibben, Paxton. *Henry Ward Beecher.* New York, 1927.

Higginson, Mary Thatcher, Editor. *Letters and Journals of Thomas Wentworth Higginson.* Boston, 1921.

Howe, Julia Ward. *Reminiscences.* Boston, 1900.

Hudson, Frederic. *Journalism in the United States from 1690-1872.* New York, 1873.

Hutchinson, John Wallace. *Story of the Hutchinsons.* Boston, 1896.

Johnson, Oliver. *William L. Garrison and His Times.* Boston, 1881.

Macy, Jesse. *The Anti-Slavery Crusade.* New Haven, 1919.

Mumford, T. J. *Memoir of Samuel Joseph May.* Boston, 1873.

Parton, J. *The Life of Horace Greeley.* New York, 1885.

Pickard, Samuel T. *Life and Letters of John Greenleaf Whittier.* Boston, 1907.

Reports of Woman's Rights Conventions, 1848-53.

Rourke, Constance M. *Trumpets of Jubilee.* New York, 1927.

Ruddy, Ella Giles, Editor. *The Mother of Clubs, Caroline M. Seymour Severance.* Los Angeles, 1906.

Sachs, Emanie. *The Terrible Siren, Victoria Woodhull.* New York, 1928.

Sears, Lorenzo. *Wendell Phillips.* New York, 1909.

Seitz, Don C. *Horace Greeley, Founder of the New York Tribune.* Indianapolis, 1926.

Shaw, Anna Howard. *The Story of a Pioneer.* New York, 1915.

Stanton, Elizabeth Cady. "Anna Elizabeth Dickinson." In *Eminent Women of the Age.* Hartford, 1869.

———. *Eighty Years and More.* New York, 1898.

———. "Susan B. Anthony." In *Our Famous Women.* Hartford, 1884.

———. *The Woman's Bible,* New York, 1895, 1898. 2 vols.

———. "The Woman's Rights Movement and Its Champions in the United States." In *Eminent Women of the Age.* Hartford, 1869.

Stanton, Elizabeth Cady, Susan B. Anthony, and Rachel Avery. *Report of the International Council of Women.* Washington, 1888.

Stanton, Elizabeth Cady, Susan B. Anthony, Matilda Joslyn Gage, and Ida Husted Harper. *The History of Woman Suffrage.* 1881-1922. 6 vols.

Stanton, Henry B. *Random Recollections*. New York, 1887.
———. *Sketches of Reforms and Reformers of Great Britain and Ireland*. New York, 1850.
Stanton, William A. *A Record, Genealogical, Biographical, Statistical, of Thomas Stanton, of Connecticut, and His Descendants, 1635-1891*. Albany, 1891.
Tilton, Theodore, vs. Henry Ward Beecher. Action for criminal conduct. Verbatim Report by the official stenographer. New York, 1875. 3 vols.
Tilton, Theodore. "Elizabeth Cady Stanton." In *Eminent Women of the Age*. Hartford, 1869.
———. *Victoria C. Woodhull. A Biographical Sketch*. New York, 1871.
Train, George Francis. *My Life in Many States and in Foreign Lands*. New York, 1902.
———. *The Great Epigram Campaign of Kansas*. Leavenworth, 1867.
Whittier, John Greenleaf. *Poems*. Philadelphia, 1838.
Willard, Frances E. and Mary A. Livermore, Editors. *A Woman of the Century*. New York, 1893.
Woman's Rights Documents. 1848-72. 2 vols.
Wright, Elizur. *Myron Holley*. Boston, 1882.
Wyman, Lillie Buffum Chace. *American Chivalry*. Boston, 1913.

NEWSPAPERS AND MAGAZINES

Arena
Boston Weekly Museum
Carpet Bag
Chicago Tribune
Free Thought Magazine. Elizabeth Cady Stanton Memorial Number. Chicago, January 1903.
Godey's Magazine and Lady's Book
Golden Age
Liberator
Lily
New Era. Elizabeth Cady Stanton Number. Chicago, November 1885.
New York American
New York Herald
New York Sun
New York Times
New York Tribune
North American Review
Revolution
Una
Westminster Review
Woman's Journal
Woman's Tribune
Woodhull & Claflin's Weekly